Statistics

Concepts and Controversies

Statistics
Concepts and Controversies

David S. Moore
Purdue University

W. H. Freeman and Company
San Francisco

Sponsoring Editor: Peter Renz
Project Editor: Dick Johnson
Production Coordinator: M. Y. Mim
Illustration Coordinator: Cheryl Nufer
Line Art: Tim Keenan
Original Cartoons: John Johnson
Compositor: Holmes Composition Service
Printer and Binder: The Maple-Vail Book Manufacturing Group.

Library of Congress Cataloging in Publication Data

Moore, David S.
     Statistics: concepts and controversies.

     Includes bibliographical references and index.
     1. Statistics. I. Title.
QA276.12.M66   001.4'22   78–12740
ISBN 0–7167–1022–6
ISBN 0–7167–1021–8 pbk.

AMS (MOS) Subject Classification 6201; Statistics, elementary exposition of.

———————————————————————

Does not He see my ways,
    and number all my steps?
                      Job

But even the hairs of your head
    are all numbered.
                      Jesus

Hell is inaccurate.
    Charles Williams

Contents

To the Teacher

In Japan, October 18 is National Statistics Day. The Japanese, with their usual thoroughness, have made public and official what is quietly recognized elsewhere: that statistics, no longer satisfied to be the assistant of researchers and government planners, now forces herself into the consciousness of students of every discipline and citizens of every occupation. This book is written for those students and citizens. There are texts on statistical theory and texts on statistical methods. This is neither. It is a book on statistical ideas and their relevance in public policy and in the human sciences from medicine to sociology.

I have developed this material during six years of teaching students (usually freshmen and sophomores) from Purdue's School of Humanities, Social Science, and Education. The students come from many disciplines and are fulfilling a dreaded mathematical sciences requirement. Future psychology and sociology majors often choose the course as preparation for later study of statistical methods; the other students will probably never again encounter statistics as a discipline. My intention is to make statistics accessible by teaching verbally rather than symbolically, and to bring statistics out of the technician's closet by discussing applications and issues of broad public concern. I have also used much of this material as supplementary reading in more traditional statistics courses, which usually neglect many of the concepts and issues discussed here.

So the book is popular, written for readers interested in ideas rather than technique. Yet this appellation requires several qualifications. First, readers will find genuine intellectual content, probably more than in a technique-laden methods course. I have even included several simple techniques (use of random digits for sampling and for simulation, computation of simple descriptive statistics and of index numbers) on the grounds that talking about a median without ever computing one may be empty. Second, I have been positive in my approach to statistics. I am annoyed that so many popular presentations suggest that statistics is a subcategory of lying. Third, this is a text, organized for study and provided with abundant exercises at the end of each chapter. I hope that this organization will not deter those admirable individuals who seek pleasure and learning in uncompelled reading.

I am grateful to many colleagues for comments and suggestions. Professors William Erickson of the University of Michigan and Paul Speckman of the University of Oregon used the first draft in their classes and graciously provided both their own reactions and those of their students. They will forgive me if I proved at times hard to sway. The mathematicians and statisticians who have taught from the first draft noted the challenge of teaching nonmathematical material. I have tried to provide detailed guidance for teachers in the Instructor's Manual. Here, only a few suggestions are in order. First, try to establish a "humanities course" atmosphere, with much discussion in class. Many of the exercises involve discussion and can be modified to ask "Come prepared to discuss" rather than seek written answers. There are of course techniques to be learned, but classes should not be primarily problem-oriented. Second, use the collection of readings *Statistics: A Guide to the Unknown,* by J. M. Tanur et al. (eds.), as supplementary material. It is referred to often in the text, and complements this book well.

Statistics is a subject of growing importance to general audiences, and statisticians are increasingly aware of the need to introduce their subject to a wider public. There is as yet no consensus on how this should be done. It is my opinion that words remain as effective as computer terminals. I enjoy teaching this material as much as any. The orientation toward discussion brings students and teachers closer than in a more technical course. I hope that you also enjoy it.

Introduction

Most of us associate "statistics" with the words of the play-by-play announcer at the end of the sports broadcast, "And we thank our statistician, Alan Roth. . . ." We meet the statistician as the person who compiles the batting averages or yards gained. Statisticians do indeed work with numerical facts (which we call *data*), but usually for more serious purposes. Statistics originated as *state*-istics, an accessory to governments wanting to know how many taxable farms or military-age men their realms contained. The systematic study of data has now infiltrated most areas of academic or practical endeavor. Here are some examples of statistical questions.

1. The Bureau of Labor Statistics reports that the unemployment rate last month was 6.5%. What exactly does that figure mean? How did the government obtain this information? (Neither you nor I were asked if we were employed last month.) How accurate is the unemployment rate given?

2. The Gallup Poll reports that 42% of the American public currently approve the President's performance in office. Where did that information come from? How accurate is it?

3. What kind of evidence links smoking to increased incidence of lung cancer and other health problems? You may have heard that much of this evidence is "statistical."

4. A medical researcher claims that vitamin C is not effective in reducing the incidence of colds and flu. How can an experiment be designed to prove or disprove this claim?

5. Do gun control laws reduce violent crime? Both proponents and opponents of stricter gun legislation offer numerical arguments in favor of their position. Which of these arguments are sense and which are nonsense?

The aim of statistics is to provide insight by means of numbers. In pursuit of this aim, statistics divides the study of data into three parts:

I. Collecting data

II. Describing and presenting data

III. Drawing conclusions from data

This book is organized into three parts following this same pattern. The second of these divisions is often called *descriptive statistics*; the third is often called *statistical inference*. I hasten to add that we will not leave the interesting business of drawing conclusions to the end of the book. Collecting and organizing data usually suggest conclusions (not always correct conclusions), and we will have much to say about these informal inferences in the first two parts of our study.

Your goals in reading this book should be threefold. First, reach an understanding of statistical ideas in themselves. The basic concepts and modes of reasoning of statistics are major intellectual accomplishments (almost all developed within this century) worthy of your attention. Second, acquire the ability to deal critically with numerical arguments. Many persons are unduly credulous when numerical arguments are used; they are impressed by the solid appearance of a few numbers and do not attempt to penetrate the substance of the argument. Others are unduly cynical; they think numbers are liars by nature and never trust them. Numerical arguments are like any others. Some are good, some are bad, and some are irrelevant. A bit of quantitative sophistication will enable you to hold your own against the number-slinger. Third, gain an understanding of the impact of statistical ideas on public policy and in your primary area of academic study. The list of statistical questions given above hints at the considerable impact of statistics in areas of public policy. I will only add that the impact is sometimes aimed at your pocketbook. For example, each 1% rise in the Consumer Price Index automatically triggers a billion dollar increase in government spending on such things as social security payments. You pay a share of that billion dollars, and you should know something about the Consumer Price Index and other creatures in the statistical zoo. The invasion of many academic areas by statistics is even more dramatic. For example, two political scientists recently compiled the percentage of articles appearing in a leading political science journal that made use of numerical data. Here are their results.[1]

1946–1948	12%	of all articles used numerical data
1950–1952	16%	” ” ” ” ” ”
1963–1965	40%	” ” ” ” ” ”
1968–1970	65%	” ” ” ” ” ”

It is clear that a political scientist must now be prepared to deal with statistics.

Economists, psychologists, sociologists, and educators have long considered statistics a basic part of their tool kit. Not even historians and literary scholars can ignore statistical methods. It is now common, for example, to attempt to decide the authorship of a disputed historical or literary document by analyzing quantitative characteristics of writing style (sentence length, vocabulary counts, frequency of certain grammatical constructions, etc.). Comparing these characteristics of the disputed document with documents by known authors often leads to a decision about authorship of the disputed document. An outstanding investigation of this type concerned the authorship of 12 of the papers originally published in *The Federalist.* These papers were published anonymously in 1787–1788 to persuade the citizens of New York State to ratify the Constitution. There is general agreement as to the authors of most of those papers: John Jay wrote 5, James Madison wrote 14, and Alexander Hamilton wrote 51. The disputed 12 may belong to either Madison or Hamilton. A statistical study of the style of these papers gave good reason to think that all were written by Madison.*

I hasten to state that one need not entirely approve of the infiltration of fields such as political science and history by quantitative methods. One might well agree with the remarks of Lewis A. Coser, president of the American Sociological Association in 1975, who warned the Association's annual meeting that "if concepts and theoretical notions are weak, no measurement, however precise, will advance an explanatory science."[2] In other words, it may be misleading to attempt to measure what you don't understand. But whether we like or dislike the increasing use of statistical arguments, we must be prepared to deal with them. Even if you wish only to rebut your local statistician, this book aims to give you the conceptual tools to do so.

NOTES

1. James L. Hutter, "Statistics and Political Science," *Journal of the American Statistical Association,* Volume 67 (1972), p. 735.
2. Reported in *The New York Times,* August 30, 1975.

*See Frederick Mosteller and David L. Wallace, "Deciding Authorship," in J. M. Tanur et al. (eds.), *Statistics: A Guide to the Unknown* (San Francisco: Holden-Day, 1972). This book of readings contains many outstanding examples of the uses of statistics, and we shall refer to it often.

Statistics

Concepts and Controversies

Part I

Collecting Data

Before numbers can be used for good or evil, we must collect them. Of course we could make up data, a common enough practice. Leaving invention aside, many statistical studies are based on *available data,* that is, data not gathered specifically for the study at hand, but lying about in files or records kept for other reasons. Available data must be used with caution. Here is an example.

> The American Cancer Society, in a booklet called "The Hopeful Side of Cancer," claims that about one in three cancer patients is now cured, while in 1930 only one in five patients was cured. That's encouraging. But where does this encouraging estimate come from? From the state of Connecticut. Why Connecticut? Because it is the only state that kept records of cancer patients in 1930. It is a matter of available data. But Connecticut is not typical of the entire nation. It has no large cities, and few blacks. Cancer death rates are higher in large cities than in rural locations, and higher among blacks than among whites. We are left without clear knowledge of the national trend in cancer cures.*

Historians must rely on available data. The rest of us can make an effort to obtain data that bear directly on the questions we wish to ask. Such data are obtained by either *observation* or *experiment.* Observation is passive: The observer wishes to record data without interfering with the process being observed. Experimentation is active: The experimenter attempts to completely control the

---

*This example is taken from a *Newsday* dispatch that appeared in the *Lafayette Journal and Courier* of January 29, 1977.

experimental situation. The difference is illustrated by the work of Tycho Brahe and Galileo at the beginning of the Scientific Revolution. Brahe devoted his life to recording precisely the positions of stars and planets, and left records from which Kepler deduced his laws of planetary motion. This was observation. Galileo studied motion under the influence of gravity by rolling balls of various weights down inclined planes of various lengths and angles. This was experiment.

Neither observation nor experiment is as simple as you might think, especially when we turn from stars and inclined planes to political opinions and the effectiveness of drugs. The first part of this book concerns the statistical ideas used to arrange observations or experiments. Statistics gives *designs* (patterns or outlines) for collecting data that can be applied in any area of study. Chapter 1 studies the design of *samples* (selecting units for observation), and Chapter 2 presents the design of *experiments*. Each chapter explores key statistical ideas, important examples of their use, and other topics including the ethical problems of collecting data about people. Chapter 3 completes the topic of collecting data by addressing the process of *measurement* by which numbers are finally obtained.

Chapter 1

Sampling

B oswell quotes Samuel Johnson as saying, "You don't have to eat the whole ox to know that the meat is tough." That is the essential idea of sampling: to gain information about the whole by examining only a part. Here is the basic terminology used by statisticians to discuss sampling.

Population—the entire group of objects about which information is wanted.

Unit—any individual member of the population.

Sample—a part or subset of the population used to gain information about the whole.

Sampling Frame—the list of units from which the sample is chosen.

Variable—a characteristic of a unit, to be measured for those units in the sample.

Notice that population is defined in terms of our desire for information. If we desire information about all U.S. college students, that is our population even if students at only one college are available for sampling. It is important to define clearly the population of interest. If you seek to discover what fraction of the American people favor a ban on private ownership of handguns, you must specify the population exactly. Are all U.S. residents included in the population, or only citizens? What minimum age will you insist on? In a similar sense, when you read a pre-election poll, you should ask what the population was: all adults, registered voters only, Democrats or Republicans only?

The distinction between population and sample is basic to statistics. Some examples will illustrate this distinction and introduce some major uses of sampling. These brief descriptions also indicate the variables to be measured for each unit in the sample. They do not state the sampling frame. Ideally, the sampling frame should be a list of all units in the population. But, as we shall see, obtaining such a list is one of the practical difficulties in sampling.

Example 1. *Public opinion polls,* such as those conducted by the Gallup and Harris organizations, are designed to determine public opinion on a variety of issues. The specific variables measured are responses to questions about public issues. Though most noticed at election time, these polls are conducted on a regular basis throughout the year. For the Gallup Poll,

Population: U.S. residents 18 years of age and over.
Sample: About 1800 persons interviewed weekly.

Example 2. *Market research* is designed to discover consumer preferences and usage of products. Among the better known examples of market research are the television rating services. One of these services uses as its sampling frame households listed in telephone directories. Note that a unit here is a household, not an individual person.

Population: All U.S. households.
Sample: About 1200 households weekly that agree to keep a "TV diary" when contacted by phone.

Example 3. *The decennial census** is required by the constitution. An attempt is made to collect basic information (number of occupants, their age, race, sex, and family relationship, etc.) from each household in the country. Much other information is collected, but only from a sample of households.

Population: All U.S. households.
Sample: The entire population (as far as possible) for basic information; only 5%, or 15%, or 20% of the population for other information.

Example 4. *Acceptance sampling* is the selection and careful inspection of a sample from a large lot of a product shipped by a supplier. On the basis

*"Decennial" means every ten years. A census has been taken every ten years since 1790. But beginning in 1985, a census also will be taken in the middle of each decade. Thus does the government's hunger for data grow. For more information on sampling by the Bureau of the Census, see Morris H. Hansen, "How to Count Better: Using Statistics to Improve the Census," in J. M. Tanur et al. (eds.), *Statistics: A Guide to the Unknown.* San Francisco: Holden Day, 1972.

of this, a decision is made whether to accept or reject the entire lot. The exact acceptance sampling procedure to be followed is usually stated in the contract between the purchaser and the supplier.

Population: A lot of items shipped by the supplier.
Sample: A portion of the lot that the purchaser chooses for inspection.

Example 5. *Sampling of accounting data* is a widely accepted accounting procedure. It is quite expensive and time-consuming to verify each of a large number of invoices, accounts receivable, spare parts in inventory, and so forth. Accountants therefore use a sample of invoices or accounts receivable in auditing a firm's records, and the firm itself counts its inventory of spare parts by taking a sample of it. A good example of this business use of sampling is the procedure for settling accounts among airlines for interline tickets. The passenger who takes a trip involving two or more carriers pays the first carrier, which then owes the other carriers a portion of the ticket cost. It is too expensive for the airlines to calculate exactly how much they owe each other, so only a sample of tickets is examined and accounts are settled on that basis.

Population: All interline air tickets purchased in a given month.
Sample: About 10% of these tickets used to settle accounts among
  airlines.

There are many more uses of sampling, some bordering on the bizarre. For example, a radio station that plays a song owes the song's composer a royalty. The organization of composers (called ASCAP) collects these royalties for all its members by charging stations a license fee for the right to play members' songs. But how should this income be distributed among the 20,000 members of ASCAP? By sampling: ASCAP tapes about 60,000 hours of local radio programs across the country each year. The tapes are shipped to New York, where ASCAP employs monitors (professional trivia experts who recognize nearly every song ever written) to record how often each song was played. This sample count is used to split royalty income among composers, depending on how often their music was played. Sampling is a pervasive, though usually hidden, aspect of modern life.

1.   The Need for Sampling Design

A *census* is a sample consisting of the entire population. If information is desired about a population, why not take a census? The first reason should be clear from the examples we have given: If the population is large, it is too expensive and time-consuming to take a census. Even the federal government, which can afford a census, uses samples to collect data on prices, employment, and many other variables. Attempting to take a census would result in this month's unemployment rate being available next year rather than next month.

There are also less obvious reasons for preferring a sample to a census. In some cases (such as acceptance sampling of fuses or ammunition) the units in the sample are destroyed. And in other cases a relatively small sample yields more accurate data than a census. This is true in developing nations that lack adequate trained personnel for a census. Even when personnel are available, a careful sample of an inventory of spare parts will almost certainly give more accurate results than asking the clerks to count all 500,000 parts in the warehouse. Bored people do not count accurately. The experience of the Census Bureau itself reminds us that a more careful definition of a census is "An *attempt* to sample the entire population." The Bureau estimates that the 1970 census missed 2.5% of the American population. These missing persons included an estimated 7.7% of the black population, largely in inner cities. So a census is not foolproof, even with the legal and financial resources of the government behind it.

Nevertheless, only a census can give detailed information about *every* small area of the population. For example, block-by-block population figures are required to create election districts with equal population. It is the main function of the decennial census to provide this local information.

So sample we must. Selecting a sample from the units available often seems simple enough, but this simplicity is misleading. If I were a supplier of oranges who sold your company several crates per week, you would be wise to examine a sample of oranges in each crate to determine the quality of the oranges supplied. You find it convenient to inspect a few oranges from the top of each crate. But these oranges may not be representative of the entire crate if, for example, those on the bottom are damaged more often in shipment. Your method of sampling might even tempt me to be sure that the rotten oranges are packed on the bottom with some good ones on top for you to inspect. Selection of whichever units of the population are easily accessible is called *convenience sampling*. Samples obtained in this way are often not representative of the population and lead to misleading conclusions about the population.

Convenience sampling occurs in situations less obvious than squeezing the oranges on the top of the crate. Suppose that we obtain a sample of public opinion by hiring interviewers and sending them to street corners and shopping centers to interview the public. The typical interviewer is a white middle-class female. She is unlikely to interview many working-class males, blacks, or others who are unlike her. Even if we assign the interviewer quotas by race, age, and sex, she will tend to select the best-dressed and least threatening members of each group. The result will be a sample that systematically overrepresents some parts of the population (persons of middle-class appearance) and underrepresents others. The opinions of such a convenience sample may be very different from those of the population as a whole. When a sampling method produces results that consistently and repeatedly differ from the truth about the population in the same direction, we say that the sampling method is *biased*. Convenience samples are often biased. Here are other examples of convenience sampling.

> **Example 6.** *Voluntary response* to a mail or television questionnaire elicits the opinions of those who feel strongly enough to respond. The opinions of this group are often systematically different from those of the population as a whole. For example, in 1972 a local television station asked viewers to send postcards indicating whether they favored or opposed President Nixon's decision to mine Haiphong harbor. Of those who responded, 5157 agreed with the decision and 1158 disagreed. It later developed that Nixon campaign workers had mailed about 2000 responses agreeing with his decision. "That type of voluntary poll is the most stackable thing," the Associated Press quoted a campaign spokesman as saying. "When you're involved in an election, you do what you can."[1]

> **Example 7.** The spacecraft Mariners 4, 6, and 7 flew past Mars in 1965 and the following years, photographing about 10% of that planet's surface. On the basis of this sample of its surface, Mars appeared to be a dead planet similar to the moon. Then in 1971–1972, Mariner 9 orbited Mars and photographed 85% of its surface. Mars was revealed as a varied world with natural features that appear to have been shaped by water. The earlier Mariner observations had been concentrated in an area of Mars not representative of the entire planet.

2.   Simple Random Sampling

A remedy for the "favoritism" usually caused by a convenience sample is to take a *simple random sample*. The essential idea is to give each unit in the sampling frame the same chance to be chosen for the sample as any other unit. For reasons to be explained later, the precise definition is slightly more complicated. Here it is.

> **A *simple random sample* of size n is a sample of n units chosen in such a way that every collection of n units from the sampling frame has the same chance of being chosen.**

We will abbreviate simple random sample as SRS. Notice that the definition concerns a property of the method for choosing the sample: A SRS is obtained by a method that gives *every* possible sample of size n the same chance of being the sample actually chosen. A SRS has a clear advantage over a convenience sample: It is fair or *unbiased.* No part of the sampling frame has any advantage over any other in obtaining representation in the sample. The definition of a SRS is designed to correct the overrepresentation of one part of the population often produced by convenience sampling.

Very well then, if a SRS is so useful a commodity, how do we actually obtain one? One way is to use *physical mixing:* Identify each unit in the sampling frame on an identical tag, mix the tags thoroughly in a box, then draw one blindly. If the mixing is truly complete, every tag in the box has the same chance of being chosen. The unit identified on the tag drawn is the first unit in our SRS. Now draw another tag without replacing the first. Again, if the mixing is thorough, every remaining tag has the same chance of being drawn. So every pair of tags has the same chance of being the pair we have now drawn; we have a SRS of size 2. To obtain a SRS of size *n,* we continue drawing until we have *n* tags corresponding to *n* units in the sampling frame. Those *n* units are a SRS of size *n.*

Physical mixing and drawing convey clearly the idea of a SRS. You should now grasp what it means to give each unit and each possible set of *n* units the same chance of being chosen. Physical mixing is even practiced on some occasions. But it is surprisingly difficult to achieve a really thorough mixing, as those who spend their evenings shuffling cards know. Physical mixing is also awkward and time-consuming. There is a better way, which I now introduce.

Picture a wheel (such as a roulette wheel) rotating on a smooth bearing so it does not favor any particular orientation when coming to rest. Divide the circumference of the wheel into ten equal sectors and label them 0, 1, 2, 3, 4, 5, 6, 7, 8, 9. Fix a stationary pointer at the wheel's rim and spin the wheel. Slowly and smoothly it comes to rest. Sector number 2 (say) is opposite the pointer. Spin the

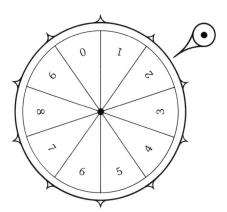

wheel again. It comes to rest with (say) sector number 9 opposite the pointer. If we continue this process, we will produce a string of the digits 0, 1, . . ., 9 in some order. On any one spin, the wheel has the same chance of producing each of these ten digits. And because the wheel has no memory, the outcome of any one spin has no effect on the outcome of any other. We are producing a table of random digits.

A *table of random digits* is a list of the ten digits 0, 1, 2, 3, 4, 5, 6, 7, 8, 9 having the following properties.

  1. **The digit in any position in the list has the same chance of being any one of 0, 1, 2, 3, 4, 5, 6, 7, 8, 9.**
  2. **The digits in different positions are independent in the sense that the value of one has no influence on the value of any other.**

Table A at the back of the book is a table of random digits. The division into groups of five digits and into numbered rows makes the table easier to read and use but has no meaning. The table is just a long list of digits having properties 1 and 2. The table of random digits was produced by a very careful physical mixing process, much more elaborate than the wheel I used to illustrate random digits. We can think of random digits as the result of someone else's careful physical mixing; our goal is to use their work in choosing a SRS rather than doing our own physical mixing. To use the table, we need the following facts about random digits, which are consequences of the basic properties 1 and 2.

  3. **Any *pair* of digits in the table has the same chance of being any of the 100 possible pairs 00, 01, 02, . . . , 98, 99.**
  4. **Any *triple* of digits in the table has the same chance of being any of the 1000 possible triples 000, 001, 002, . . . , 998, 999.**
  5. **And so on for groups of four or more digits from the table.**

How to use Table A to choose a SRS is best illustrated by a sequence of examples.

Example 8. A dairy products manufacturer must select a SRS of size 5 from 100 lots of yogurt to check for bacterial contamination. We proceed as follows.

(a) Label the 100 lots 00, 01, 02, . . . , 99 in any order.

(b) Enter Table A in any place and read systematically through it. We choose to enter line 111 and read across:

81486   69487   60513   09297.

(c) Read groups of two digits. Each group chooses a label attached to a lot of yogurt. Our SRS consists of the lots having labels

81, 48, 66, 94, 87.

This example illustrates the basic technique: Give the units in the sampling frame numerical labels and use Table A to choose a SRS of these labels. *It is essential that each label consist of the same number of digits.* In the example, each label consists of two digits. By property 3 of random digits, each pair of digits in Table A is then equally likely to choose any label. Two-digit labels are adequate for a sampling frame containing between 11 and 100 units. (If no more than 10 units must be labeled, one-digit labels can be used. If 101 to 1000 units must be labeled, three-digit labels are needed.) *Always use as few digits as possible in labels.* That is why we labeled the first lot of yogurt 00 instead of 01; there are 100 labels 00, 01, . . . , 99, so 100 units can be labeled with two digits if we start with 00. It is good practice to begin at zero rather than one even when all labels are not needed.

Suppose that the line of Table A used in the example had read

$$81486 \qquad 68186 \qquad 60513 \qquad 09297.$$

The first three lots chosen are those with labels 81, 48, and 66, as before. The next pair of digits in the table is 81. Because lot 81 is already in the sample, we *ignore repeated groups of digits* and go on to choose lots 86 and 60 to complete a SRS of size 5. You are now ready for a more difficult example.

> **Example 9.** A SRS of size 5 must be chosen from a group of 300 convicts who have volunteered to take part in a medical experiment. We proceed as follows.
>
> (a) List the convicts in some order (such as alphabetically). This list is the sampling frame.
>
> (b) Label the convicts 000, 001, . . . , 299.
>
> (c) Enter Table A at (say) line 116 and read across in three-digit groups. Each three-digit group 000 to 299 chooses a convict; each three-digit group 300 to 999 is not a label and is ignored. The result is:
>
> | | |
> |---|---|
> | 144 | 803 ignore |
> | 592 ignore | 716 ignore |
> | 605 ignore | 510 ignore |
> | 631 ignore | 362 ignore |
> | 424 ignore | 253 |
>
> and so on.

This example illustrates the fact that we must *ignore unused labels.* But we examined ten three-digit groups and succeeded in choosing only two convicts. It is much more efficient to give several labels to each unit in the sampling frame, being sure to give each unit the same number of labels. Let us redo the last example.

Example 10. A SRS of size 5 must be chosen from a group of 300 convicts who have volunteered to take part in a medical experiment. We proceed as follows.

(a) List the convicts in some order.

(b) Label the first convict 000, 300, and 600.

Label the second convict 001, 301, and 601.

- •
- •
- •

Label the last convict 299, 599, and 899.

(c) Enter Table A at line 116 and read across in three-digit groups. Choose a convict for the sample if any of his labels occur. The result is

144	convict 144 is in the sample
592	convict 292 is in the sample
605	convict 005 is in the sample
631	convict 031 is in the sample
424	convict 124 is in the sample.

Notice that the three labels given each convict in Example 10 are

1. the original label, between 000 and 299
2. the original label plus 300 (the number of units in the sampling frame)
3. the original label plus 600.

So label 592 is the same as label 592 − 300 = 292 and label 605 is the same as label 605 − 600 = 005. The labels 900 to 999 are not used, and are ignored if we come upon them in Table A.

3. Population Information from a Sample

Ann Landers once asked her readers, "If you had it to do over again, would you have children?" She received nearly 10,000 responses, almost 70% saying "NO!" Now this is an egregious example of voluntary response, as you should have recognized in doing Exercise 6 in Section 1. How egregious was suggested by a professional nationwide random sample commissioned by *Newsday*. That sample polled 1373 parents and found that 91% would have children again. To which a newspaper reporter responded, "Far be it from us to question the

"Hey, Pops, what was that letter you sent off to Ann Landers yesterday?"

validity of any statistic that we read in the papers, but in 1974 there were 54,917,000 families in America. This means we are talking somewhere in the neighborhood of a 1-in-50,000 sampling."[2] Leaving aside the reporter's poor arithmetic (1373 out of 54,917,000 families is 1-in-40,000, not 1-in-50,000), he has raised a perceptive question. We know why convenience sampling is unreliable, but why is a SRS reliable, especially when so small a fraction of the population is sampled?

Well, a SRS has no bias. In this case, the *Newsday* poll gave all parents the same chance of responding, rather than favoring those who were mad enough at their children to write Ann Landers. But lack of favoritism alone is not enough when we are asked to draw conclusions about 55 million families from results on only 1400 of them. We need to think more carefully about the process of gaining information about a population from a sample, starting with some new vocabulary.

The conclusions we wish to draw from a sample usually concern some numerical characteristic of the population, such as the fraction of American parents who would have children again, the average lifetime of General Electric 40-watt standard light bulbs, or the fraction of Princeton alumni who approve of coeducation. As always, we must distinguish between population and sample.

A *parameter* is a numerical characteristic of the *population*. It is a fixed number, but we usually do not know its value.

A *statistic* is a numerical characteristic of the *sample*. The value of a statistic is known when we have taken a sample, but it changes from sample to sample.

Put simply, parameter is to population as statistic is to sample. Both parameters and statistics are numbers. The distinction lies entirely in whether the number describes the population (then it is a parameter) or a sample (then it is a statistic). The fraction of all American parents who would have children again is a parameter describing the population of parents. Call it p. Alas, we do not know the numerical value of p. We usually use a sample statistic to estimate the unknown value of a population parameter. *Newsday,* in an attempt to estimate p, took a sample of 1371 parents. The fraction (call it $\hat{p}$) of the sample who would have children again is a statistic. If 1249 of this sample of size 1373 would do it again, then

$$\hat{p} = \frac{1249}{1373} = 0.91.$$

It is reasonable to use this sample proportion $\hat{p} = 0.91$ as an estimate of the unknown population proportion p, and that is exactly what *Newsday* did. But if *Newsday* took a second sample of size 1373, it is almost certain that there would *not* be exactly 1249 positive responses. So the value of $\hat{p}$ will vary from sample to sample. This is called *sampling variability.*

Aha! So what is to prevent one random sample from finding that 91% of parents would have children again and a second random sample from finding that 70% would not? After all, we just admitted that the statistic $\hat{p}$ wanders about from sample to sample. We are saved by a second property of random sampling, a property even more important than lack of bias: A sample statistic from a SRS has a predictable pattern of values in repeated sampling. This pattern is called the *sampling distribution* of the statistic. Knowledge of the sampling distribution allows us to make statements about how far the sample proportion $\hat{p}$ is likely to wander from the population proportion p owing to sampling variability.

To illustrate a sampling distribution, let us do an experiment. We will assume for now that the sampling frame contains *every* unit in the population. I have a box containing a large number of round beads, identical except for color. These beads are a population. The fraction of dark beads in the box is

$$p = 0.20,$$

and this number is a parameter describing this population of beads. I also have a paddle with 25 bead-sized indentations in it, so when I thrust it into the beads in the box, it selects a sample of 25 beads. If the beads in the box are well mixed, this is a SRS of size 25. Ask yourself a few questions about this SRS of size 25 from a population containing 20% dark beads.

- How many dark beads do you expect to appear in the sample?

- If I take several SRS's, do you expect to find a sample with 25 dark beads? One with no dark beads? One with as many as 15 dark beads?

You might reasonably expect about 20% of the beads in the sample to be dark, that is, about 5 dark beads among the 25 beads in the sample. But we will not always get exactly 5 dark beads. If we get (say) 4 dark beads, then the statistic

$$\hat{p} = \frac{4}{25} = 0.16$$

is still a good estimate of the parameter $p = 0.20$. But if we draw a sample with 15 dark beads, then

$$\hat{p} = \frac{15}{25} = 0.60$$

is a very bad estimate of p. How often will we get such poor estimates from a SRS?

I carried out this bead-sampling experiment 200 times and recorded the number of dark beads in each sample. (I was careful to return the sample to the population and stir the population after each repetition.) The results are shown in a table and pictorially in Figure 1. None of the 200 samples contained more

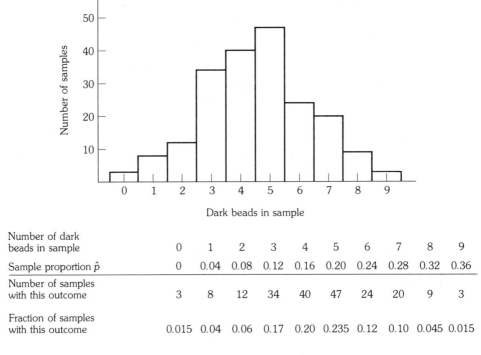

Number of dark beads in sample	0	1	2	3	4	5	6	7	8	9
Sample proportion $\hat{p}$	0	0.04	0.08	0.12	0.16	0.20	0.24	0.28	0.32	0.36
Number of samples with this outcome	3	8	12	34	40	47	24	20	9	3
Fraction of samples with this outcome	0.015	0.04	0.06	0.17	0.20	0.235	0.12	0.10	0.045	0.015

Figure 1. Results of 200 simple random samples of size 25 when $p = 0.20$.

than 9 dark beads. The sample proportion $\hat{p}$ did indeed vary from sample to sample; it ranged from 0 (no dark beads) to 0.36 (9 dark beads) when all 200 samples were examined. But estimates as bad as $\hat{p} = 0$ or $\hat{p} = 0.36$ (remember that the true p is 0.20 for this population) did not occur often. Of the 200 samples, 55% had either 4, 5, or 6 dark beads ($\hat{p}$ of 0.16, 0.20, or 0.24) and 83% had 3, 4, 5, 6, or 7 dark beads ($\hat{p}$ between 0.12 and 0.28).

In our experiment, we knew p. If p were not known, the same facts would hold. We could not guarantee that the sample statistic $\hat{p}$ is close to the unknown p (because of sampling variability), but we could be confident that it is close (because most of the time a SRS gives a $\hat{p}$ close to p). So the results of a SRS not only show no favoritism, but they tend to be repeatable from sample to sample. We need a final bit of vocabulary to describe the fact that lack of repeatability (the sample result wanders all over the barnyard) is as serious a flaw in a sampling method as is favoritism.

Because a sample is selected for the purpose of gaining information about a population, we mean by error in a sample an incorrect estimate of a population parameter by a sample statistic. Two basic types of error are associated with any method of collecting sample data.

Bias is consistent, repeated divergence of the sample statistic from the population parameter in the same direction.

Lack of precision means that in repeated sampling the values of the sample statistic are spread out or scattered. The result of sampling is not repeatable.

A common misunderstanding is to confuse bias in a sampling method with a strong trend in the population itself, especially if that trend is a reflection of prejudice or "bias" in the ordinary sense of that word. If, for example, 93% of a population of corporate personnel directors are opposed to the federal government's Affirmative Action hiring program, this is *not* bias in the statistical sense. It is simply a fact about this population.

We can think of the true value of the population parameter as the bullseye on a target, and of the sample statistic as a bullet fired at the bullseye. *Bias* means that our sight is misaligned and we shoot consistently off the bullseye in one direction. Our sample values do not center about the population value. *Lack of precision* means that repeated shots are widely scattered on the target. That is, repeated samples do not give similar results but differ widely among themselves.

This target illustration of the results of repeated sampling is shown in Figure 2. Notice that high precision (repeated shots are close together) can accompany high bias (the shots are consistently away from the bullseye in one direction). Notice also that low bias (the shots center on the bullseye) can accompany low precision (repeated shots are widely scattered). A good sampling scheme, like a good shooter, must have both low bias and high precision.

The sampling distribution of a statistic describes both its bias and its precision.

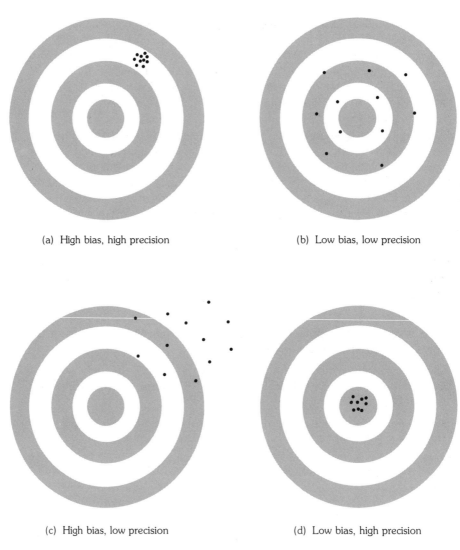

(a) High bias, high precision

(b) Low bias, low precision

(c) High bias, low precision

(d) Low bias, high precision

Figure 2. Bias and lack of precision in sample results.

For example, the precision of $\hat{p}$ as an estimator of p in Figure 1 can be expressed by a statement like "55% of SRS's of size 25 have a value of $\hat{p}$ within $\pm$ 0.04 of the true value of p." The shape of the distribution of values shown in Figure 1 is typical of a SRS. These distributions can be studied mathematically to save us the work of experimentation. As you might guess, such studies (and experiments as well) show that *increasing the size of the sample increases the precision of sample statistics.* If in our experiment we had used samples of size 100, about 74% of these samples would have sample proportions $\hat{p}$ within $\pm$ 0.04 of p.

Only one other fact about precision is needed to apply the coup de grâce to that newspaper reporter's skepticism about 1-in-40,000 samples: *The precision of a sample statistic does not depend on the size of the population, as long as the population is much larger than the sample.* In other words, the pattern of results from repeatedly thrusting my 25-bead paddle into a large box of beads does not depend on whether the box contains 1000 beads (as it did in my experiment) or 10,000 beads. The precision does depend on how many beads the paddle selects (sample size) and, to a lesser extent, on the fraction *p* of dark beads in the population.

This is good news for *Newsday*. Their sample of size 1373 has high precision because the sample size is large. That only 1-in-40,000 in the population were sampled is irrelevant. It is almost certain—Ann Landers to the contrary—that close to 91% of American parents would have children again. But the fact that the precision of a sample statistic depends on the size of the sample and not on the size of the population is bad news for anyone planning an opinion poll in a university or small city. For example, it takes just as large a SRS to estimate the proportion of Purdue University students who favor legalizing marijuana as to estimate with the same precision the proportion of all U.S. residents 18 and over who favor legalization. That there are about 30,000 Purdue students and about 150 million U.S. residents 18 and over does *not* mean that equally precise results can be obtained by taking a smaller SRS at Purdue.

The facts acquired here are the foundation for an understanding of the uses of sampling. In review, those facts are as follows.

1. **Despite the *sampling variability* of statistics from a SRS, the values of those statistics have a *known distribution* in repeated sampling.**

2. **When the sampling frame lists the entire population, simple random sampling produces *unbiased* estimates—the values of a statistic computed from a SRS neither consistently overestimate nor consistently underestimate the value of the population parameter.**

3. **The *precision* of a statistic from a SRS depends on the size of the sample and can be made as high as desired by taking a large enough sample.**

I have a closing confession to make: *Newsday* did not use a SRS to refute Ann Landers. Opinion polls use more complicated sampling methods—just how complicated will be seen in Section 5. But these sampling methods share the three basic properties listed, so that our conclusions about the Newsday poll are unchanged. The exact shape of the sampling distribution and the exact precision for any sample size depend on the sampling method. For a real-life example, consider Table 1, which describes the precision of the Gallup Poll's sampling procedure.

Table 1

PRECISION OF THE SAMPLING PROCEDURE
USED BY THE GALLUP POLL AS OF 1972*

Population percentage	Sample size						
	100	200	400	600	750	1000	1500
near 10	7	5	4	3	3	2	2
near 20	9	7	5	4	4	3	2
near 30	10	8	6	4	4	4	3
near 40	11	8	6	5	4	4	3
near 50	11	8	6	5	4	4	3
near 60	11	8	6	5	4	4	3
near 70	10	8	6	4	4	4	3
near 80	9	7	5	4	4	3	2
near 90	7	5	4	3	3	2	2

SOURCE: George Gallup, *The Sophisticated Poll Watcher's Guide* (Princeton Opinion Press, 1972), p. 228.

*The table shows the range, plus or minus, within which the sample percentage $\hat{p}$ falls in 95% of all samples. This margin of error depends on the size of the sample and on the population percentage p. For example, when p is near 60%, 95% of all samples of size 1000 will have $\hat{p}$ between 56% and 64% because the margin of error is ±4%.

4.   Sampling Can Go Wrong

The conclusions of the last section seem too good to be true. Most of us are aware of times when samples led to erroneous results, as when opinion polls predicted that Thomas Dewey would defeat Harry Truman in the 1948 presidential election. Alas, the glowing conclusions of the last section say only that errors from one source can be made small by properly conducted random sampling. These are *random sampling errors,* the deviations between sample statistic and population parameter caused by chance in selecting a random sample. When we are sampling beads or ball bearings or laboratory rats, random sampling error is our main problem, and it is an easy problem to deal with. That was the good news of Section 3. But, when we turn from sampling beads to sampling public opinion, consumer preferences, or personal habits, other sources of error become more serious than random sampling error in all but the smallest samples.

> **Sampling errors are errors caused by the act of taking a sample. They cause sample results to be different from the results of a census.**
>
> **Nonsampling errors are errors not related to the act of selecting a sample from the population and that might be present even in a census.**

Random sampling error is one kind of sampling error. *Nonrandom sampling errors* arise from improper sampling and have nothing to do with the chance selection in a SRS. One source of nonrandom sampling error is a biased sampling method, such as convenience sampling. Another common source of nonrandom sampling error is a sampling frame which itself differs systematically from the population. Even a SRS from such a frame will give biased conclusions about the population. Here are some examples of improper sampling.

> **Example 11.** *Telephone directories.* The two principal television rating services select their sample households at random from telephone directories. This sampling frame omits households having no telephone and those with unlisted numbers. Roger Rice, a San Francisco television station operator, charged several years ago that this sampling system underrepresents the poor and therefore that television ratings are biased; they underestimate the audience for programs of special interest to minorities.[3] Rice noted that in the San Francisco-Oakland area, about 62% of households have listed telephones, 25% have unlisted phones, and 13% have no telephone service. He said that the 1970 census for this area reported that about 57% of the population was white, whereas one of the television rating services used a sample which was 78% white. Chicano residents made up 14% of the population but only 1.2% of the rating service sample.

> **Example 12.** *Volunteer subjects.* Much behavioral research, especially in areas such as sexual habits, can use only subjects who volunteer to discuss their behavior or otherwise participate in the research. Although it is naturally hard to study persons who refuse to volunteer, there is evidence that the behavior of volunteers and nonvolunteers is quite different in many respects. Conclusions about a population that are based on a sample of persons in the population willing to volunteer may therefore be biased.[4]

Nonsampling errors, those which plague even a census, are often rooted in the perversity and complexity of human behavior. I will mention four types of nonsampling error: missing data, response errors, processing errors, and the effect of the data-collection procedure.

Missing data are due to inability to contact a subject or to the subject's refusal to respond. If subjects who cannot be contacted or who refuse to respond differ from the rest of the population, bias will result. For example, a survey conducted entirely during ordinary working hours will fail to contact households in which all adults work. Refusal to respond to survey questions is becoming more common. The American Statistical Association has estimated that in the 1960s about 15–20% of persons sampled refused to respond to nongovernmental surveys, but that 35–40% refused to respond in the mid 1970s. This growing emphasis on privacy is in many ways praiseworthy, but it threatens even random samples with the same bias caused by use of volunteer subjects.

Response errors concern the subject's own response. The subject may lie about her age or income. Or he may remember incorrectly when asked how many packs of cigarettes he smoked last week. Or a subject who cannot understand a question may give a faulty response out of fear of showing ignorance.

Processing errors are mistakes in such mechanical tasks as doing arithmetic, punching responses on computer cards, or coding the data (i.e., assigning numerical values to responses for data-processing purposes). These can be minimized by rechecking every mechanical task.

The effect of the method used to collect data can be large. Sometimes this effect clearly leads to errors in conclusions drawn about the population, as when black subjects speak less openly about their views on race relations to a white interviewer than they would to a black interviewer. Other times the effect of the data collection method cannot be called an error. The timing of a survey, for example, often affects its results. Thus in 1971 the National Football League sponsored a poll that showed football to be the nation's favorite spectator sport. The Commissioner of Baseball pointed out that the poll was taken a week before the Superbowl, and disputed its conclusions. Yet it is quite possible that the favorite spectator sport of Americans is football a week before the Superbowl and baseball during the World Series, so the poll was accurate even though its conclusions depend in part on timing.[5]

One important decision about the method of collecting data once a sample is chosen concerns the exact wording of questions. It is surprisingly difficult to word questions so they are completely clear. (A survey that asked about "ownership of stock" once found that most Texas ranchers owned stock, probably not the kind traded on the New York Stock Exchange.) What is more, small changes in the wording of questions can significantly change the responses received. In fact, it is easy to introduce a definite bias into a sample survey by slanting the questions. A favorite trick is to ask if the subject favors some policy as a means to a desirable end. "Do you favor banning private ownership of handguns in order to reduce the rate of violent crime?" and "Do you favor restoring capital punishment in order to reduce the rate of violent crime?" are loaded questions that draw positive responses from persons worried about crime.

Finally, a survey taker must decide whether to use mail, telephone, or personal interview to contact subjects. Mail surveys often have a low response rate. Because people with strong feelings on an issue are most likely to respond, a serious bias can result. Yet more people will express strongly negative opinions or "socially unacceptable" opinions by mail. Telephone surveys are fast, but 11% of American households have no telephone and AT&T estimates that 16% of all residential phones have unlisted numbers. What is more, many people will not speak openly about controversial issues or express negative opinions by telephone. Personal interviews allow a skillful interviewer to establish rapport with the subject; this results in a higher response rate and clearer communication of the questions. Personal interviews are much more expensive than mail or telephone contact, but with carefully trained interviewers this method introduces less bias than other methods of collecting data. Personal contact is used by

"Do I own any stock, Ma'am? Why, I've got 10,000 head out there."

government agencies to collect such information as unemployment rates, by the
major public opinion polls, and by most university survey workers.*
    Here are some examples of nonsampling errors.

> **Example 13.** *Race of interviewer.* In 1968, one year after a major racial
> disturbance in Detroit, a sample of black residents were asked:
>
> > "Do you personally feel that you can trust most white people, some
> > white people, or none at all?"
>
> Of those interviewed by whites, 35% answered "Most" while only 7% of
> those interviewed by blacks gave this answer. (Many questions were asked
> in this experiment. Only on some topics, particularly black-white trust or
> hostility, did the race of the interviewer have a strong effect on the answers

---

*Nonetheless, there is a surprising variation in the responses obtained by different interviewers. For
an account of this interviewer effect on responses to the decennial census, see Morris H. Hansen's
article in *Statistics: A Guide to the Unknown.*

given. Most sample surveys try to match the race of the interviewer to that of the subject.)[6]

Example 14. *Wording of questions.* To demonstrate the large effect sometimes caused by small changes in the wording of questions, a researcher asked a sample of citizens their opinion about a proposal to modify the Constitution to limit the president to one term in office. Some citizens were asked if they favored "adding to" the Constitution a one-term limit: 50% said "No." Others were asked if they favored "changing" the Constitution to include a one-term limit: 65% said "No."[7]

Example 15. *Mail versus interview.* In 1971 a sample of Boston Catholics were asked whether they favored making contraceptives available to unmarried women. Some subjects were interviewed in person, and 44% of these answered "Yes." Others were questioned by telephone or mail, and 75% of these answered "Yes." This is an example of reluctance to give a socially unacceptable response in a personal interview, but we might also suspect that fewer adherents to traditional Catholic morality returned the mail questionnaire.[8]

Example 16. *Processing error.* A famous professor of child development once did a study in which subjects were asked to respond to a question with one of

> strongly agree
>
> agree
>
> indifferent
>
> disagree
>
> strongly disagree.

These responses were coded as 0, 1, 2, 3, 4 in that order, and the data were analyzed by computer. The results were different from what was expected. Only after announcing these results at a professional meeting did the famous professor discover that by mistake his assistant had coded the responses in the reverse order: 4, 3, 2, 1, 0. The computer had obediently given conclusions that reversed the truth.

The moral of this presentation of possible errors in a conclusion drawn from sample is not that sampling is unreliable and untrustworthy. The moral is that great care is required in sampling human subjects, and that the statistical idea of using a SRS is not the cure for all possible ills. (It is an essential part of the cure, and for sampling ball bearings or accounting data it is most of the cure.) When you read or write an account of a sample survey, be sure that answers to the following questions are included.

- What was the *population?* That is, whose opinions were being sought?
- How was the sample *selected?* Look for mention of random sampling or probability sampling.
- What was the *size* of the sample? It is even better to give a measure of precision, such as the margin of error within which 95% of all samples drawn as this one was would fall.
- How were the subjects *contacted?* Personal interview is best.
- *When* was the survey conducted? Was it just after some event which might have influenced opinion?
- What were the *exact questions* asked?

The code of ethics of the American Association for Public Opinion Research (AAPOR) requires disclosure of this information. The major opinion polls always answer these questions in their press releases when announcing the results of a poll. But newspaper editors have the bad habit of cutting out the paragraphs containing these facts and printing only the lead paragraphs announcing the sample result. Government and academic surveys also always make this information available. If a politician or advertiser announces the results of a private poll without these facts, be suspicious.

5.   More on Sampling Design

By now you have absorbed the message that a reliable sample survey depends both on statistical ideas (random sampling) and on practical skills (wording questions, skillful interviewing, etc.). When our goal is to sample a large human population, using a SRS is good statistics but bad practice. First, a sampling frame is rarely available. Second, if we choose a SRS of 1600 U.S. residents for a public opinion poll, it would be a bit expensive to send interviewers off to Beetle, Kentucky and Searchlight, Nevada to find the lucky persons chosen. The solution to these practical difficulties is to use a sampling design more complicated than a SRS and "to sample not people but the map."[9]

Thus an opinion poll or market researcher or government office usually proceeds somewhat as follows. First select a SRS of counties, then a SRS of townships or wards within each county chosen. There is no difficulty in obtaining lists of counties and wards to serve as sampling frames for these two steps. Now, using a map or aerial photograph as the sampling frame, select a SRS of small areas (such as city blocks) within each ward chosen earlier. Finally, select a SRS of households in each small area chosen. This can be done by sending interviewers to the area to compile a list of households if none is available. Interview one adult from each household selected.

Such a *multistage sampling design* overcomes the practical drawbacks of SRS. We do not need a list of all U.S. households, only a list of households in the small areas arrived at by sampling counties, then wards, then areas within wards. Moreover, all the households in the sample are *clustered* within these few small areas, thus making it much cheaper to collect the data.

It is clear that the details of complicated sampling designs should be left to experts. (Strike a blow against poverty—hire a statistician.) But do note that such designs use the SRS as a building block. Our understanding of the basic ideas of sampling variability and sampling distributions applies to all properly designed sampling schemes. The all-inclusive statistical framework for sampling is called the *probability sample*.

> A *probability sample* is a sample chosen in such a way that every unit in the sampling frame has a known nonzero chance (or probability) of being chosen.

In a SRS, each unit has the *same* chance of being chosen. So a SRS is a probability sample, but there are other kinds of probability samples, many of which do not give each unit the same chance to be chosen. As long as each unit has a known chance, the results of repeated probability sampling have the same kind of predictability described for the SRS in Section 3. Let's illustrate the usefulness of probability samples by a much used sampling method.

> To obtain a *stratified random sample,* proceed as follows.
>
> *Step 1.* Divide the sampling frame into groups, called *strata,* of units. The strata are chosen because we have a special interest in these groups within the population or because the units in each stratum resemble each other.
>
> *Step 2.* Take a separate SRS in each stratum and combine these to make up the stratified random sample.

In a stratified random sample, units do not usually have equal chances to be chosen. Some strata are usually deliberately overrepresented in the sample. For example, if a poll of student opinion at a Big Ten university used a SRS of moderate size, there would probably be too few blacks in the sample to draw separate conclusions about black student opinion. By stratifying, we can take a SRS of black students and a separate SRS of other students and then combine them to make up the overall sample. If the university has 30,000 students, of which 3000 are black, we would expect a SRS of 500 students to contain only about 50 blacks. (Because 10% of the population is black, we expect about 10%

of a SRS to be black. Remember those beads in Section 3?) So we might instead take a stratified random sample of 200 blacks and 300 other students. The 200 blacks allow us to study black opinion with fair precision. You know how to choose the sample if you remember how to take a SRS: Use Table A to select a SRS of 200 of the 3000 blacks; then use Table A a second time to select a SRS of 300 of the other 27,000 students. Because 200 of the 3000 black students are selected, the chance that any one black student is chosen is

$$\frac{200}{3000} = \frac{1}{15}.$$

The chance that any one nonblack student is selected is

$$\frac{300}{27,000} = \frac{1}{90}.$$

So each student has a known chance to be chosen, but that chance is different for blacks and others. This is a probability sample, but not a SRS.

Stratified samples have two advantages. First, they allow us to gather separate information about each stratum. Second, if the units in each stratum are more alike in the variable measured than is the population as a whole, estimates from a stratified sample will be more precise than from a SRS of the same size. To grasp this, think about the extreme case when all the units in each stratum are exactly alike. Then a stratified sample of only one unit from each stratum would completely describe the population, but a SRS of the same size would have very low precision. Because of these advantages, stratified samples are widely used. The results of the Gallup Poll and the monthly unemployment rate are obtained from the kind of multistage sampling design we encountered earlier, but with stratified samples rather than SRS's at each stage. Counties, for example, might be stratified by population density and geographic location.

Another common use of stratification is in sampling economic units. Because the largest corporations, or farms, or bills payable are especially important, economic surveys usually stratify by size and sample a higher proportion of the larger units. Sometimes *all* the large units are chosen and only a sample of the smaller ones. This is a stratified sample where a census is taken in one stratum.*

There is a cloud over this beautiful landscape. If we deliberately overrepresent blacks in a sample of student opinion, or large corporations in a sample of business practices, won't that bias the sample results? Yes, indeed. Fortunately, because we arranged the sample, we can correct for this overrepresentation when we analyze the data. When properly analyzed, any probability sample

---

*See John Neter, "How Accountants Save Money by Sampling," in J. M. Tanur et al. (eds.), *Statistics: A Guide to the Unknown*, for an example of the use of such a sampling design by the Chesapeake and Ohio Railroad.

(multistage, with stratification and clustering, or whatnot) gives unbiased information about the sampling frame. Our conclusion: Any probability sample shares the essential characteristics of a SRS. These characteristics are twofold: sampling variability when repeated samples are drawn and long-run predictability, including lack of bias and increasing precision as the size of the sample increases.

The details of estimating a population parameter from sample data depend on the sampling method and can be quite complicated. Example 17 illustrates the estimation procedure for a stratified sample. The more important lesson to be learned from this example is that data can be analyzed correctly only when we know how they were collected.

Example 17. The Internal Revenue Service is said to use a stratified sampling design to choose income tax returns to be audited. (This is in addition to the auditing of suspicious returns.) The strata are groups of returns showing similar adjusted gross incomes. Suppose that a district IRS office has 1000 returns divided into three strata as follows:

Stratum	Size of stratum	Size of sample	Returns in sample showing fraud
1. (Under $15,000)	800	8	1
2. ($15,000—50,000)	190	7	1
3. (Over $50,000)	10	5	3
	1000	20	5

As the table shows, a stratified sample is selected by taking a SRS of 8 of the 800 returns in stratum 1, a SRS of 7 of the 190 returns in stratum 2, and a SRS of 5 of the 10 returns in stratum 3. In all, 20 of the 1000 returns are chosen. The last column in the table shows that five fraudulent returns were found in the audit of this sample.

It is foolish to estimate that because 5/20 or 25% of the returns in the sample showed fraud therefore about 25% of all 1000 returns show fraud. This is biased upward because we did not use a SRS but deliberately overrepresented the high-income returns, which appear to have a higher incidence of fraud. Instead, we analyze these data as follows:

1. Estimate the proportion of fraud in each stratum separately by using the SRS for that stratum.

$$\text{Stratum 1: Estimate } \hat{p} = 1/8.$$
$$\text{Stratum 2: Estimate } \hat{p} = 1/7.$$
$$\text{Stratum 3: Estimate } \hat{p} = 3/5.$$

2. Now estimate the *number* of fraudulent returns in each stratum by multiplying the estimated fraction of fraudulent returns by the size of the stratum. Add these together to estimate the total *number* of fraudulent returns in the population.

Stratum 1: Estimate $(800)(1/8) = 100$ bad returns.

Stratum 2: Estimate $(190)(1/7) = 27.2$ bad returns.

Stratum 3: Estimate $(10)(3/5) = 6$ bad returns.

Total estimate is $100 + 27.2 + 6 = 133.2$ bad returns. (We round this off to 133 returns.)

3. Now the estimated *proportion* of fraudulent returns in the population is

$$\hat{p} = \frac{133}{1000} \text{ or } 13.3\%.$$

This is much lower than the incorrect estimate of 25%, because we corrected for the overrepresentation of high-income returns in the sample. This method of estimation is *unbiased*—it will be correct on the average in many samples.*

It may be that you will never have the good fortune to participate in the design of a sample survey. But if you work in sociology, politics, advertising, marketing, or use government economic and social data, you will surely have to use the results of surveys. We can summarize our study in an outline of the steps in designing a sample survey.

Step 1. *Determine the population,* both its extent and the basic unit. If you are interested in buyers of new cars, your unit could be new car registrations, new car owners (individuals), or households that purchased new cars. You must also be specific about the geographic area and date of purchase needed to qualify a unit for this population.

Step 2. *Specify the variables to be measured* and prepare the questionnaires or other instruments you will use to measure them. Your decisions here are

---

*Some lovers of algebra might appreciate a formula for estimating a population proportion p from a stratified sample. Here it is. Suppose that a population of N units is divided into k strata, with stratum i containing N_i units. (So $N_1 + \cdots + N_k = N$.) We take a SRS of n_i units from stratum i and then combine these k SRS's to form a stratified random sample. The SRS from stratum i contains f_i fraudulent returns (or whatever it is we are counting). The estimate of p from this stratified sample is

$$\hat{p} = [\frac{N_1 f_1}{n_1} + \cdots + \frac{N_k f_k}{n_k}]/N$$

I do not wish to stress the technique of Example 17, let alone this formula. I do stress the importance of knowing how data were gathered.

related to those made at Step 1. If you seek information about the income of households buying new cars (so household income is your variable), then the unit must be a household rather than an individual or a new car.

Step 3. *Set up the sampling frame.* This again is related to Step 1. If you use a list of new car registrations as a sampling frame (because this list is easy to obtain), households who bought several new cars will appear several times on the list. So a SRS of registrations will not be a SRS of households. (I bought a new car in 1974. The retiring president of General Motors, to express his confidence in the industry in a year of poor sales, bought *five* new GM cars that year. His household is five times as likely as mine to appear in a SRS of 1974 new car registrations.)

Step 4. *Do the statistical design* of the sample, specifying how large the sample will be and how it will be chosen from the sampling frame.

Step 5. *Attend to details* like training interviewers and arranging the timing of the survey.

Much more might be said about each of these steps. A good deal is known about how to word questions, how to train interviewers, how to increase response in a mail survey, and so on. Much of this is interesting, and some is slightly amusing; for example, colorful commemorative stamps on the outer and return envelopes greatly increase the response rate in a mail survey. But a sample survey would show that you already know more about sampling than 99.9% of U.S. residents aged 18 or over. Enough is enough.

6. Opinion Polls and the Political Process

Public opinion polls, especially pre-election "For whom would you vote?" polls, are the most visible example of survey sampling. They are also one of the most controversial. Most people are happy that sampling methods make employment and unemployment information rapidly available, and few people are upset when marketers survey consumer buying intentions. But the sampling of opinion on candidates or issues is sometimes strongly attacked as well as strongly praised. We will briefly explore three aspects of polls and politics. First, polls of public opinion on issues. Second, polls as a tool used by candidates seeking nomination or election. Third, pre-election polls for public consumption, designed to satisfy our curiosity as to who's ahead and by how much.

Polls on public issues (defense spending, gun control, legalization of marijuana) are praised as the only way our representatives can know what the people think. You now have the background to understand why other means (such as mail for and against) are unreliable, and why surveys such as the Gallup Poll give accurate information about public opinion. Legislators are constantly under pressure by special interest groups who back their interests with lobbyists and campaign contributions. Opinion polls give the general public a chance to

*"Seventy-three percent are in favor of one through five,
forty-one percent find six unfair, thirteen percent are opposed
to seven, sixty-two percent applauded eight, thirty-seven percent . . ."*

offset this pressure. As George Gallup says, "The modern poll can beam a bright and devastating light on the gap which too often exists between the will of the people and the translation of this will into law by legislators."* Not only that, but such open-ended questions as "What do you consider to be the most urgent problems facing our country today?" can reveal areas of public concern that otherwise would be only vaguely sensed. In short, public opinion is an essential part of democratic government. Polls express this opinion accurately; the alternative is vague impressions and the loud voices of special interests.

_____

*George Gallup, "Opinion Polling in a Democracy," in *Statistics: A Guide to the Unknown.*

Intelligent arguments against polling do not dispute that modern sampling methods guarantee that the polls will give results close to the results we would get if we put the poll questions to the entire population. Some would argue against opinion polls on the ground that we elect representatives to use their best judgment, not to slavishly follow public opinion. This seems to be no argument against polls; they only inform our governors what the opinion of the governed is and cannot force them to follow it.

More thoughtful critics ask what the opinions revealed by the polls are worth. Leo Bogart has written a provocative book that raises this very question.[11] He points out that many citizens will not have thought about an issue until a poller questions them. Unwilling to appear ignorant or uncaring, they will give hasty and uninformed answers. A question put by an interviewer who appears at the door as you were planning supper, a question with no responsibility attached to answering it, will get a low quality opinion. As Bogart says, "We are likely to answer questions differently when we know the decision is really up to us." He doubts that the 62% of Americans who favored using atomic artillery shells against the Chinese Communists in a 1954 Gallup Poll would give the same answer if seriously faced with starting a nuclear war. If not all opinions are of equal weight, because some are uninformed and some are flippant, then "public opinion" is not the sum of individual opinions reported by the polls.

What is more, public opinions and attitudes are complex, not easily gauged by a few questions. Because of this (and because some of our answers to a poll lack serious thought), polls sometimes produce contradictory answers to related questions. Bogart points out that in 1969 over half of one sample favored President Nixon's anti-ballistic missile program, but over half of a second sample thought the money could be better spent on education, health, and other needs. What *is* public opinion, anyway? That's a question worth pondering.

Opinion polls conducted privately by candidates are now a common tool of campaign strategy. This is the second area of impact of polls on politics. The purpose of these polls is information for more effective campaigning. In what areas and with what groups of voters is the candidate weak? Where are large numbers of uncommitted voters to be found? Which of the opponent's views are liabilities to be exploited? What arguments are most effective in advocating the candidate's views? You might argue that campaigners have always sought such information, and that sampling methods only replace vague impressions and intuition by reliable estimates.

Yet polls are sometimes viewed as part of the transformation of campaigns into exercises in marketing—selling the candidate to the consumers. By market research (sample surveys), the campaign manager discovers what the voters want, then, using all the devices of advertising and sales promotion, cleverly presents the candidate as satisfying those wants.

Most political professionals feel that attempting to present the candidate in a false light to fit voter preferences will fail. It is better politics to use poll results as guides in presenting the candidate's real views and concerns most effectively. If this is true, we as voters need not be alarmed by survey sampling as a campaign tool. As with any tool, it can be used unethically, but the ethical problem is the user rather than the tool. With attention, we should be able to accurately judge the candidate's programs and intentions.

Polls as election predictors are the third, and most dubious, political use of polls. I speak here of the results that fill the news before each election, informing us that Senator so-and-so is the choice of 58% of Ohio voters. Such polls are certainly popular, as they speak to our wish to know the future. The public is entitled to have its wants satisfied (within reasonable limits), so pre-election polls will probably always be with us. Notice also that election polls do not have the drawbacks of opinion research. In an election poll, as in the voting booth, we are presented with a clear choice in an area where the decision is really up to us.

But election forcasts are somewhat shaky statistically, and some people think they have undesirable political effects. Let us examine both of these problems.

The key question asked in pre-election polls takes the form "If the election were held today, would you vote for X or Y?" Here is the exact question from the 1976 Gallup Poll presidential election questionnaire:

Suppose you were voting TODAY for President and Vice President of the United States. Here is a Gallup Poll Secret Ballot listing the candidates for these offices. Will you please MARK that secret ballot for the candidates you favor today—and then drop the folded ballot into the box.

"Suppose you were voting today. . .". Modern sampling methods give us great confidence that the sample result for the Gallup Poll of October 27, 1972 (59% would vote for Nixon and Agnew, 36% would vote for McGovern and Shriver, and 5% are undecided) was close to the truth about the population on that date. But the election is not being held today, and minds may change between the poll and the election. What is more, some of those who said for whom they would vote today will not take the trouble to vote for anyone on election day. Gallup and other pollsters make great efforts to determine how strongly their respondents hold their preferences and how likely they are to vote. For example, the 1976 Gallup Poll questionnaire included such questions as:

- Where do people who live in this neighborhood go to vote?
- Are you NOW registered so that you can vote in the election this November?
- Do you, yourself, plan to vote in the election this November, or not?

But the problems of changing opinions and low voter turnout cannot be entirely avoided, especially in primary elections. Election forecasting is one of the less satisfactory uses of sampling.

Changing opinions were a major cause of the polls' famous failure in the 1948 Dewey–Truman election. The last poll was conducted three weeks before the election. It is likely (as the polls indicated) that Dewey was leading at the time, but Truman was gaining fast and continued to gain, winning an extremely close election. The other major cause of error was the sampling method. Interviewers were given quotas of voters by age, race, sex, and economic status, but selection of individual subjects was left to the interviewer. Such quota samples are far better than "straw polls" that depend on voluntary response, but they are not probability samples. We saw in Section 1 that such quotas favor the well dressed and respectable. In political terms, such a poll has a Republican bias. Gallup and others overestimated the Republican vote in every election from 1936 to 1948, and in the close 1948 election this bias caused an incorrect forecast of a Republican victory.

The opinion polls switched to probability samples after 1948, and computers now enable the final poll to be taken three days rather than three weeks before the election. Despite the problem of failure to vote, election forecasts are now quite accurate; though when the margin of sampling error is taken into account, the election may still be too close to call.

The political effects of election forecasts are much debated. Nobody maintains that they have any major beneficial effects. Here are some of the alleged disadvantages. Voters may decide to stay home if the polls predict a landslide—why bother to vote if the result is a foregone conclusion? There is little evidence for this claim. But there is clear evidence that contributions dry up when the polls show that a candidate is weak. In particular, polls taken far in advance can make it difficult for a little-known candidate to gather resources for primary election campaigns. Such a candidate may do well if, despite the polls, resources are found for an effective campaign that captures the attention of the voters. The charge is that the effect of polls on both candidates and contributors may be to encourage them to act on practical calculations rather than on their convictions.

In reply, note that voters and contributors are likely to react only when the polls show a one-sided contest—a state of affairs that is clear even without polls. Potential contributors surely know that an unknown candidate is unknown. McGovern or Goldwater supporters surely knew that they were the minority. I see no substantial reason to fret over the effects of election forecasts. What is your opinion?

7. Random Selection as Public Policy

On January 23, 1976 the draft died, remembered but not mourned by the 50 million men who had been registered since Selective Service was initiated in 1948. Of these 50 million men, less than 5 million were inducted into the armed forces between 1948 and the end of inductions in 1972. Because only about 1 in 10 were actually drafted, how should the choice be made? For many years an involved system of deferments, exemptions, and quotas was followed, with final decisions lying in the hands of local draft boards. But beginning in 1970 a draft lottery was introduced to choose draftees by random selection.

The idea of random selection is that of drawing lots—or of taking a SRS. The goal is to treat everyone identically by giving all the same chance to be selected. Random selection for military service was used during parts of World Wars I and II, and lotteries have been employed or proposed for other public policy purposes. A panel of the National Heart and Lung Institute predicted in 1973 that artificial hearts might be available within 10 years. Because as many as 50,000 patients a year might be helped by such a device, which might cost $25,000 (installed), the demand will exceed the supply. Who should receive them? The panel recommended that recipients be selected randomly from the pool of persons meeting similar medical criteria. Random selection has been used already to allot space in public housing to eligible applicants when there are more applicants than available housing units.

When should random selection decide public issues? I claim that this is a policy question, not a statistical question. Random selection does treat everyone identically; it is fair or unbiased in that sense. If a policy of identical treatment is desired, random selection is the tool that will implement that policy. Debate over random selection should concentrate on whether or not distinctions among persons are desirable in a certain situation. With the draft, Congress felt that distinctions ought not to be made, and so requested random selection. In the case of allotting public housing, a federal court has ruled that random selection is allowed only when applicants are equally needy. Distinctions *are* to be made among different degrees of need, so random selection is inappropriate for the entire pool of eligible applicants.

How is random selection carried out? In principle, the same way that a SRS is selected: Label everyone in the pool and use a table of random digits to select at random as many persons from the pool as are needed. In practice, random digits are not used. Instead, physical mixing and drawing of labels is used, for public relations reasons. Because few people understand random digits, the draft lottery looks fairer if a dignitary chooses capsules from a glass bowl in front of the TV cameras. This also prevents cheating; no one can check the table of random digits in advance to see how cousin Joe will make out in the selection.

Physical mixing *looks* random, but you may recall from Section 2 that it is devilishly hard to achieve a mixing that *is* random. There is no better illustration of this than the 1970 draft lottery. Because a SRS of all eligible men would be hopelessly awkward, the draft lottery aimed to select birth dates in a random order. Men born on the date chosen first would be drafted first, then those born on date number 2, and so on. Because 1952 (the birth year of men who turned eighteen in 1970) was a leap year, 366 birth dates were to be drawn. Here is an account of the 1970 lottery.[11]

> They started out with 366 cylindrical capsules, one and a half inches long and one inch in diameter. The caps at the ends were round.
> The men counted out 31 capsules and inserted in them slips of paper with

the January dates. The January capsules were then placed in a large square wooden box and pushed to one side with a cardboard divider, leaving part of the box empty.

The 29 February capsules were then poured into the empty portion of the box, counted again, and then scraped with the divider into the January capsules. Thus, according to Captain Pascoe, the January and February capsules were thoroughly mixed.

The same process was followed with each subsequent month, counting the capsules into the empty side of the box and then pushing them with the divider into the capsules of the previous months.

Thus, the January capsules were mixed with the other capsules 11 times, the February capsules 10 times and so on with the November capsules intermingled with others only twice and the December ones only once.

The box was then shut, and Colonel Fox shook it several times. He then carried it up three flights of stairs, a process that Captain Pascoe says further mixed the capsules.

The box was carried down the three flights shortly before the drawing began. In public view, the capsules were poured from the black box into the two-foot deep bowl.

You can guess what happened. Dates in January tended to be on the bottom, while birth dates in December were put in last and tended to be on top. Newspaper reporters noticed at once that men born later in the year seemed to receive lower draft numbers, and statisticians soon showed that this trend was so

"So you were born in December too, eh?"

strong that it would occur less than once in a thousand years of truly random lotteries. An inquiry was made, which produced the account quoted.

What's done is done, and off to Vietnam went too many men born in December of 1952. But for 1971, the captain and the colonel were given other duties, and statisticians from the National Bureau of Standards were asked to design the lottery. Their design was worthy of Rube Goldberg. The numbers 1 to 365 (no leap year in 1953) were placed in capsules in a random order determined by a table of random digits. The dates of the year were placed in another set of capsules in a random order determined again by the random digit table. Then the date capsules were put into a drum in random order determined by a third use of the table of random digits. And the number capsules went into a second drum, again in random order. The drums were rotated for an hour. The TV cameras were turned on, and the dignitary reached into the date drum: Out came September 16. He reached into the number drum: Out came 139. So men born on September 16 received draft number 139. Back to both drums: Out came April 27 and draft number 235. And so on. It's awful, but it's random.[12] You can now rejoice that in choosing samples we have Table A to do the randomization for us.

8.   Some Ethical Questions

Whenever our activities impinge on others (as they usually do), those activities should be carried on with sensitivity to their effects. Sampling of human populations is therefore a possible source of ethical problems. In general, the ethical problems posed by sample surveys are much less severe than those arising in experimentation with human subjects. This is because an experiment imposes some treatment (such as a new drug for a medical symptom), while a sample survey only seeks information or opinion from the respondents. Many ethical problems of survey work concern *deceiving respondents;* very rarely is any physical harm possible.

At one extreme of deceit is the use of false pretenses, as when encyclopedia salespersons pretend to be taking a survey in order to gain access to homes. This fraud has little to do with actual survey work and is detested by users of sample surveys because it increases resistance to genuine polling. Another extreme is covert collection of information. Covert operations are not limited to spy rings. Social psychologists, for example, have gathered data by "infiltrating" small religious groups under the pretense of sincere membership. Spies and researchers both give the same rationale for violation of privacy: The information they desire cannot be obtained by other methods. The moral problem is to decide when the information sought justifies such deceit.

Some withholding of information from subjects is often essential to avoid bias. A political poll sponsored by a candidate cannot tell subjects who is paying, for knowing that a representative of the Senator X Committee stood before us would influence our answers. Academic survey workers sometimes cannot tell subjects the full purpose of their research for the same reason. This withholding of information does not amount to active deceit, but certain safeguards are called for. The political poll representative should provide subjects with the name, address, and telephone number of the polling organization so the subject has an avenue of recourse if the poll or its taker are offensive. (The polling organization must have a neutral name to avoid bias. This is easy if the candidate has hired a professional pollster, and is otherwise accomplished by setting up a polling office separate from the campaign office.) The academic researcher can inform subjects of the full purpose (and sometimes the results) of the research after the fact, thus providing the information that could not be given in advance. In any case, potential respondents always must be told how much time the interview will require, what kinds of information are wanted, and how widely this information will circulate with or without personal identification. Only then can the subject make an informed decision to participate or not.

A second area of ethical problems in sampling work is *anonymity and confidentiality*. These are not identical. Anonymity means that the respondent is anonymous; his or her name is not known even to the sampler. Anonymity causes severe problems because it is then not known who responded to a poll and who did not. This means that no follow-up work can be done to increase the

"I realize the participants in this study are to be anonymous, but you're going to have to expose your eyes."

response rate. And of course anonymity is usually possible only in mail surveys, where responses can be mailed in without any identification.

Confidentiality means that each individual response will be kept confidential, that only sample statistics from the entire sample or parts of it will be made public. Confidentiality is a basic requirement of most survey work, and any breach of confidentiality is a serious violation of professional standards. The best practice is to separate the identity of the respondent from the rest of the data at once and use the identification only to check on who did or did not respond.

Some common practices, however, seem to promise anonymity while actually delivering only confidentiality. Market researchers often use mail surveys that do not ask the respondent's identity but contain hidden codes on the questionnaire that do identify the respondent. Invisible ink coding and code numbers hidden under the flap of the return envelope are the usual techniques. A false claim of anonymity is clearly unethical; but if only confidentiality is promised, is it also unethical to hide the identifying code, thus perhaps causing respondents to believe their replies are anonymous? Here is a story to frame the question.

In 1975, *The National Observer* hired a survey firm to mail a detailed questionnaire to a sample of that newspaper's subscribers. The paper desired information about the tastes and lifestyle of its audience to aid its planning and advertising. The survey form was headed "A confidential survey" and was accompanied by a letter from the editor, Henry Gemmill, stating: "Each individual reply will be kept confidential, of course, but when your reply is combined with others from all over this land, we'll have a composite picture of our subscribers." Confidentiality was promised and observed. But because name and address were not requested, an impression of anonymity was created. One member of the sample, an optics professor, used ultraviolet light to detect an invisible ink code and wrote Gemmill a letter of complaint. Gemmill did not know that a hidden code had been used, and he reacted with outrage. He called it "slick trickery" in an article apologizing to subscribers. Gemmill also discovered that most market researchers felt that hidden codes were ethical as long as confidentiality was promised and observed. University survey researchers felt that hidden identification was not ethical, and that open identification of respondents should be used to make follow-up possible. Some of the market researchers felt that this would reduce the response rate. What do you think?[13]

The *use of information* is the final area I wish to question. A rigorous standard would require public availability of all poll results. Otherwise, the possessors of poll results can use the information gained to their own advantage. This may involve acting on the information, releasing only selected parts of it, or timing the release for best effect. Private polls taken for political candidates are often used in these ways. Is it unrealistic to ask complete disclosure of poll results?

Whatever our response to this question, some aspects of disclosure are agreed upon. The information about the sampling process required by the AAPOR code of ethics (examined at the end of Section 4) should be revealed whenever a sample result is announced. Most survey workers think that who paid for the poll should also be announced, though this is not required by the AAPOR code. After all, we might more carefully inspect a poll paid for by a political party or other interest group than a poll sponsored by a news organization or other neutral party.

Potential abuses certainly exist in sampling, and we shall meet more difficult ethical problems in studying statistically designed experiments. These abuses and problems should not blind us to the fact that decisions based on incorrect information surely cause far more hardship. Because the statistical ideas we have met reduce the chance of incorrect information being used by decision makers, their overall ethical impact seems to me to be positive.

NOTES

1. Associated Press dispatch appearing in the *Lafayette Journal and Courier* of April 26, 1973.
2. From an article by Michael Kernan of *The Washington Post,* printed in the *Lafayette Journal and Courier* of August 19, 1976.
3. Rice's speech reported in *The New York Times* of February 19, 1974.
4. The evidence on this issue is discussed at length in Robert Rosenthal and Ralph L. Rosnow, *The Volunteer Subject* (New York: Wiley, 1975).
5. This controversy is discussed in an article in *The New York Times* of February 1, 1972.
6. Reported in *Public Opinion Quarterly,* Volume 35 (1971–1972), p. 54.
7. Reported by Charles Roll and Albert Cantrill, *Polls—Their Use and Misuse in Politics* (New York: Basic Books, 1972), p. 107.
8. Reported in *Public Opinion Quarterly,* Volume 36 (1972), p. 107.
9. These are the words of John B. Lansing and James N. Morgan, *Economic Survey Sampling* (Institute for Social Research, The University of Michigan, 1971). This book is an excellent source of practical advice on carrying out sample surveys.
10. Leo Bogart, *Silent Politics: Polls and the Awareness of Public Opinion* (New York: Wiley-Interscience, 1972).
11. From *The New York Times* of January 4, 1970. Quoted with extensive discussion by Stephen E. Fienberg, "Randomization and Social Affairs: The 1970 Draft Lottery," *Science,* Volume 171 (1971), pp. 255–261.
12. It's even a little more complicated than I've described. For all the details, see Joan R. Rosenblatt and James J. Filliben, "Randomization and the Draft Lottery," *Science,* Volume 171 (1971), pp. 306–308.
13. The details in the text are taken from Henry Gemmill, "The Invisible Ink Caper," in *The National Observer* of November 1, 1975.

Exercises

Section 1

In each of Exercises 1–4, briefly identify the *population* (what is the basic unit and which units fall in the population?), the *variables* measured (what is the information desired?), and the *sample*. If the situation is not described in enough detail to completely identify the population, complete the description of the population in a reasonable way. Be sure that from your description it is possible to tell exactly when a unit is in the population and when it is not.

Moreover, each sampling situation described in Exercises 1–4 contains a serious source of probable bias. In each case, discuss the *reason* you suspect that bias will occur and also the *direction* of the likely bias. (That is, in what way will the sample conclusions probably differ from the truth about the population?)

1. A national newspaper wanted Iowa's reaction to President Johnson's agricultural and foreign policy in early 1968. A reporter interviewed the first 50 persons willing to give their views, all in a single voting precinct. The headline on the resulting article read "Johnson Policies Disenchant Iowa," and the reporter wrote that he would lose an election in Iowa if one were held then.

2. A Congressman is interested in whether his constituents favor a proposed gun control bill. His staff reports that letters on the bill have been received from 361 constituents and that 283 of these oppose the bill.

3. A flour company wants to know what fraction of Minneapolis households bake some or all of their own bread. A sample of 500 residential addresses is taken, and interviewers are sent to these addresses. The interviewers are employed during regular working hours on weekdays, and interview only during those hours.

4. The Chicago Police Department wants to know how black residents of Chicago feel about police service. A questionnaire with several questions about the police is prepared. A sample of 300 mailing addresses in predominantly black neighborhoods is chosen, and a police officer is sent to each address to administer the questionnaire to an adult living there.

5. You have probably seen the printer's filler ETAOINSHRDLU resulting from running a finger across a linotype keyboard. These are said to be the most frequently occurring letters in English. How do English and German differ in the frequency with which these letters occur? Open a book of English prose and a book of German prose haphazardly. Record how often each of these 12 letters occurs in the first 100 letters on the page you open to in each book.

    What is the population in this sampling exercise? What is the sample? What are the variables measured? Does the sampling method contain any serious sources of bias?

6. The advice columnist Ann Landers was once asked by a young couple whether having children was worth the problems involved. She asked her readers, "If you had it to do over again, would you have children?" A few weeks later, her column was headlined "70% OF PARENTS SAY KIDS NOT WORTH IT," for indeed 70 percent of the parents who wrote said they would not have children if they could make the choice again. (From the *Lafayette Journal and Courier* of January 23, 1976.) Do you think that this sample is biased? Why, and in what direction?

Section 2

1. Use Table A (Random Digits, p. 308) to select a SRS of 3 of the following 25 volunteers for a drug test. Be sure to say where you entered the table and how you used it.

Agarwal	Garcia	Petrucelli
Andrews	Healy	Reda
Baer	Hixson	Roberts
Berger	Lee	Shen
Brockman	Lynch	Smith
Casella	Milhalko	Sundheim
Frank	Moser	Wilson
Fuest	Musselman	
Fuhrmann	Pavnica	

2. A food processor has 50 large lots of canned mushrooms ready for shipment, each labeled with one of the lot numbers below.

A1109	A2056	A2219	A2381	B0001
A1123	A2083	A2336	A2382	B0012
A1186	A2084	A2337	A2383	B0046
A1197	A2100	A2338	A2384	B0123
A1198	A2108	A2339	A2385	B0124
A2016	A2113	A2340	A2390	B0125
A2017	A2119	A2351	A2396	B0138
A2020	A2124	A2352	A2410	B0139
A2029	A2125	A2367	A2411	B0145
A2032	A2130	A2372	A2500	B0151

A SRS of 5 lots must be chosen for inspection. Use Table A to do this, beginning at line 139.

3. A SRS of 25 of 440 voting precincts in a metropolitan region must be chosen for special voting-fraud surveillance on election day. Explain clearly how you would label the precincts. Then use Table A to choose the SRS, and list the precincts you selected. Enter Table A at line 117.

4. The following page contains a population of 80 circles. (They might represent fish in a pond or tumors removed in surgery.) Do a sampling experiment as follows.

    (a) Label the circles 00, 01, . . . , 79 in any order, and use Table A to draw a SRS of size 4.

    (b) Measure the diameter of each circle in your sample. (All of the circles have diameters that are multiples of 1/8 inch for convenience. So record the diameters as 1/8, 2/8, 3/8, etc.) Now compute the *mean*

diameter of the four circles in your sample. (The mean of the diameters d_1, d_2, d_3, d_4 is the ordinary average

$$\frac{d_1 + d_2 + d_3 + d_4}{4}.$$

Because (4) (8) = 32, it is easiest to record the mean in 1/32 of an inch.)

(c) Now repeat steps (a) and (b) three more times (four times in all) by using different parts of Table A. Was any circle chosen more than once in your four SRS's? How different were the mean diameters for the four samples?

(d) Now draw a SRS of size 16 from this population by taking a part of Table A not yet used in this exercise. Measure the diameters of the 16 circles in your sample and find the mean (average) diameter. (Because (16) (8) = 128, it is easiest to record this mean in 1/128 of an inch.) Your results for SRS's of size 4 and 16 can be combined with those of the rest of the class to produce two pictures like Figure 1. These pictures show less sampling variability for means of samples with size 16 than for samples with size 4.

5. Another way to sample the population of circles in Exercise 4 is as follows. Close your eyes and drop your pencil point at random onto the page. Do this until you have hit 4 circles.

(a) Is this (at least approximately) a SRS of size 4? Why or why not?

(b) Think of these circles as cross sections of trees at breast height above the ground. Foresters who want to estimate the total volume of wood in a woodlot use a sampling method that has the same effect as dropping a pencil point onto the circles. Can you explain why this is done?

6. Figure 3 is a map of a census tract in Cedar Rapids, Iowa. [I took this map from *A Student's Workbook on the 1970 Census* (U.S. Department of Commerce, 1975), p. 8. Statistics buffs will find this thin booklet interesting.] Census tracts are small, homogenous areas averaging 4000 in population. A SRS of blocks from a census tract is often the penultimate stage in a sample survey. Use Table A beginning at line 125 to choose a SRS of 5 blocks from this tract. Note that each block has a Census Bureau identification number on the map.

Section 3

Each boldface number in Exercises 1–3 is the value of either a *parameter* or a *statistic*. In each case, state which is correct.

1. The Bureau of Labor Statistics announces that last month it interviewed a

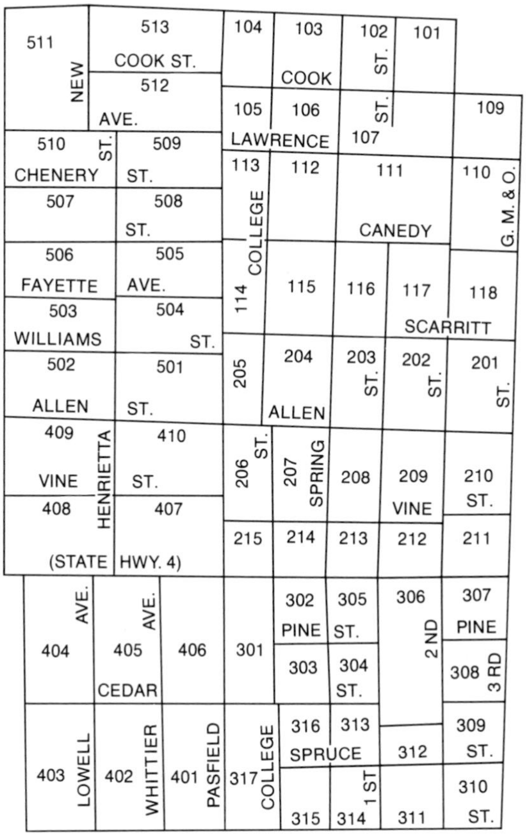

Figure 3

sample of 50,000 members of the labor force, of which **6.5%** were unemployed.

2. A carload lot of ball bearings has an average diameter of **2.503** cm. This is within the specifications for acceptance of the lot by the purchaser. But the acceptance sampling procedure happens to inspect 100 bearings from the lot with an average diameter of **2.515** cm. This is outside the specified limits, so the lot is mistakenly rejected.

3. A telephone sales outfit in Los Angeles uses a device that dials residential phone numbers in that city at random. Of the first 100 numbers dialed, **23** are unlisted numbers. This is not surprising because **38%** of all Los Angeles residential phones are unlisted.

4. Figure 1 is a graph of the values of a sample statistic in 200 samples when the population parameter has the same value. Bias and lack of precision can be seen pictorially in such a graph of the sampling distribution as well as in the

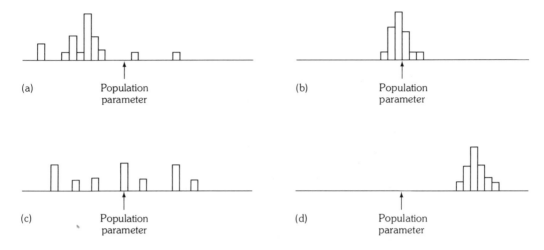

(a)   Population parameter

(b)   Population parameter

(c)   Population parameter

(d)   Population parameter

Figure 4

target illustration of Figure 2. Label each of the sampling distributions in Figure 4 as high or low bias and as high or low precision.

5. I confess with some feelings of guilt that Figure 1 shows that my sampling procedure has a tendency to underestimate the true proportion, p, of dark beads in the population. How is this visible in the graph? Give a numerical measure of this bias by counting the number of samples that underestimated p and the number that overestimated it. (I don't know the cause of this bias. I suspected that the dark and light beads were of slightly different sizes, but not even with a micrometer could I verify this. Well, I *said* it is hard to get a true SRS by physical mixing and drawing.)

6. An agency of the federal government plans to take a SRS of residents in each state to estimate the proportion of owners of real estate in each state's population. States range from California (over 20 million) to Wyoming (under 400,000) in number of inhabitants.

   (a) Will the precision of the sample proportion change from state to state if a SRS of size 2000 is taken in each state? Explain your answer.
   (b) Will the precision of the sample proportion change from state to state if a SRS of 1/10 of 1% (0.001) of the state's population is taken in each state? Explain your answer.

7. A news article on a Gallup Poll noted that "28 percent of the 1,548 adults questioned felt that those who were able to work should be taken off welfare." The article also said (this information is usually cut out by editors), "The margin of error for a sample size of 1,548 is plus or minus three percentage points." Explain carefully what "margin of error" means here. *Hint:* It came from a table like Table 1. (From *The New York Times* of June 20, 1977.)

8. A poll of 1000 voters uses the Gallup Poll's sampling method, which has precision described in Table 1. Although 52% of those polled say they will vote for Ms. Caucus, the polling organization announces that the election is too close to call. Explain carefully why this is the proper conclusion.

9. Not every household fills out the same form in the decennial census of the United States. Basic questions about the number of people in the household and their age, sex, race, and so on appear on all the forms. Other questions appear on only a sample of 20% (or even 15%, or 5%) of the forms. The Census Bureau publishes summary statistics for various geographic areas. For the questions that appear on all forms, these statistics are published for areas with as few as 100 households. But for questions appearing on the 20% sample, the bureau does not publish statistics for areas with fewer than about 2000 households. Can you think of possible reasons for this policy?

Section 4

1. Below is a newspaper report of a public opinion poll, reprinted from *The New York Times* of June 2, 1977. (Copyright 1977 by the New York Times Company. Reprinted by permission.) At the end of Section 4 are some questions that should be answered by a careful account of a sample survey. Which of these questions does this newspaper report answer, and which not? Give the answers whenever the article contains them.

Only About Half of Public Knows U.S. Has to Import Oil, Gallup Survey Shows

Only a little more than half of the American public is aware that the United States must import oil to meet its energy needs, according to the latest Gallup Poll.

Thirty-three percent of 1,506 adults interviewed April 29 through May 1 in more than 300 communities indicated they believed the country was self-sufficient in oil while 15 percent said they would not venture a guess.

Of those who were aware of the need to import oil, the Gallup organization reported, about a third (9 percent of all adults) knew that the amount shipped into the United States last year was 42 percent.

In the poll, Gallup found that residents of the Northeast and Midwest were more aware of the need to import oil than were people living in the warmer climates of the South and West.

Gallup said that the poll indicated that those who were best informed on the oil situation appeared to be most receptive to the call from President Carter for energy conservation and sacrifice.

For example, the polling organization said, among those who believe that Mr. Carter's proposals call for too many sacrifices on the part of the public 41 percent think "we have enough oil in this country."

Responding to the question, "From what you have heard or read, do you think we produce enough oil in this country to meet our present energy needs or do we have to import some oil from other countries," 52 percent replied "must import," 33 percent replied "produce enough" and 15 percent said "don't know."

2. Read in *Statistics: A Guide to the Unknown* the articles by Hansen, "How to Count Better," and Taeuber, "Information for the Nation from a Sample Survey." Both articles describe a use of sampling and mention several practical difficulties and possible sources of error in the sampling application described. Describe in one sentence each such difficulty you find mentioned. Are there any that were not mentioned in the text?

3. Much market research is based on samples chosen from telephone directories and contacted by telephone. The sampling frame therefore omits households having unlisted numbers and those without phones.

   (a) What groups of people do you think will be underrepresented by such a sampling procedure?
   (b) Can you think of any way to include in the sample households with unlisted telephone numbers?
   (c) Can you think of any way to include in the sample households without telephones?

4. We have seen that the method of collecting the data can influence the accuracy of sample results. The following methods have been used to collect data on television viewing in a sample household.

   (a) *The diary method.* The household is asked to keep a diary of all programs watched and who watched them for a week, then mail in the diary at the end of the week.
   (b) *The roster-recall method.* An interviewer shows the subject a list of programs for the preceding week and asks which programs were seen.
   (c) *The telephone-coincidental method.* The household is telephoned at a specific time and asked if the television is on, which program is being watched, and who is watching it.
   (d) *The automatic recorder method.* A device attached to the set records what hours the set is on and which channel it is tuned to. At the end of the week, this record is removed from the recorder.

   For each method, discuss its advantages and disadvantages, especially any possible sources of error associated with each method. Method (a) is most commonly used. Do you agree with that choice? Explain. (Do not discuss choosing the sample, just collecting data once the sample is chosen.)

5. You wish to determine whether students at your school think that faculty are sufficiently available to students outside the classroom. You will select a SRS of 800 students.

   (a) Specify the exact population. (Will you include part-time students? Graduate students?)
   (b) How will you obtain a sampling frame?
   (c) How will you contact subjects? (Is door-to-door interviewing allowed in campus residence halls?)
   (d) What specific question or questions will you ask?

6. The monthly unemployment rate is estimated from the Current Population Survey (CPS), a probability sample of about 55,000 households each month conducted by the Bureau of the Census. It would be cheaper to choose one probability sample and re-interview the adults in the chosen households each month for a year or more. This is called using a *panel*. Because we are interested most of all in changes over time for employment and unemployment, a panel also has the advantage of following these changes for a group of people over time. Can you think of any disadvantages of the panel method?

7. The CPS uses a modified panel method. The sample is changed every month, but not completely. Once chosen, a household stays in the sample for four months, drops out for eight months, then returns for four more months before finally dropping from the sample. Which of the disadvantages you listed in Exercise 6 will be partly overcome by this rotation system?

8. We have seen that the exact wording of questions can influence sample survey results. Two basic types of questions are *closed questions* and *open questions*. A closed question asks the subject for one or more of a fixed set of responses. An open question allows the subject to answer in his or her own words; the responses are written down verbatim by the interviewer and sorted later. For example, here are an open and a closed question on the same issue, both asked by the Gallup Poll within a few years of each other (Recorded in *Public Opinion Quarterly,* Volume 38 (1974–75), pp. 492–493).

OPEN. "In recent years there has been a sharp increase in the nation's crime rate. What steps do you think should be taken to reduce crime?"

CLOSED. "Which two or three of the approaches listed on this card do you think would be the best ways to reduce crime?

Cleaning up social and economic conditions in our slums and ghettos that tend to breed drug addicts and criminals.

Putting more policemen on the job to prevent crimes and arrest more criminals.

Getting parents to exert stricter discipline over their children.

Improving conditions in our jails and prisons so that more people convicted of crimes will be rehabilitated and not go back to a life of crime.

Really cracking down on criminals by giving them longer prison terms to be served under the toughest possible conditions.

Reforming our courts so that persons charged with crimes can get fairer and speedier justice."

What are the advantages and disadvantages of open and closed questions? Use the example just given in your discussion.

9. Comment on each of the following as potential sample survey questions. If any are unclear or slanted, restate the question in better words.

    (a) "Does your family use food stamps?"

    (b) "Which of these best represents your opinion on gun control?

        (1) The government should confiscate our guns.

        (2) We have the right to keep and bear arms."

    (c) "In view of escalating environmental degradation and predictions of serious resource depletion, would you favor economic incentives for recycling of resource-intensive consumer goods?"

10. Response to a proposal often varies with its source. Try the following. Tell several of your friends (don't burden yourself with selecting a SRS) that you are collecting opinions for a course. Ask some:

Thomas Jefferson said, "I hold that a little rebellion, now and then, is a good thing, and as necessary in the political world as storms are in the physical." Do you generally agree or generally disagree with this statement?

Ask others the same question, but replace "Thomas Jefferson said" by "Lenin said." (Be sure to ask each privately. To avoid bias, randomize the question you ask each person by tossing a coin.) Record the opinions you obtain and be prepared to discuss your results.

11. The noted scientist Dr. Iconu wanted to investigate attitudes toward television advertising among American college students. He decided to use a sample of 100 students. Students in freshman psychology (PSY 001) are required to serve as subjects for experimental work. Dr. Iconu obtained a class list for PSY 001 and chose a simple random sample of 100 of the 340 students on the list. He asked each of the 100 students in the sample the following question:

    "Do you agree or disagree that having commercials on TV is a fair price to pay for being able to watch it?"

Of the 100 students in the sample, 82 marked "Agree." Dr. Iconu announced the result of his investigation by saying "82% of American college students are in favor of TV commercials."

    (a) What is the population in this example?

    (b) What is the sampling frame in this example?

    (c) Explain briefly why the sampling frame is or is not suitable.

    (d) Discuss briefly the question Dr. Iconu asked. Is it a slanted question?

    (e) Discuss briefly why Dr. Iconu's announced result is misleading.

    (f) Dr. Iconu defended himself against criticism by pointing out that he had carefully selected a simple random sample from his sampling frame. Is this defense relevant?

Section 5

1. A university employs 2000 male and 500 female faculty members. The equal employment opportunity officer polls a stratified random sample of 200 male and 200 female faculty members.

   (a) What is the chance that a particular female faculty member will be polled?
   (b) What is the chance that a particular male faculty member will be polled?
   (c) Explain why this is a probability sample.
   (d) Each member of the sample is asked, "In your opinion, are female faculty members in general paid less than males with similar positions and qualifications?"

   > 180 of the 200 females (90%) say "Yes"
   > 60 of the 200 males (30%) say "Yes"

   So 240 of the sample of 400 (60%) answered 'Yes," and the officer therefore reports that "Based on a sample, we can conclude that 60% of the total faculty feel that female members are underpaid relative to males." Explain why this conclusion is wrong.

   (e) If we took a stratified random sample of 200 male and 50 female faculty members at this university, each member of the faculty would have the same chance of being chosen. What is that chance? Is this a SRS? Explain.

2. A club contains 25 students named

Abel	Fisher	Huber	Moran	Reinmann
Carson	Golomb	Jack	Moskowitz	Silvers
Cryer	Griswold	Jones	Neyman	Sobar
David	Hein	Kiefer	O'Brien	Thompson
Elashoff	Holland	Lamb	Potter	Vlasic

   and 10 faculty members named

Andrews	Fischang	Knoll	Moore	Rabinowitz
Besicovitch	Gupta	Lightman	Phillips	Vincent

   The club can send 4 students and 2 faculty members to a convention, and decides to choose those who will go by random selection. Use Table A to choose a stratified random sample of 4 students and 2 faculty members. (There are two strata here, faculty and students. A stratified random sample can be taken only when the strata are chosen in advance and you can identify the members of each stratum.)

3. You have alphabetized lists of the 2000 male faculty and of the 500 female faculty at the university described in Exercise 1. Explain how you would assign labels and use Table A to choose a stratified random sample of 200

female and 200 male faculty members. What are the labels of the first 5 males and the first 5 females in your sample?

4. Using the information in part (d) of Exercise 1, give an unbiased estimate of the proportion of the total faculty who feel that females are underpaid.

5. A town contains 33 supermarkets. A health inspector wants to check compliance with a new town ordinance on meat storage. Because of the time required, he can inspect only 10 markets. He decides to choose a stratified random sample and stratifies the markets by sales volume. Stratum A consists of 3 large chain stores; the inspector decides to inspect all 3. Stratum B consists of 10 smaller chain stores; 4 out of the 10 will be inspected. Stratum C consists of 20 locally owned small stores; 3 of these 20 will be inspected.

Let "Yes" mean that the store is in compliance and "No" mean that it is not. The population is as follows (unknown to the inspector, of course):

Stratum A		Stratum B		Stratum C			
Store 1	Yes	Store 1	No	Store 1	Yes	11	Yes
2	Yes	2	Yes	2	Yes	12	Yes
3	No	3	No	3	No	13	No
		4	No	4	Yes	14	Yes
		5	Yes	5	No	15	Yes
		6	No	6	No	16	No
		7	Yes	7	No	17	No
		8	No	8	Yes	18	No
		9	No	9	No	19	Yes
		10	Yes	10	No	20	Yes

(a) Use Table A to choose a stratified random sample of size 10 allotted among the strata as described above.
(b) Use your sample results to estimate the proportion of the entire population of stores in compliance with the ordinance.
(c) Use the description of the population given above to find the true proportion of stores in compliance. How accurate is the estimate from part (b)?

6. Another type of probability sample often used in sample surveys is a *systematic random sample,* which we will describe by an example. Suppose that the final area chosen in a multistage sampling design contains 500 addresses, of which 5 must be selected. A systematic random sample is chosen as follows.

Step 1. Choose one of the first 100 addresses on the list at random. (Label them 00, 01, ..., 99 and use a pair of digits from Table A to make the choice.)

Step 2. The sample consists of the address from Step 1, and the addresses 100, 200, 300, and 400 positions down the list from it.

For example, if 71 is chosen at random in Step 1, the systematic random sample consists of the addresses numbered 71, 171, 271, 371, and 471.

(a) Use Table A to choose a systematic random sample of 5 from a list of 500 addresses. Enter the table at line 130.

(b) What is the chance that a certain address will be chosen? Explain your answer. (Knowing this chance for each unit means we have a probability sample.)

(c) Is this a SRS? Explain your answer.

(d) What is the practical advantage of a systematic sample over a SRS? Can you see any possible disadvantages?

7. A group of librarians once wanted to estimate what fraction of books in large libraries falls in each of several size (height and width) categories. This information would help them plan shelving. To obtain it, they measured all of the several hundred thousand books in a library. Describe a sampling design that would have saved them time and money. That is, outline Steps 1–4 at the end of Section 5 for a sampling design (simple or complicated) you would suggest to the librarians.

8. A labor organization wishes to study the attitudes of college faculty members toward collective bargaining. These attitudes appear to be different at different types of colleges. The American Association of University Professors classifies colleges as follows.

Class I   Offer the doctorate, and award at least 15 per year

Class IIA   Award degrees above the bachelor's, but are not in Class I

Class IIB   Award only bachelor's degrees

Class III   Two-year colleges

Describe a sampling design that would gather information for each class separately, as well as overall information about faculty attitudes.

9. An important government sample survey is the monthly Current Population Survey (CPS), from which employment and unemployment statistics are produced. The sampling design of the CPS is described in Chapter 1 of the *BLS Handbook of Methods* (Bureau of Labor Statistics, 1976). Obtain the handbook from the library, and write a brief description of the multistage sample design used in the CPS.

10. Many nationwide surveys "sample the map." That is, the sampling frame consists of identifiable geographic units rather than of a list of people or places. The Statistical Reporting Service of the U.S. Department of Agriculture makes extensive use of such "area frames" in its surveys of crops, farm economics, and so forth.

(a) What are the general advantages and disadvantages of an area frame as opposed to a list of farms or mailing addresses? [Part (b) may help you here.]

(b) The Agriculture Department finds that an area frame is preferred for surveys of the acreage planted in each crop, but that a list frame is superior for surveys of farm income. Can you explain why?

11. One topic of this section has been estimation of population parameters from sample statistics in a variety of sampling designs. Estimation is much harder when a neat sampling design is not possible. As an example, read the essay by Douglas G. Chapman, "The Plight of the Whales," in *Statistics: A Guide to the Unknown.* Chapman describes three methods for estimating the size of an animal population, methods widely used in ecological studies. Which method would you use to estimate the total number of lake trout in Lake Winnebago, Wisconsin? Explain your answer.

Section 6

1. Never since the beginnings of opinion polls over 40 years ago have less than two-thirds of those sampled favored stronger controls on firearms. Specific gun control proposals have often been favored by 80% to 85% of respondents. Yet little national gun control legislation has passed, and no major national restrictions on firearms exist.

   Why do you think this has occurred? Does this mean that opinion polls on issues do not really offer the public a means of offsetting special interest groups?

2. To see whether people often give responses on subjects they are entirely ignorant about, try the following. Ask several persons (we won't ask for a SRS) the following questions:

   (a) Have you ever heard of the Taft-Johnson-Pepper bill on veteran's housing?
   (b) Have you ever heard of Midwestern Life Magazine?

   (In a study of a few years ago, 53% said yes to (a) and 25% to (b) even though neither the bill nor the magazine ever existed. The study is cited by Dennis Trewin, "Non-sampling Errors in Sample Surveys," *CSIRO Division of Mathematics and Statistics Newsletter,* June 1977.)

3. Bogart (see Sourcenote 10) reports that during the 1968 campaign George Wallace accused the polls of favoring Eastern moneyed interests and neglecting the common people. He would ask crowds at his rallies "Have any of you-all ever been asked about this here election by Mr. Harris or Mr. Gallup?" and receive shouts of "No," "Never" in reply. (*Silent Politics*, p. 39).

   If 150 million U.S. residents are of age 18 and over, and a poll selects 1500 at random, what is the chance that you will be interviewed? Suppose that the major polling organizations conduct 20 surveys during a presidential campaign. What is the chance that you will be interviewed at least once? Being interviewed by an opinion poll is an unlikely event, and no accusations of bias are needed to explain why you haven't been chosen.

4. A committee of the British Parliament suggested in 1966 that no poll results

should be published during the three days before an election. Do you feel that this is a good idea? Explain.

5. Election-night television coverage features a sampling design that often allows quite precise predictions of the outcome before the polls have closed in parts of the country. (For a brief description, read Richard F. Link, "Election Night on Television" in *Statistics: A Guide to the Unknown.*) It is sometimes charged that late voters may stay home if the networks say that the national election is decided. Therefore predictions based on samples of actual votes should not be allowed until the polls have closed everywhere in the country. Do you agree with this proposal? Explain your opinion.

6. The 1976 Gallup Poll election questionnaire cited in the text used a "secret ballot" arrangement. Why do you think that this arrangement was used?

7. In the text we briefly examined the pros and cons of public opinion polls on issues. For more background, read Gallup's essay in *Statistics: A Guide to the Unknown* and the chapter "Polling and the Concept of Public Opinion" in Bogart's book. Come to class prepared to discuss using public opinion (as reported by polls) in government.

Section 7

1. Discuss the recommendation of the National Heart and Lung Institute panel that artificial hearts be allotted at random among patients of similar medical condition. Do you favor random selection? If not, how should recipients be chosen? By ability to pay? By value to society? (As assessed by whom?) By age and family responsibilities?

2. Give an example of a situation where you definitely would *approve* random selection. Give an example of a situation where you would definitely *disapprove* random selection.

3. A basketball arena has 8000 student seats, but 18,000 students would like to watch basketball games. Design a system of allotting tickets that seems fair to you. (All students can see some of the 12 home games if you use a rotation system. Will you give upperclassmen some preference? How many tickets may an individual buy? Will you use random allotment, and how? If your school actually does use a random drawing to allot seats, describe the details of the official system and discuss any changes you favor.)

Section 8

1. In what circumstances is collecting personal information without the subject's consent permitted? Consider the following cases in your discussion.

   (a) A government agency takes a random sample of income tax returns to obtain information on the average income of persons in different occupations. Only the incomes and occupations are recorded from the returns, not the names.

    (b) A psychologist asks a random sample of students to fill out a question-naire; he explains that their responses will be used to measure several personality traits so he can study how these traits are related. The psychologist does not inform the students that one trait measured by the test is how prejudiced they are toward other races.

    (c) A social psychologist attends public meetings of a religious sect to study the behavior patterns of members.

    (d) The social psychologist pretends to be converted to membership in a religious sect and attends private meetings to study and report the behavior patterns of members.

2. A researcher suspects that orthodox religious beliefs tend to be associated with an authoritarian personality. A questionnaire is prepared to measure authoritarian tendencies and also ask many religious questions. Write a description of the purpose of this research to be read to potential respondents. You must balance the conflicting goals of not deceiving respondents as to what the questionnaire will tell about them and of not biasing the sample by scaring off certain types of people.

3. Does having an abortion affect the health of mother or child in any future live births? To study this question, The New York State Health Department traced the reproductive histories of 21,000 women who had abortions in New York in 1970–1971 and compared them with 27,000 women who gave birth to living children in the same period. The comparison was carried out entirely with Health Department records, beginning in 1970 and tracing any later maternity records for these 48,000 women through 1977.

    Do you consider this study an invasion of privacy? If you do, do you think the information to be gained and the difficulties in asking consent justify the study anyway?

4. The federal government, unlike opinion polls or academic researchers, has the legal power to compel response to survey questions. The 1960 and 1970 Census both contained the following question:

H21. **How many bathrooms do you have?**

A complete bathroom is a room with flush toilet, bathtub or shower, and wash basin with piped water.

A half bathroom has at least a flush toilet or bathtub or shower, but does not have all the facilities for a complete bathroom.

    ○ No bathroom, or only a half bathroom

    ○ 1 complete bathroom
    ○ 1 complete bathroom, plus half bath(s)

    ○ 2 complete bathrooms
    ○ 2 complete bathrooms, plus half bath(s)

    ○ 3 or more complete bathrooms

(This is reproduced from an informational copy of the 1970 census form provided by the Census Bureau.)

Some members of Congress felt that this was an invasion of privacy, and that the Census Bureau should be prohibited from asking such questions. The bureau replied that as with all census data, no individual information would be released, only averages for various regions, and that lack of plumbing is the best single measure of substandard housing, and the government needed this information to plan housing programs.

Do you feel that this question is proper? If not, when do you think that the government's need for information outweighs a citizen's wish to withhold personal facts? If you do think the plumbing question is proper, where does the citizen's right to withhold information begin?

5. If only confidentiality is promised, and confidentiality is carefully observed, are hidden codes that identify respondents ethical? Do you agree with Mr. Gemmill that this is "trickery" or with those who claim that this practice serves a necessary purpose and does not violate the assurances given respondents?

6. Discuss how anonymity can be preserved while still recording who did and who did not respond to a survey. (See Exercise 6 in Section 6 for one idea.)

7. A radical critique of polling is given by Herbert I. Schiller, "Polls are Prostitutes for the Establishment," *Psychology Today,* July 1972, p. 20. His arguments, which apply to almost any sample survey, are

   (a) The poller exercises power over the respondent by wording questions and restricting alternatives in answering.
   (b) Polls provide information about the respondent to the poller with no reciprocal flow of information in the other direction. They give power to the poller by allowing him to choose the uses of this information.

   Thus Schiller feels that polls are an instrument of manipulation, enabling the poller to manipulate respondents. (Read his complete article if possible.) Discuss Schiller's position and give your reasons for agreeing or disagreeing.

8. Do you favor requiring complete disclosure of the methods, sponsorship, and results (sample statistics only, never individual responses) of all sample surveys? In your discussion you must balance any benefits of this policy against the cost of carrying it out and the resulting restriction on your ability to ask questions of other people.

9. One of the best discussions of the ethics of sampling is by Lester R. Frankel, "Statistics and People—the Statistician's Responsibilities," *Journal of the American Statistical Association,* Volumes 71 (1976), pp. 9–16. Mr. Frankel was then president of the American Statistical Association, and works for a firm specializing in sample surveys.

   Read this article as an example of the ethical standards that survey statisticians currently hold. Make a list of the areas in which Frankel suggests guidelines for the behavior of survey takers.

Chapter 2

Experimentation

E xperimentation differs from sample surveys (and other forms of observation) in that an experimenter controls or manipulates the environment of the units. In an experiment, researchers actively intervene by administering a treatment in order to study its effects. The great advantage of experimentation is that we can study the effects of the specific treatments that interest us, rather than simply observe units as they occur "in nature." Imagine the frustration of a researcher trying to study the effects of prolonged sleeplessness on reaction time by finding persons who just happen to have been awake for at least 48 hours. Instead, she performs the experiment of keeping volunteer subjects awake for 48 hours and then measuring their reaction time. She can even keep the subjects awake for 36, 48, 60, and 72 hours and measure their reaction times for each duration of sleeplessness. This kind of experimentation makes possible conclusions about the effect of sleeplessness on reaction time.

The intent of most experiments is to study the effect of changes in one variable (such as hours without sleep) on another variable (such as reaction time). We distinguish response, or *dependent,* variables from *independent* variables that the experimenter manipulates. Experiments often have several of each kind of variable. We might, for example, wish to study the effect of hours awake (independent variable A) and noise level (independent variable B) on reaction time (dependent variable 1) and score on a test of manual dexterity (dependent variable 2). The idea behind this terminology is that the dependent variables depend on the independent variables.

A sample survey may also study the effect of some variables (which thus become independent variables) on others (the dependent variables). A survey of natural deaths, for example, might study the relationship between the smoking habits of the deceased and the cause of death. It is clear that a sample survey may show a relationship between smoking and death from lung cancer, but it cannot show that smoking causes lung cancer. In principle, experiments can establish causation: If we change the value of an independent variable with no other changes in the experimental conditions, any resulting changes in a dependent variable must be caused by the changing independent variable. This ideal is not often achieved in real experiments. It is devilishly hard to arrange an experiment so nothing affects the dependent variables except changes in the independent variables. Nonetheless, experimentation is far better than observation when we wish to conclude that one variable really does explain another. Sample surveys, on the other hand, are better suited for describing a population. Here is a summary of the vocabulary of experimentation.

Units—the basic objects on which the experiment is done. When the units are human beings, they are called *subjects.*

Variable—a measured characteristic of a unit.

Dependent variable—a variable whose changes we wish to study; a response variable.

Independent variable—a variable whose effect on the dependent variables we wish to study. An independent variable in an experiment is called a *factor.*

Treatment—any specific experimental condition applied to the units. A treatment is usually a combination of specific values (called *levels*) of each of the experimental factors.

Here is an example that illustrates our terminology.

Example 1. A fabrics researcher is studying the durability of a fabric under repeated washings. Because the durability may depend on the water temperature and the type of cleansing agent used, the researcher decides to investigate the effect of these two factors on durability. Factor A is water temperature, and has 3 levels—hot (145°F), warm (100°F), and cold (50°F). Factor B is the cleansing agent and also has 3 levels—regular Tide, low-phosphate Tide, and Ivory Liquid. A treatment consists of washing a piece of the fabric (a unit) 50 times in a home automatic washer with a specific combination of water temperature and cleansing agent. The dependent variable is strength after 50 washes, measured by a fabric-testing machine that forces a steel ball through the fabric and records its breaking strength.

In this example there are 9 possible treatments (choices of a temperature and a cleansing agent). By using them all, the researcher obtains a wealth of information on how temperature alone, washing agent alone, and the two in combination affect the durability of the fabric. For example, water temperature may have no effect on the strength of the fabric when regular Tide is used, but after 50 washings in low-phosphate Tide the fabric may be weaker when cold water instead of hot water is used. This kind of combination effect is called an *interaction* between cleansing agent and water temperature. Interactions can be important, as when a drug that ordinarily has no unpleasant side effects interacts with alcohol to knock out the patient who drinks a martini. Because an experiment can combine levels of several factors, interactions between the factors can be observed.

So experiments allow us to study factors of interest to us, either individually or in combination. And, an experiment can show that these factors actually cause certain effects. For these reasons, experimentation is the favored method of collecting data whenever our goal is to study the effects of variables rather than simply to describe a population. Experiments are universal in the physical and life sciences. They are carried out whenever possible in the social sciences. (That's quite often in psychology, but less often in sociology or economics.) Some experiments influence the lives of all of us. For example, the safety of food additives and the safety and effectiveness of drugs must be demonstrated by experiment before public use is allowed.

In this chapter we are concerned with the statistical ideas of experimental design. The *design* of an experiment is the pattern or outline according to which treatments are applied to units. The basic concepts of experimental design apply to experiments in all areas, whether they study agricultural fertilizers, vaccines, or teaching methods.

1.   The Need for Experimental Design

Laboratory experiments often have a simple design such as

(1)   Treatment⟶ Observation

in which a treatment is applied (often to several units) and its effect is observed. If before-and-after measurements are made, the design is

(2)   Observation 1⟶ Treatment⟶ Observation 2.

Statistical ideas are not used in the design of such simple experiments. (These experiments are "simple" in their design or pattern, even though the treatment may be quite complex.) When experiments are conducted outside the controlled environment of a laboratory, simple designs such as (1) and (2) often yield *invalid* data; we cannot tell whether the treatment had an effect on the units. The same sad tale must often be told of observational studies such as sample surveys. Some examples will show what can go wrong.

Example 2. In 1940, a psychologist conducted a study of the effect of propaganda on attitude toward a foreign government. He devised a test of attitude toward the German government, and administered it to a group of American students. After reading German propaganda material for several months, the students were tested again to see if their attitude had changed. This experiment had a design of the form (2), namely,

$$\text{Test of} \atop \text{attitude} \xrightarrow{\quad} \text{Reading of} \atop \text{propaganda} \xrightarrow{\quad} \text{Retest of} \atop \text{attitude}$$

Unfortunately, Germany attacked and conquered France while the experiment was in progress. There was a profound change of attitude toward the German government between the test and the retest, but we shall never know how much of this change was due to the independent variable (reading propaganda) and how much to the historical events of that time. The data are invalid; they give no information about the effect of reading propaganda.

Example 3. A high school Latin teacher wished to demonstrate the favorable effect of studying Latin on mastery of English. She therefore obtained from the school records the scores of all seniors on a standard English proficiency examination. The average score for seniors who had studied Latin was much higher than the average score for those who had not. The Latin teacher concluded that "The study of Latin greatly improves one's command of English." But students elect whether or not to study Latin. Those who elect Latin are probably (on the average) both smarter and more interested in language than those who do not. This self-selected group would have a higher average English proficiency score whether or not they studied Latin. Whether studying Latin raised their English scores yet more we cannot tell; the data are invalid for this purpose. (This is a census of the school's seniors, not an experiment. But it is similar to Example 2 in that the effect of the independent variable on the dependent variable cannot be discovered.)

No valid conclusion can be drawn in either of these examples because the effect of the independent variable cannot be distinguished from the effect of factors outside the study. Variables not of interest in a study that nonetheless influence the dependent variable are *extraneous factors*. In Example 2, reading propaganda is the experimental factor (the independent variable), and the events of current history are an extraneous factor. In Example 3, study of Latin is the independent variable and the innate ability of the students is an extraneous factor.

The effects of two variables (independent variables or extraneous factors) on a dependent variable are said to be *confounded* when they cannot be distinguished from each other.

In Example 2, the effect of reading propaganda was confounded with the effect of historical events; the influences of these two factors on attitude toward Germany cannot be separated. In Example 3, the effect of studying Latin was confounded with the ability of the students; both influence English proficiency scores and their influences cannot be separated.

Confounding of different factors (mixing up of their effects) often obscures the true effect of independent variables on a dependent variable. Here are some additional examples.

> **Example 4.** An article in a women's magazine reported that women who nurse their babies feel warmer and more receptive toward the infants than mothers who bottle feed. The author concluded that nursing has desirable effects on the mother's attitude toward the child. But women choose whether to nurse or bottle feed, and it is possible that those who already feel receptive toward the child choose to nurse, while those to whom the baby is a nuisance choose the bottle. The effect on the mother's attitude of the method of feeding is confounded with the already existing attitude of the mother toward the child. Observational studies of cause and effect, such as this one, rarely lead to clear conclusions because confounding with extraneous factors almost always occurs.

> **Example 5.** A particularly important example of confounding occurs in clinical trials of drugs and other medical treatments. Many patients respond positively to *any* treatment, even a dummy medication such as a sugar pill. This is presumably a psychological reaction to receiving personal attention, and especially to the authority of the doctor who administers the treatment. Dummy medications are called *placebos,* and the response of patients to any treatment in which they have confidence is called the *placebo effect.* Psychological or not, the placebo effect is not confined to the patient's imagination. Not only subjective effects ("My pain is less") but objectively measured responses often occur. In a clinical trial of the effectiveness of vitamin C in preventing colds, patients who were given a placebo that they thought was vitamin C actually had fewer colds than patients given vitamin C who thought it was a placebo! There is no doubt that faith healing works (sometimes).
>
> Experiments of the designs (1) and (2), therefore, are often useless in testing drugs or other medical treatments. The placebo effect is confounded with the effect of the treatment; the patients might have responded as well to a sugar pill as they did to the drug being tested.

"I want to make one thing perfectly clear, Mr. Smith. The medication I prescribe will cure that run-down feeling."

So both observation and simple experiments often yield invalid data owing to confounding with extraneous factors. This situation is difficult to remedy when only observation is possible. Experiments offer the possibility of escaping the effects of confounding in ways not possible by observation alone. The first goal of experimental design is to make possible valid conclusions—to enable us to say how the independent variables affected the dependent variables. It is now clear that some new ideas are needed to reach this goal.

2. First Steps in Statistical Design of Experiments

The central idea in avoiding confounding of experimental with extraneous factors is *comparative experimentation*. If we can set up two equivalent groups of units, then give the treatment to only one group (the experimental group) while treating the other group (the control group) exactly the same in every way except that it does not receive the treatment, then any differences between the groups at the end of the experiment must be due to the effect of the treatment. Any extraneous factors influence *both* groups, while the experimental treatment influences only one; so by comparing the two groups, the effect of the treatment can be discovered. If two treatments—two drugs, or two fertilizers, for example—are to be compared, we can give one to each of two equivalent groups and no control group is needed.

Comparative studies need not be experiments. We might, for example, assess the safety of various surgical anesthetics by analyzing hospital records to compare death rates during surgery when the different anesthetics are used. But the groups being compared are not equivalent. For some anesthetics tend to be used in serious operations, or on patients who are old or in poor physical condition, while others are used in less risky situations. A high death rate may mean only that this anesthetic is used in high-risk operations.* If comparison is to eliminate such confounding, we must have equivalent groups of subjects. Arranging for equivalent groups to receive the treatments is the kind of active intervention that distinguishes experiments from other types of studies.

Comparative experimentation was first used in earnest in agricultural research, beginning in the nineteenth century. Agronomists tried to obtain equivalent groups of units (small plots of land) by carefully matching plots in fertility, soil type, and other factors. It is difficult to match units in all important extraneous factors—especially because the experimenter may not think of them all ahead of time! What is more, experimenter judgment in assigning units to groups opens the door to bias. A medical researcher may unconsciously tend to assign more seriously ill patients to the standard treatment and leave less serious cases to the new and untried treatment. The moral is clear: If comparative experimentation is to be effective, we need a better way of assigning units to groups.

The better way was provided in the 1920s by R. A. Fisher, a statistician working for an English agricultural experiment station.† Fisher realized that equivalent groups for experimental use can be obtained by *randomly assigning* units to groups. Just as a simple random sample is likely to be representative of the population, so a random selection of (say) half the units available is likely to create two groups (the one selected and the one left behind) similar in *every* respect. We have now reached the simplest statistically designed experiment:

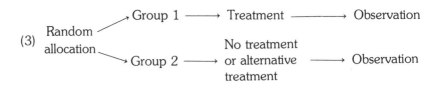

*An account of the most important study of this problem appears in Lincoln E. Moses and Frederick Mosteller, "Safety of Anesthetics," in J. M. Tanur et al. (eds.), *Statistics: A Guide to the Unknown* (San Francisco: Holden-Day, 1972). Because the hospital records contained information on the kind of surgery and type of patient, it was possible to correct for the effects of these extraneous factors.

†Sir Ronald Aylmer Fisher (1890–1962) was one of the century's greatest scientists in two fields, genetics and statistics. He invented statistical design of experiment and much else besides.

This is the replacement for the design (1), which involved no comparison. If before-and-after observations are made, as in design (2), we simply make them on each group:

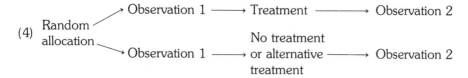

(4) Random allocation

Observation 1 ⟶ Treatment ⟶ Observation 2

No treatment

Observation 1 ⟶ or alternative ⟶ Observation 2
treatment

Let us study some examples of simple designed experiments.

Example 6. Suppose that we wish to give an experimental design for the propaganda study (Example 2 on p. 59) that will allow valid conclusions to be drawn. There are 100 subjects available. We first choose a SRS of 50 subjects in the usual way: Label the subjects 00, 01,. . . ,99 and use the table of random digits to choose 50. If we enter the table in line 136, we obtain

Group 1

08	42	14	47	53	77	37	72	87	44
75	59	20	85	63	79	09	24	54	64
56	68	12	61	78	36	60	91	73	98
48	11	45	92	66	83	16	89	40	22
15	58	13	35	86	17	70	69	28	55

Group 2 consists of the 50 remaining subjects. All 100 subjects are tested for attitude toward the German government. The 50 subjects in Group 1 then read German propaganda regularly for several months, while the 50 subjects in Group 2 are instructed not to read German propaganda; otherwise, both groups go about their normal lives. Then all 100 subjects are retested. This experiment has the design (4):

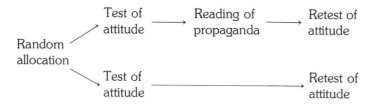

Test of ⟶ Reading of ⟶ Retest of
attitude   propaganda   attitude

Random allocation

Test of ⟶ Retest of
attitude   attitude

If Group 1 shows a more positive (or less negative) change in attitude toward Germany between test and retest, we can attribute this difference to the effect of reading propaganda.

Some comments on Example 6 are in order. First, notice that "random allocation" to Groups 1 and 2 is done by selecting a SRS from the available units to be Group 1. Please check the use of the table of random digits in Example 6 if you are unsure of how to do this. The purpose of randomization is to create groups that are equivalent prior to the experiment. Many factors (sex, age, race, religion, political opinion) may influence a subject's reaction to German propaganda. Random allocation should "average out" the effects of these extraneous factors by dividing them evenly between the groups. Moreover, random allocation will average out the effects of extraneous factors we have not thought of, as well as those we have listed.

Second, notice how randomization and *control* ensure that valid conclusions can be drawn. The control group shares the experiences of the experimental group except for propaganda reading. The fall of France, for example, influences the attitudes of both groups. The groups were equivalent prior to the experiment (we can check this by comparing their average scores on the first test). And the groups were identically treated except that Group 1 read propaganda while Group 2 did not. So any difference in the average change in the attitudes of the two groups must be due to the effect of the propaganda. It might happen, for example, that the attitude of both groups becomes much more negative after the fall of France, but that the attitude of Group 1 changes less in the negative direction that does the attitude of Group 2. This would show the effect of the propaganda read by Group 1 but not by Group 2.

Example 7. It has been claimed, most notably by the double Nobel laureate Linus Pauling, that large doses of vitamin C will prevent colds. An experiment to test this claim was performed in Toronto in the winter of 1971–1972. About 500 volunteer subjects were randomly allocated to each of two groups. Group 1 received 1 gram per day of vitamin C, and 4 grams per day at the first sign of a cold. (This is a large amount of vitamin C; the recommended daily allowance of this vitamin for adults is only 45 milligrams, or 45/1000 of a gram.) Group 2 served as a control group, and received a placebo pill identical in appearance to the vitamin C capsules. Both groups were regularly checked for illness during the winter. The experimental design is (3):

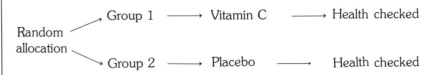

Random allocation → Group 1 ⟶ Vitamin C ⟶ Health checked
Random allocation → Group 2 ⟶ Placebo ⟶ Health checked

Some of the subjects dropped out of the experiment for various reasons, but 818 completed at least two months. Groups 1 and 2 remained well matched in age, occupation, smoking habits, and other extraneous factors. At the end of the winter, 26% of the subjects in Group 1 had not had a cold, as opposed to 18% in Group 2. Thus vitamin C does appear to prevent colds better than a placebo—but not much better. [1]

Again, in Example 7, confounding has been avoided so the effect of the treatment can be separated from the effects of extraneous factors, including the placebo effect. If Group 2 had received nothing, the effect of vitamin C would still have been confounded with the placebo effect, because Group 1 might be responding to being given any treatment at all. As it is, *both* groups receive pills, and both were equivalent before the experiment began, so the chemical effect of vitamin C is the only difference between the groups. So we should be able to draw valid conclusions as to whether vitamin C prevents colds better than a placebo does.

Examples 6 and 7 show how valid data can be obtained in the settings of Examples 2 and 5 by a simple experimental design. Examples 3 and 4 are observational studies. Simple experiments also would yield valid data in those settings. But such experiments would mean randomly assigning students to study or avoid Latin, and women to nurse or bottle feed their children. These treatments cannot be imposed for practical and moral reasons. It is only when experimentation is not possible that we try (often without success) to study cause and effect by observation alone.

Randomization in an experiment is the analog of probability sampling in a sample survey, and serves the same purposes. Randomization is a fair or unbiased way of assigning units to experimental groups, just as a SRS is a fair or unbiased way of selecting units from a population. As in sampling, randomization in experimental design has a less obvious but equally important function. Recall that probability sampling produces sample statistics having a known sampling distribution, so we know how likely the statistic is to fall within any given distance of the population parameter. In a similar sense, if experimental units are randomly allocated to treatments, we know how likely is any degree of difference among the groups. For example, in the Toronto vitamin C experiment, a difference between the groups of 26% versus 18% illness-free was observed. Because of the use of randomization, we can say that if the two treatments (vitamin C, placebo) have the same effect, a difference at least this large would occur in less than 1% of a large number of experiments. We therefore can be confident that the difference is due to the differing effects of the treatments. Randomization as the basis for drawing conclusions will receive much attention in Chapter 8. At this point, we concentrate instead on randomization as a means of eliminating possible bias by averaging extraneous factors and creating equivalent groups that allow valid comparison of treatments.

Increasing the number of units assigned to each group has the same effect as increasing the size of a sample. In both cases, a greater number of observations produces less variable (more precise) results. That is, we can be more confident that a repetition of the experiment would give results that differ little from those we obtained. Thus we can be more confident that our experimental results reflect the effect of the treatments and are not just an accident arising from bad luck in the random assignment of units to groups. Let us sum up the analogy between random sampling and randomized experiments.

1. **Random sampling has no bias; it favors no part of the population in choosing a sample. Random allocation of experimental units to groups has no bias; units with special properties are not favored in choosing any group.**

2. **The sample obtained by random sampling varies in repeated sampling and may be unrepresentative of the population. The experimental groups obtained by randomization vary in repeated trials and may fail to be closely equivalent.**

3. **Using larger random samples decreases the variability of the result and increases our confidence that the sample is representative of the population. Using larger randomly chosen groups of experimental units decreases the variability of the result and increases our confidence that the groups are equivalent before treatments are applied.**

How well does randomization work in practice? Here is an example in which this question was investigated.

Example 8. When the University Group Diabetes Program, a major medical experiment on treatments for diabetes, produced evidence that the drug tolbutamide was ineffective and perhaps unsafe, the design of the experiment was questioned. In response, the statistician Jerome Cornfield wrote a detailed account of the conduct of the study that includes a look at the effectiveness of the randomization.[2] Subjects were randomly assigned to four treatments. The tolbutamide group showed higher cardiovascular mortality (i.e., more subjects died of heart attacks) than the other groups. Could this have happened because the tolbutamide group contained higher risk subjects? Cornfield examined how patients with each of eight "risk factors" that increase the chance of a heart attack were distributed among the groups. These risk factors were: age 55 or older, high blood pressure, history of digitalis use, history of chest pains, abnormal electrocardiogram, high cholesterol level, overweight, and calcification of the arteries. The results appear in Table 1. The groups do appear quite equivalent in these risk factors. For example, 84.9% of the patients assigned to placebo had one or more risk factors, compared to 86.8% of those assigned to tolbutamide. "All in all," Cornfield commented, "the luck of the draw does not seem to have been too bad." He reminded his medical readers that randomization achieves groups also comparable in other extraneous factors, such as a patient's smoking history, for which information was not available.

Table 1

NUMBER OF SUBJECTS IN THE UNIVERSITY GROUP DIABETES PROGRAM
HAVING EACH NUMBER OF RISK FACTORS*

Number of risk factors	Group 1 (placebo)	Group 2 (tolbutamide)	Group 3 (insulin standard)	Group 4 (insulin variable)
0	28	25	22	15
1	60	50	62	76
2	59	58	60	57
3	26	34	34	30
4	10	17	8	4
5	2	4	8	4
6	0	1	1	1
Total number of subjects	185	189	195	187

SOURCE: Jerome Cornfield, "The University Group Diabetes Program," *Journal of the American Medical Association,* September 20, 1971, pp. 1676–1687. Copyright 1971, American Medical Association.

*This table covers the 756 subjects (out of a total of 823) for which information on all eight risk factors was available.

The simplest kind of randomization allocates experimental units at random among *all* treatments. Such experimental designs are called *completely randomized designs.* They correspond to the SRS in sampling. The designs (3) and (4) are completely randomized designs with two groups. If more treatments are to be compared, we can randomly divide the units into more groups. It is not necessary to allot the same number of units to each group, but the data are

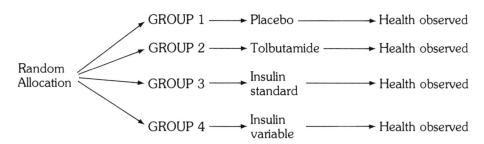

Figure 1. The University Group Diabetes Program, a completely randomized experimental design with four groups and about 200 subjects in each group.

easier to use when this is done. The University Group Diabetes Study (Example 7) was a completely randomized design with four groups. This design is illustrated in Figure 1.

3.   Difficulties in Experimentation

Just as probability sampling does not ensure accurate results from a sample survey, so statistically designed experiments are not a total solution to the problem of obtaining valid experimental data. In this section, we increase our understanding of experimentation by looking at some common difficulties in drawing valid conclusions.

Difficulty 1: To What Population Do the Conclusions Apply?

If you've seen one alpha particle, you've seen them all. So experimental conclusions about alpha particles reached in Denmark in 1923 remain true in Berkeley in 1973. The physical sciences often work with essentially identical experimental units. This has two heavenly consequences: Random assignment is not needed to create equivalent groups when all units are identical, and conclusions about one set of units generalize to the population of all such units. In other areas of study, the units are often highly variable. This may be due to variation in the units themselves or to the effects of extraneous variables. We know that random assignment can, on the average, create equivalent groups from variable units. Now we must ask how widely one can apply the conclusions from such an experiment. An example will convey the difficulty.

> **Example 9.** A psychologist selects as experimental subjects students enrolled in freshman psychology, PSY 001, at Upper Wabash University. Because two treatments are being compared, the students are assigned at random to two groups; that is, design (3) of Section 2 is used. There is a large difference in the average response of the two groups, too large to be reasonably due to the accidents of random assignment. The psychologist therefore concludes that the effects of the two treatments on the units differ.

For what population is this conclusion valid? In a strict sense, only for the group of students who served as subjects. If they are not representative of some larger population, the experimental conclusions are not valid for any larger population. The situation is quite similar to taking a SRS from a sampling frame that is not representative of the population. To take an extreme example, an experiment on psychological reactions to a pain-relieving drug, however well designed, will not give valid conclusions about adults in general if the subjects are mental patients.

What shall we do? The ideal solution is clear: Take a SRS from the population of interest to obtain the experimental subjects, and then apply the random assignment needed for the experiment. This ensures (or at least makes it very likely) that the experimental subjects are representative of the larger population. Such an ideal solution is almost never possible in practice. What is possible is to use a SRS from the pool of available subjects. The psychologist, for instance, should draw a SRS of PSY 001 students rather than allow students to choose which of a list of experiments they will participate in. If, for example, his experiment concerns the effect of watching pornographic movies, the reactions of students who choose to watch may differ sharply from the reactions of randomly selected students. (Of course, telling randomly selected students they must watch pornography is morally objectionable. So student choice of experiments rather than random selection is often necessary. It's enough to make psychologists envy physicists.)

If the experimental subjects are a SRS of a pool of available units, the experimental results are surely valid for that pool. Our psychologist can now draw conclusions about the population of students in PSY 001 this semester. No doubt he had grander things in mind. So he must start being persuasive. He must persuade us that his experimental subjects are representative of some larger population. Here he draws on his understanding of his subject matter, not on statistics. If the experiment involved eye movements in response to visual stimuli, the experimenter can probably persuade us that the conclusions are valid for all persons with normal vision. If the experiment involved response to pornographic films, it is not clear that conclusions drawn from student subjects can be generalized to executives. If the subjects were volunteers, this limits still more the population to which the conclusions apply.

Validity of the conclusions of a study for the subjects of the study themselves is sometimes called *internal validity*. Generalizability of the conclusions of a study to a larger population is sometimes called *external validity*. Internal validity depends largely on statistical ideas. External validity depends largely on knowledge of the particular field of the study.

Difficulty 2: Lack of Realism

Our psychologist, let us say, is interested in response to frustration. His experiment requires the subjects to play a game rigged against them. The game demands team cooperation, and the experimenter will observe the relations among team members as they repeatedly lose. This is an artificial situation, and the PSY 001 students know it's "only an experiment," even if they don't know that the game is rigged. Do their reactions in this situation give information about their response to genuine frustration outside the laboratory? As with Difficulty 1, the question involves how much the experimental conclusions can be generalized. But the barrier to general conclusions here is the lack of realism of the experimental treatment. Once again the experimenter must try to persuade us. And once again the eye movements expert has a better case than the student of pornography or frustration. Inability to apply realistic treatments is a serious barrier to effective experimentation in many areas of the social sciences.

Lack of realism in experiments is an issue that touches our health and prosperity more than do the frustrations of social scientists. Food additives are required, not unreasonably, to be safe. The Food and Drug Administration (FDA) is charged with seeing that they are safe. The FDA's exercise of judgment is restricted by laws, in particular by the famous Delaney amendment of 1958, an all-or-nothing statement that outlaws additives found to cause cancer in man *or animal*. A typical trial of a food additive involves adding large amounts of the substance to the diet of laboratory rats. If significantly more tumors appear in this experimental group than in the control group of rats fed an additive-free diet, the additive is guilty and must be banned.

THE DELANEY AMENDMENT

Sec. 409 (c) (3) (A). No additive shall be deemed to be safe if it is found to induce cancer when ingested by man or animal, or if it is found, after tests which are appropriate for the evaluation of the safety of food additives, to induce cancer in man or animal.
—Federal Food, Drug and Cosmetic Act, 1958

Now such an experiment can provide strong evidence that large doses of an additive over a short period do (or don't) induce cancer in rats. We would really like to know whether small doses over a long period induce cancer in people. As the list of condemned additives grows (cyclamates, the food color Red 2, saccharin, . . .), so does the grumbling. Part of the grumbling is about the all-or-nothing character of the law. Surely, some say, if so useful a substance as saccharin causes just a little cancer, we ought to allow it in our colas, cookies, and cakes. That's a policy question, not a scientific question, and I leave you to choose your own poison. But part of the grumbling concerns the realism of rat experiments as indicators of human health hazards.

Informed opinion holds that the rats can be trusted in general. But *every* species has its peculiarities, and the case of the universally used sweetener saccharin may ride on a peculiarity of rats. Saccharin caused bladder tumors in rat trials, and the bladders of rats are special. Rats concentrate their urine very highly before excreting it. Saccharin is not metabolized, but is excreted unchanged. So the saccharin sits there in the rat bladders for a long time, in raw form and in high concentration, waiting for the rat to get around to urinating.

Some respectable scientists think that all that saccharin could cause tumors by physically irritating the bladder. Only in rats, or course, not in people.

There are ways to check this hypothesis that saccharin is dangerous only to rats. Trials on monkeys or hamsters, for example. Such experiments on people are frowned on, but it is possible to observe if bladder cancer occurs more frequently in heavy users of saccharin. The verdict is not yet in, but it appears that these alternative studies may find saccharin not guilty.[3]

This and many another example point to a clear principle. Rarely does a single experiment definitely establish that A causes B. There is almost always some flaw. (What flaws there might be is the subject of this section.) Repeated experiments, perhaps combined with other kinds of studies, are usually needed to found a conclusion on rock rather than sand.

Difficulty 3: Avoiding Hidden Bias

Many of our warnings about sources of bias in sample surveys concerned the need for care in areas other than the statistical design. There is an art to wording questions; there are special techniques to increase the response rate. In experimentation, there are also special techniques and precautions that go beyond the statistical design. We will mention two common precautions: the double-blind technique and randomization for purposes other than assigning units to treatments.

> **Example 10.** *Double-blind experiments.* In the vitamin C trial (Example 7 on p. 64), the health of the subjects was checked regularly and a judgment was made as to whether each was illness-free. These judgments are necessarily somewhat subjective, especially because the experiment concerned mild illnesses such as the common cold. The physician making the judgment may be unconsciously influenced by knowledge of what treatment the subject received, especially if he or she knows that the treatment was a placebo and so "ought" to have no effect. (Keep in mind that this is not a deliberate bias, simply an unconscious influence similar to the placebo effect in patients.) Therefore the diagnosing physician is kept ignorant of which treatment each subject received, so the diagnosis cannot be different for subjects in the two groups. This is called the *double-blind technique.* If only the subjects are ignorant of which treatment they are given, we have a single-blind experiment. When, as here, both the subjects and those who evaluate the outcome are ignorant of which treatment was given, we have a double-blind experiment. Only the director of the experiment knows which patients received vitamin C pills and which received sugar pills.

The double-blind procedure is used whenever possible in medical trials because experience has shown that even careful investigators can be influenced by knowledge of the treatments used. Such ideas ought to be used in other experi-

"Dr. Burns, are you sure this is what the statisticians call a double blind experiment?"

mental settings whenever they are appropriate. For example, in a common ESP (extrasensory perception) experiment, the experimenter looks at cards printed with various shapes (star, square, circle, etc.) invisible to the subject. The subject guesses the shapes, and the experimenter records whether the guesses are correct. It was noticed that the experimenter often recorded some incorrect guesses as correct. This does not necessarily show deliberate distortion but may be a result of the experimenter's desire to discover ESP. The remedy is to have the subject's guesses recorded by a third party who cannot see the cards and does not know whether a guess is right or wrong. The written record of guesses is later compared with a written record (made before the experiment) of the shape of each card in the shuffled deck used. Failure to use blind experimentation often invalidates "experiments" set up to prove a point.

Example 11. *More randomization.* In experiments on nutrition, it is common to use newly weaned male white rats as experimental units. Rats are randomly assigned to the diets to be compared, thus assuring that the stronger rats are not somehow assigned to one diet. Weight gain over a several-week period is observed. Now it turns out that rats placed in top cages gain weight somewhat faster than rats housed in bottom cages.* If rats fed diet A were placed in the bottom row, those fed diet B in the row above, and those fed diet C in the top row, the effects of diet and cage location would be confounded. The remedy is to assign rats to cages at random. Note that this is not the same as the random assignment to diets used in the experimental design. It is quite common to use additional randomization somewhere in carrying out an experiment.

The design of the ESP experiment also can be improved by an additional randomization. Instead of using a deck of cards, we might place cards bearing different shapes on a table in front of the "sender" with a light next to each. The lights are lit in an order determined by a table of random digits. The sender concentrates on the card whose light is on. The subject being tested for ESP sits in another room with the shapes in front of him, and pushes a button under the shape he thinks the sender is concentrating on. Score is kept automatically by an electronic device that sees whether the button pushed by the subject matches the sender's light. The use of a table of random digits prevents the subject from picking up patterns in a reshuffled deck, and keeps the sender "blind." The entire format is designed to prevent communication between sender and subject.

No precaution is too elaborate in such an experiment, for many professional "psychics" are clever frauds, and many "researchers" on psychic phenomena want so badly to find paranormal effects that they unconsciously collaborate with the psychic. It is not surprising that the most publicized "scientific experiments" on psychic phenomena have been arranged by physicists, who are naive where human subjects are concerned. As one skeptic put it, "Electrons and rats don't cheat. Professional psychics do."[4] Anyone planning to test the powers of psychics should have at least a psychologist present, and preferably a professional magician who knows the tricks of the trade. (Houdini made a regular practice of exposing phony spiritualist "mediums," and contemporary magicians perform like services.)

Difficulty 4: Attention to Detail

Even when your subjects are not as slippery as psychics, no data collection design can survive lack of attention to detail. It is surprising how often sloppiness infects even important experiments. In 1976, the FDA banned Red 2, the food

---

*See Example 14 in this Chapter for a more detailed study of this example, which is based on Elisabeth Street and Mavis B. Carroll, "Preliminary Evaluation of a New Food Product," in J. M. Tanur et al. (eds.), *Statistics: A Guide to the Unknown* (San Francisco: Holden-Day, 1972). This fact about rats appears on p. 222.

color most widely used in the United States, as a potential cause of cancer. Here is a quote from an account of the experiment that led to the ban. [5]

> **Example 12.** The study involved feeding Red 2 to four different groups of rats, each at a different dosage level, and then comparing the health of these treated groups with the health of a control group. There were 500 rats in all—seemingly enough for a solid evaluation. But the study was left unsupervised for a long period of time after a scientist was transferred, and it developed two serious flaws. To begin with, the animal handlers managed to put some of the rats back in the wrong cages part way through the experiment, so that an undetermined number of rats were shifted among the control group and the four treated groups. Second, the animal handlers were lackadaisical about retrieving dead rats from their cages and rushing them off to the pathologist for examination. As a result, virtually all of the rats that died during the course of the experiment were so badly decomposed as to be of little use for evaluation. Only those rats that survived to the end of the experiment and were killed—some 96 in all— were available for detailed histopathological examination, "It was the lousiest experiment I've seen in my life," commented one scientist who reviewed the data.

A decision had to be made, and a clever statistician managed to rescue some information. But careless supervision prevented the kind of clear conclusion that properly designed experiments are intended to produce. The detailed statement of exactly how the experiment is to be conducted is called (especially in clinical trials) the *protocol* of the experiment. Writing a careful protocol and making certain that it is followed is part of an experimenter's job.

4.   More on Experimental Design

The basic ideas of statistical design of experiments are *randomization* and *control*.

> **Randomization** is the random allocation of experimental units among treatments, most simply by assigning a SRS of units to each treatment.

> **Control** is taking account of extraneous factors in the experimental design, most simply by the use of equivalent groups for comparison.

Completely randomized designs use both randomization and control in their simplest form, allocating the units at random among all the treatments. The examples in Section 2 were particularly simple in that the treatments were levels of a single factor, such as "drug administered" in the University Group Diabetes Program. Many experiments have more than one factor so interactions among the factors can be studied. Here is an example with two factors and six treatments.

Example 13. A food products company is preparing a new cake mix for marketing. It is important that the taste of the cake not be changed by small variations in baking time or temperature. An experiment is done in which batches of batter are baked at 300°, 320°, and 340°F, and for 1 hour and 1 hour and 15 minutes. All possible combinations are used, resulting in six treatments that can be outlined as follows

		Factor A (temperature)		
		300°	320°	340°
Factor B (time)	1 hr	1	2	3
	1¼ hr	4	5	6

Sixty batches of batter—ten for each treatment—will be prepared from the mix and baked. The batches should be assigned at random to the treatments. This can be done by rolling a fair die repeatedly. If the first roll gives a 4, the first cake prepared is baked under treatment 4 (300° for 1¼ hours), and so on until 10 cakes have been baked under each treatment. It is also possible to choose a SRS of size 10 from the numbers 01 to 60 to obtain the positions in which cakes will receive Treatment 1 on baking, then a SRS of the remaining 50 numbers to obtain the baking positions for Treatment 2 and so on. After baking, each cake will be scored for taste and texture by a panel of tasters. These scores are the dependent variables.

It would be a serious mistake in this example to first prepare 10 batches of batter to bake under Treatment 1, then 10 under Treatment 2, and so on. Any factor changing systematically over time, as room humidity might, would be confounded with the experimental treatments. Notice that there are two experimental factors (baking time and oven temperature). Each treatment is a combination of a particular level of each factor. This design is somewhat more complex than those with only one experimental factor, but it is completely randomized because the 60 units (batches of batter) are assigned completely at random to the six treatments.

Control appears in completely randomized designs only in the basic idea of comparative experimentation. Much of the advanced study of experimental design concentrates on more elaborate ways of controlling extraneous factors. We will introduce only one additional experimental design to illustrate the use of control in experiments.

> **Example 14.** It is common in nutrition studies to compare diets by feeding them to newly weaned male rats and measuring the weight gained by the rats over a 28-day period.* If 30 such rats are available and 3 diets are to be compared, each diet will be fed to 10 rats. Random assignment of rats to diets will average the effect of extraneous factors such as the health of the rats. It is nonetheless wise to take additional steps to produce equivalent groups of rats for each diet. For example, standard strains of laboratory rats are available; this minimizes hereditary differences among the rats.
>
> We can also redesign the experiment. The initial weight of the rats is an extraneous factor that is especially important as an influence on weight gain. Rather than randomly assign 10 rats to each diet, we therefore first divide the animals into 10 groups of 3 rats each based on weight. The three lightest rats form the first group, the next lightest three form the second group, and so on, with the tenth group consisting of the three heaviest rats. These groups of rats of similar weight are called *blocks*. Now we randomly assign one rat from each block to each diet. The blocks help to create equivalent groups of 10 rats to be fed each diet, because the rats in each block are approximately equal in weight and one of them is assigned to each diet.

In Example 14, we did *not* use the completely randomized design described by

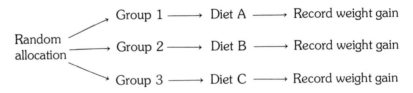

A completely randomized design handles all extraneous factors by randomization. If the weight gained by individual rats varies a lot from rat to rat, the groups fed diets A, B, and C will have quite different average weight gains just because of this individual variation. Thus it will be hard to detect the systematic effect of the diets. One remedy is to add more rats to each group to obtain less variable average results. That's expensive. Another remedy is to take account of the worrisome extraneous factor in the layout of the experiment, that is, to control

---

*For more information on this example, see Elisabeth Street and Mavis B. Carroll, "Preliminary Evaluation of a New Food Product," in J. M. Tanur et al. (eds.), *Statistics: A Guide to the Unknown* (San Francisco: Holden-Day, 1972).

for the effect of initial weight directly rather than simply relying on randomization to average the effect. This was done in Example 14. First divide the rats into blocks consisting of rats of about the same weight. This is *not* random, but is based on a particular extraneous factor, the initial weight of the rats. Then randomize, but only within the blocks, by randomly assigning one of the three rats in each block to each diet. This is called a *randomized complete block design*. It has the pattern shown in Figure 2.

There are still three experimental groups of ten rats each, one fed each of diets A, B, and C. Each group contains one rat from each of the ten blocks, so the initial weights of the rats in the three groups closely match. This matching greatly reduces the variation in average weight gain among the groups owing to different initial weights. It is now much easier to detect any difference in weight gain resulting from the different diets.

Blocking in experimental design is similar to stratification in sampling. Both require judgment to classify units into groups (blocks or strata) in such a way that units within a group show less variability than the entire population of units. Randomization is then used only within each block or stratum. That is, the randomization no longer is "complete" as in a completely randomized design but is restricted to each block separately.

The definition of *control* as taking account of extraneous factors in the experimental design is now clearer. The blocks in a randomized complete block design are groups of units that agree in some extraneous factor important to the outcome of the experiment. The term "block" originated in agricultural experimentation, where it refers to a compact plot of land with little variation in soil type, fertility, and so forth. In experiments on fertilizers or cultivation methods,

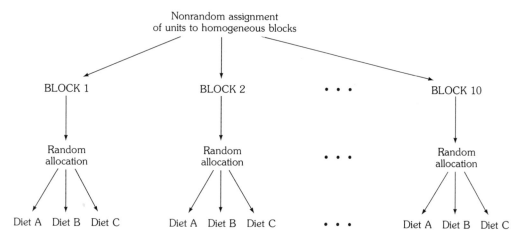

Figure 2. Randomized complete block design. In such a design, judgment is used to form blocks of similar units, and randomization is applied within each block separately.

we are not interested in extraneous factors such as soil type and fertility. Random assignment of treatments (fertilizers or whatever) to small plots of ground (experimental units) within the same block gives equivalent units for comparison of treatments. Several blocks give a larger number of observations, and also provide data on more than one soil type and fertility. In Example 14, a block consisted of animals of approximately equal weight. We are interested in the effect of diet, not of initial weight. Because animals within a block have the same initial weight, it should be easier to detect the effect of diet when these animals are fed different diets. We use several blocks to obtain more observations; data on three rats would not be precise even if all had the same initial weight. In summary, blocks are a way of holding fixed an extraneous variable that would otherwise cause large variations in the experimental results. A randomized complete block design therefore will give more precise (more repeatable) results than a completely randomized design with the same number of units.

Completely randomized designs and simple random samples employ random selection from the entire available set of units. Randomized complete block designs and stratified random samples restrict random selection to predetermined blocks or strata that are less variable than the entire population. More elaborate experimental designs further restrict the groups of units within which random selection is made. Because these groups often are formed by taking account of extraneous variables, restrictions on randomization frequently are associated with control of extraneous factors.

Extraneous factors can be dealt with by either randomization or control. Completely randomized experiments rely exclusively on the averaging effects of randomization, while randomized complete block experiments include an extraneous factor directly in forming blocks. Elaborate experimental designs often deal with many factors by control. In a general sense, factors with a large influence on the outcome should be controlled. Others can be randomized. Using a completely randomized design in place of a randomized complete block design is not wrong in the sense of producing invalid results. But it is inefficient. That is, the more elaborate design requires fewer experimental units to give equally precise results. In Section 1 I stated that the first goal of experimental design was to obtain valid results, to discover the true effects of the treatments. The second goal is to do this as efficiently as possible, to use as few units as possible for a given degree of precision. The randomized complete block design hints at how this second goal is pursued.

5.   Social Experiments

The effectiveness of a new fertilizer or a new drug is always tested by a controlled and randomized experiment. And for good reason: A well-designed experiment can provide clearer answers than any other method of study. What about testing the effectiveness of a new welfare program or health care system or preschool education program? Public policy decisions in these areas have usually been based on much supposition and little knowledge. It is tempting to try an experiment in the hope of finding clear answers. Such *social experiments* have been done during the past decade. I will describe one such experiment and comment on this method of testing social programs.

Many proposals for change in the present welfare system have been made. Supporters of these changes argue that new welfare programs would provide stronger incentives for welfare families to seek work and for families to stay together. Opponents argue that the new programs would be expensive and of doubtful effectiveness. In response to these arguments, the Federal government has sponsored five experiments to test alternative welfare policies. One of these, the New Jersey Income-Maintenance Experiment, was conducted in four urban areas in New Jersey and Pennsylvania, beginning in 1968. [6]

The policy tested in this experiment comprised a guaranteed annual income and a negative income tax that the government pays to (rather than collects from) low-income families. Just as the ordinary income tax rises by some percentage of earned income, the payment made under the negative income tax drops by some percentage of earned income. There are two factors in this scheme: the guarantee level and the tax rate. The guarantee is the amount the government pays a family having no earned income. The tax rate states how fast the welfare payments fall as earned income increases. Suppose, for example, that the guarantee is $3000 and the tax rate is 30%. A family with no earned income receives $3000 (the guarantee) in welfare payments. If the family earns $2000, the welfare payment decreases by 30% of this, or $600. Now the family receives $2400 in welfare ($3000 less $600) plus the $2000 it earned, or $4400 in all. Figure 3 shows that as the family earns more, the welfare payments decrease but total income always increases. Under the present system, payments end abruptly at a certain income level, so taking a job may lower a recipient's income. The negative income tax is intended to provide an incentive for welfare recipients to find jobs.

This social experiment had nine treatments, including the current welfare system as a control. The eight experimental treatments are shown in Table 2. The guarantee is expressed as a percent of the poverty lines established by the Social Security Administration. The actual dollar amounts guaranteed depended on the size of the family, and were raised during the four years of the study as rising prices pushed up the poverty line. Notice that not all possible combinations of the two factors were used as treatments.

The population from which units for the experiment were selected consisted of low-income households containing at least two persons, one of them a healthy male between 18 and 58 years old. This requirement eliminates many poverty-stricken families in which no employable male is present. This population was chosen because of special interest in the effects of the new welfare system on working-age males, an interest aroused not so much by sexism as by the fact that working-age males generally cannot collect welfare under the present system and so might have less incentive to work under a new system that

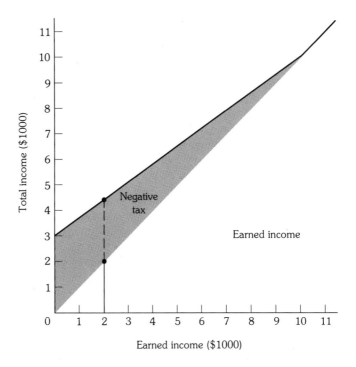

Figure 3. The negative income tax. As a family's earned income grows, the negative tax (shaded region) decreases but total income increases. A family earning $2000 (solid line) also receives $2400 in negative tax payments (broken line), for a total income of $4400. The graph assumes a $3000 base and a 30% tax rate.

would provide welfare benefits to them. None of the four income-maintenance experiments funded by the Federal government in other parts of the country required that a male worker be present.

As recommended in Section 3, experimental units were chosen from the population by sampling. Poverty areas in four cities were selected from census data and on-site inspection. Then blocks were selected at random within these areas, and field workers sent out to make lists of all dwelling units in each block selected. From these, a sample of households was chosen. Interviewers visited these households to see if they belonged to the target population and to explain the experiment. Now came the fun—dark stairwells, vicious dogs, hostile local politicians, and militant community groups. These were dealt with. But 10% of the dwelling units were empty. Of the remaining households, 19% were never at home (in five tries) and 18% refused to speak to the interviewer in four visits. The initial sample of 48,000 households yielded 27,000 who were interviewed. Of these, only 3124 were eligible to participate in the experiment; low income families with able-bodied men present are not common in urban areas. Another 425 families had vanished by the time interviewers returned to invite them to

Table 2

EXPERIMENTAL TREATMENTS FOR THE NEW JERSEY
INCOME-MAINTENANCE EXPERIMENT

		Factor A (guarantee as percent of poverty line)			
		50	75	100	125
Factor B	30	X	X		
(tax rate	50	X	X	X	X
in percent)	70		X	X	

join the experiment. The life of an experimenter out there in the real world has its frustrations. But at last 1357 families were chosen, and agreed, to participate.

You might well ask if this sample is representative of the population after all those refusals and never-at-homes. Comparing characteristics of the sample with characteristics of all families in their neighborhoods (courtesy of the 1970 Census) suggests, amazingly enough, that the sample is quite representative in income, family composition, and so on. Whether the noncooperators and never-at-homes are different in less tangible ways that would affect their reaction to a negative income tax remains unanswered.

Now for the random assignment of units to treatments. Well, not quite yet. First the sample households were divided into three blocks of 400 to 500 families each, depending on their normal income. Random assignment to the nine treatments took place separately within each block. The use of blocks was due to a reason not mentioned in Section 4: The experiment could not afford to assign too many of the lowest-income families to the most expensive (high guarantee and low tax rate) treatments. It would simply cost too much, because the gap between these families' normal earned income and that promised by the new welfare scheme was so great. So the randomization did not make all treatments equally likely. Indeed, the chance of being assigned to a specific treatment was different in each of the three blocks. But each family had a known chance of being assigned to each treatment, and these chances were the same for every family in a block. It was a complicated bit of randomization, much akin to moving from a SRS to a general probability sample.

This experimental design is more involved than any we met earlier, in three ways. First, it makes use of blocks in a two-factor experiment. Second, not all of the possible combinations of the two factors were used. And third, different randomization patterns, none of them giving a household the same chance of landing in all nine groups, were employed in each block. You would call a statistician before entering such a jungle, but a glimpse of this statistical jungle is one motive for the tale I have told in this section. A second motive is to remind you once again of how much harder experiments are in the slums of Trenton than on the statistician's desk. The third, and most important, of my motives is to instill the idea of using statistically designed experiments to answer questions about public policy. The advantages of social experimentation are clear: There is a real possibility that experiments will give a better picture of the effects of a new welfare policy than any amount of debate. The new welfare system tested in the New Jersey experiment succeeded in increasing the income of poverty-level families without reducing the employment rate of the husbands. But the new system did lower the employment of their wives; the wives in the experimental groups worked 23% fewer hours per week than the controls. (Because these families had an average of four children, the wives were working hard at home.) These and other effects of the negative income tax are illuminated by the experiment.

The disadvantages of social experiments are also clear. They take a long time and are expensive. The New Jersey experiment lasted four years, cost $8 million, and the detailed results are just being published. Often problems of validity arise; for example, participating in an experiment may change the behavior of welfare families. Moreover, conditions may so change between the planning of an experiment and release of first results five years later that the answers given by the experiment no longer respond to the right questions.

Public policy decisions affect us all, either directly or indirectly by changing our society and spending our taxes. Experimentation is a powerful tool for gathering information on the effects of treatments. Such a tool should certainly help to guide policy decisions. Social experimentation, used carefully, is an idea whose time has come.

6. Ethics and Experimentation

Carrying out experiments on human subjects raises serious ethical problems. Medical experiments (often called *clinical trials*) have been particularly controversial because the giving or withholding of medical treatment can result in direct danger to a patient. Yet comparative experiments are necessary if life-saving medical knowledge is to be obtained. Some treatments—"magic bullets" like penicillin—have effects so dramatic that properly designed experiments are not needed to detect them. But this is rare. Medicine usually advances in smaller steps: The death rate from the new operation is 10% lower than for the old one; patients given the new drug live 5% longer than those given the old. The dilemma is that medical experiments often are potentially harmful to some of the subjects, yet are needed to obtain valuable knowledge. The potential for harm must be balanced against the value of the knowledge.

All agree that medical experiments must be guided by the first principle of medical ethics, expressed in the ancient Latin motto *"Primum non nocere"* or "First of all, do no harm." That is, exposing patients to treatments *known* to be harmful is clearly unethical. Latin mottos lack teeth, however, and experimenters have only recently become sufficiently sensitive to their subjects' welfare. Here are two examples of blatant abuse of subjects.[7]

Example 15. In the early 1960s, two cancer researchers injected live cancer cells into geriatric patients without the informed consent of the patients. Their intent was to study the possibility of "infection" with cancer.

Example 16. Syphilis progresses slowly, so it is difficult to study the development of the disease. From 1932 to 1972, researchers observed two groups of subjects in Tuskegee, Alabama, one with and one without the disease. (This was an observational study with a control group, not an experiment.) In 1945, the first effective treatment for syphilis (penicillin) became known. The researchers did not treat their subjects with penicillin, but continued observing the progress of their syphilis.

The second ethical standard for clinical trials requires that the *informed consent* of the subjects be obtained. Subjects are told that they will be part of a research study, that is, that something beyond treating their illness is going on. The nature of the study and the possible risks and benefits are explained, and the patients are asked to agree to participate and to consent to random assignment to a treatment. Those who refuse are not included in the experiment, and usually receive the standard therapy. (Why cannot these patients be used as part of the control group, even though they receive the standard therapy?) Many individuals are willing to participate in random clinical trials for the future benefit of all. But many patients find the idea of being subjects in an experiment hard to accept, and the idea that their treatment will be chosen by the toss of a coin even harder to accept. In studies of serious conditions such as cancer, as many as 80% or 90% of the subjects approached sometimes refuse to participate. The strict rules on disclosure and informed consent now enforced in clinical trials cause considerable grumbling among medical researchers.

Informed consent is somewhat difficult to achieve, especially when the subjects are a dependent group rather than paying consumers of medical care. It is probably not accidental that the subjects in Example 15 were aged and institutionalized, while those in Example 16 were poor and black. Groups such as prisoners have often been volunteer subjects for medical experiments. We might doubt whether prisoners requested to "volunteer" are really free to refuse. In early 1976, the Federal Bureau of Prisons announced that medical experimentation on Federal prisoners no longer would be permitted. *The New York Times* commented in an editorial (March 8, 1976):

> *Truly voluntary consent is virtually impossible to achieve in prison and there is a large temptation to undervalue prisoners' interests during the course of such research. The new Federal policy is clearly the appropriate response to these problems and it should serve as an example to the states which still permit experiments to be conducted in their prisons.*

What all of this adds up to is that medical experimentation in the United States is subject to tight rules for the protection of subjects, rules drawn up by the

Federal agencies that pay for (and hence can control) almost all medical studies. Some doctors and statisticians say that as a result we will never learn the answers to some medical questions. That is true enough, yet it has always been true that some valuable experiments were forbidden by ethical constraints. Here is an example.

> **Example 17.** People who smoke are more likely to contract lung cancer (and many other diseases) than those who do not, and the disease is more common among long-term heavy smokers than among those who have smoked less. This may happen because smoking is a cause of lung cancer. But because people choose whether or not to smoke, some factor such as heredity might cause cancer-prone persons to choose to smoke in greater numbers than others. An experiment to settle this question is easy to imagine. Choose young subjects (say age 10) who have not smoked. Assign them at random to groups. Group 1 will begin to smoke at age 18 and smoke two packs of cigarettes a day for life. Group 2 will not smoke at all. Other groups will smoke less, or for shorter periods. All subjects will be observed for life. Such an experiment is morally impossible; we are not willing to force some subjects to smoke and others not to.

There is no easy answer to the problem of balancing the growth of knowledge and the protection of patients. I think it is fair to say that the present rules restore that balance after a period in which medical researchers were largely free to follow their natural bias in favor of gaining knowledge.

Clinical trials also present a more subtle class of moral problems: those arising from random assignment of subjects to different treatments. Here are two examples.

> **Example 18.** There is at present no vaccine for a serious viral disease. A vaccine is developed and appears effective in animal trials. Only a comparative experiment with human subjects in which a control group receives a placebo can determine the true worth of the vaccine. Is it ethical to give some subjects the placebo, which cannot protect them against the disease? (Of course, the vaccine may have undesirable side effects. It may even give a few patients the disease it is designed to protect against. So a risk accompanies the chance of protection.)

> **Example 19.** The standard surgical treatment for breast cancer has long been radical mastectomy, an operation to remove the infected breast, underlying chest muscles and lymph nodes in the arm pits. This operation is quite disfiguring, and many women would prefer a simple mastectomy (removal of the breast only) or even removal of the tumor only. But these operations cannot be more effective than a radical mastectomy, and may

be less effective, because they often leave cancer cells behind. The effectiveness of these operations can be compared only by a clinical trial. But is it ethical to randomly assign women to a treatment that cannot be more effective than the radical surgery? The other treatments should be used if they equal the effectiveness of radical surgery, since they are less disfiguring. But we cannot know whether they are equally effective without a trial.

In each case, one group of patients will receive an inferior therapy. I think that experimentation is ethical in such situations, for two reasons. First, it is not known which of the treatments is superior; if that were certain, all patients would be given the better therapy. No one is deliberately deprived of the best therapy, even though because of our ignorance one group will receive an inferior treatment. Second, I remind you again that controlled and randomized experiments are the only method of discovering which therapy is superior. Refusing to experiment is therefore not a solution to these ethical problems. The natural reluctance to "use human beings as guinea pigs" cannot be justified. For refusing to experiment would not only leave *all* present patients with an inferior treatment if the new is better, it would deprive all future patients of the better treatments which can be found only by experimentation. Dr. Bernard Fisher, director of a study of breast cancer treatments now in progress, was quoted in *The New York Times* (October 2, 1974) as follows.

> [Dr. Fisher said] . . . that random clinical trials were "ethical" and the only way to answer women's questions about breast cancer surgery. Without such trials, the current state of uncertainty will persist indefinitely, Dr. Fisher insisted, and women will continue either to be disfigured unnecessarily or to receive less than the best therapy.

When we leave the area of medical experiments, the direct risk to the subjects is often less clear, but so is the value of the knowledge gained. Consider, for example, the experiments conducted by psychologists in their study of human personality. Here is a particularly distasteful example.[8]

> **Example 20.** Stanley Milgram of Yale conducted the following experiment "to see if a person will perform acts under group pressure that he would not have performed in the absence of social inducement." The subject arrives with three others who (unknown to the subject) are confederates of the experimenter. The experimenter explains that he is studying the effects of punishment on learning. The Learner (one of the confederates) is strapped into an electric chair, mentioning in passing that he has a mild heart condition. The subject and the other two confederates are Teachers. They sit in front of a panel with switches ranging from "Slight Shock" to "Danger: Severe Shock" and are told that they must shock the

Learner whenever he fails in a memory learning task. How badly the Learner is shocked is up to the Teachers, and will be the *lowest* level suggested by any Teacher on that trial.

All is rigged. The Learner answers incorrectly on 30 of the 40 trials. The two Teacher-confederates call for a higher shock level at each failure. As the shocks increase, the Learner protests, asks to be let out, shouts, complains of heart trouble, and finally screams in pain. (The "shocks" are phony and the Learner is an actor; but the subject doesn't know this.) What will the subject do? He can keep the shock at the lowest level, but the two Teacher-stooges are pressuring him to torture the Learner more for each failure.

What the subject most often does is give in to the pressure. "While the experiment yields wide variation in performance, a substantial number of subjects submitted readily to pressure applied to them by the confederates." Milgram noted that in questioning after the experiment, the subjects often admit that they acted against their own principles and are upset by what they did. "The subject was then dehoaxed carefully and had a friendly reconciliation with the victim." [9]

Even though this experiment offends most people, we must agree that the potential harm to the subjects is not as clear as in some medical experiments. That sick feeling of knowing that you were tricked into acts you consider despicable doesn't put Dr. Milgram in the class of those who in Example 15 injected live cancer cells into aged patients. But then neither is knowledge of the behavior of individuals under group pressure as clearly valuable as knowledge of whether or not cancer can be infectious.

I am happy to mention that Milgram's experiments could no longer be performed in most universities. All universities and other research institutions now have review committees that screen all research with human subjects for potentially harmful treatments. Experiments with possibly negative emotional effects much less severe than those in Milgram's studies are regularly vetoed by the review committee at Purdue (where I teach), and presumably elsewhere. The committee system serves as a check on the consciences of individual researchers. Yet many experiments in the social sciences include treatments in the gray area where "possible emotional harm" shades into "attacks human dignity" or merely into the slippery category of "in bad taste." Solomon himself could not make decisions acceptable to all in so foggy a situation.

In addition to the question of what constitutes "possible harm to the subject," Milgram's work illustrates another problem common to studies of human behavior. The informed consent required by medical ethics is simply not possible. If the subject were aware of the true purpose of the experiment, the experiment would not be valid. So subjects are usually asked to consent to participation without being given a detailed description of the experiment and its purpose. Do such experiments amount to unjustified manipulation of the subjects, bringing out aspects of their behavior that they would prefer not to reveal to scrutiny? Or

"I'm doing a little study on the effects of emotional stress. Now, just take the axe from my assistant."

are the experiments justified by the knowledge gained, by uninformed consent, and by the fact that the treatments are not harmful? Exercises 1 and 2 afford an opportunity for you to make this judgment in some specific cases.

Experimentation is necessary for the advance of knowledge, and at least with medical trials few would deny that the knowledge gained serves the general good. Nevertheless, experimenters are often tempted to place their search for knowledge ahead of the welfare of their subjects. It is fortunate that interest in the welfare of subjects has greatly increased in recent years. Yet citizens would do well not to rely entirely on review committees and other expressions of the collective conscience of researchers. The record of experimenters on human subjects is not good enough to justify complacency.

NOTES

1. Read "Is Vitamin C Really Good for Colds?" in *Consumer Reports,* February 1976, pp. 68–70, for a discussion of this conclusion. The article also reviews the need for controlled experiments and the Toronto study.

2. Jerome Cornfield, "The University Group Diabetes Program," *Journal of the American Medical Association,* Volume 217 (1971), pp. 1676–1687.

3. The saccharin question is discussed in detail in Barbara J. Culliton, "Saccharin: A Chemical in Search of an Identity," *Science,* Volume 196 (1977), pp. 1179–1183.

Details of the data from the rat experiment that led to FDA action appear in a letter to the editor, *Science*, Volume 197 (1977), p. 320.

4. Martin Gardner, "Supergull," *New York Review of Books*, March 17, 1977. This review of two books on psychic researchers illustrates nicely the naive experiments and vague and deceptive accounts that pervade this field.

5. From Philip M. Boffey, "Color Additives: Botched Experiment Leads to Banning of Red Dye No. 2," *Science*, Volume 191 (1976), p. 450.

6. For a full account of this social experiment, see David Kershaw and Jerilyn Fair, *The New Jersey Income-Maintenance Experiment, Volume I* (New York: Academic Press, 1976). All of the specific information about that experiment cited in this section is taken from that book.

7. Both cases are reported in Bernard Barber, "The Ethics of Experimentation with Human Subjects," *Scientific American*, February 1976, pp. 25–31.

8. Stanley Milgram, "Group Pressure and Action Against a Person, " *Journal of Abnormal and Social Psychology*, Volume 69 (1964), pp. 137–143.

9. Postexperimental attitudes and the final quotation are in Stanley Milgram, "Liberating Effects of Group Pressure," *Journal of Personality and Social Psychology*, Volume 1 (1965), pp. 127–134.

Exercises

Section 1

1. A study of the effect of living in public housing on family stability and other variables in poverty-level households was carried out as follows. A list of applicants accepted for public housing was obtained, together with a list of families who applied but were rejected by the housing authorities. A random sample was drawn from each list, and the two groups were observed for several years.

   (a) Is this an experiment? Why or why not?
   (b) What are the independent and dependent variables?
   (c) Does this study contain confounding that may prevent valid conclusions on the effects of living in public housing? Explain.

2. An educator wants to compare the effectiveness of a "reading machine" with that of a standard reading curriculum. She tests the reading ability of each of a class of 4th graders, then divides them into two groups. One group uses only the machine, while the other studies a standard curriculum. At the end of the year, all students are retested and the two groups are compared for increase in reading ability.

   (a) Is this an experiment? Why or why not?
   (b) What are the independent and dependent variables?

3. In each of the situations that follow, confounding is present. Explain briefly what variables are confounded and why the conclusions drawn about the effect of the independent variable on the dependent variable are not valid.

   (a) Last year only 10% of a group of adult men did not have a cold at some time during the winter. This year all the men in the group took 1 gram of vitamin C each day, and 20% had no colds. This shows that vitamin C helps prevent colds.

(b) The educator in Exercise 2 asked for teachers who would volunteer to use the teaching machines. One group of students was taught by teachers who volunteered to use the machines, while the control group was taught by teachers who did not volunteer. At the end of the year, the machine group had improved their reading scores somewhat more than the nonmachine group.

(c) It was suspected that a daily vitamin supplement might improve the health of nursing home patients. The patients in a large nursing home were divided into two groups. One group was given a vitamin supplement each day, while the other group received no treatment. After six months, the first group had fewer days ill than the second.

4. In 1976, Pepsi-Cola ran a television advertising campaign that featured an experiment. Regular drinkers of Coca-Cola were given a glass of Coke, marked only as "Q," and a glass of Pepsi, marked only as "M." More than half of the subjects said brand "M" tasted better.

   Coca-Cola said (in less technical language) that this experiment was invalid owing to confounding of the brand of cola with an extraneous variable. Can you see where the confounding lies?

5. Professor Thomas Ryan of Pennsylvania State University told me about some poorly designed experiments he had encountered. One, for which a Ph.D. in education was awarded, compared the ethnocentrism of students in a largely white school, a largely black school, and an integrated school. But one of these was a school for the mentally retarded! The confounding in his second example is not so blatant. Discuss the following experiment, identifying the independent and dependent variables and any confounding present.

   A study of human development showed two types of movies to groups of children. Crackers were available in a bowl, and the investigators compared the number of crackers eaten by children watching the different kinds of movies. One kind was shown at 8 A.M. and another at 11 A.M.

6. Read the article "Safety of Anesthetics" by Lincoln E. Moses and Frederick Mosteller in *Statistics: A Guide to the Unknown*. Identify the independent variables, the dependent variables, and the extraneous variables confounded with the independent variable. Why is it that the data in Table 1 "cannot be trusted"?

7. After the July 1976 convention of the American Legion in Philadelphia, 29 convention-goers died of a mysterious "Legionnaires' disease." It was at first suspected that the disease might be a variety of influenza. To check this theory laboratory experimenters injected material from dead and sick Legionnaires into chick embryos and watched to see if influenza virus grew in the embryo. (The presence of small numbers of virus in the material injected would go undetected. But if they grow into many, they can be detected.) No influenza virus was found. A Yale Medical School virologist commented that

these results were not quite convincing. He said that a known dose of influenza virus should have been injected into other chick embryos as a "positive control."

Can you see the virologist's point and explain his objection in more detail?

Section 2

1. A vaccine for use against a dangerous virus has been developed. You have available 10 rats (named below), which will be exposed to the virus. Unprotected rats usually die when infected. Design an experiment to test the effectiveness of the vaccine. Use line 140 of Table A to carry out the random assignment.

Alfie	Bernie	Chuck	David	Frank
Harry	Lyman	Mercedes	Polyphemus	Zaffo

2. A group of 200 first graders is available to compare the effectiveness of method A and method B for teaching reading.

(a) Design an experiment to make this comparison.

(b) Explain carefully how you would carry out the random assignment called for in your design. Use Table A, beginning at line 137, to assign five students as a demonstration of your randomization.

3. You wish to compare three treatments for effectiveness in preventing flu: (1) flu vaccine, (2) 1 gram of vitamin C per day, (3) a placebo taken daily. Describe how you would use 600 volunteer subjects in a designed experiment to compare these treatments. (Do not actually do any randomization, but do include a diagram showing your design.)

4. To demonstrate how randomization elminates confounding, consider the following situation. A nutrition experimenter intends to compare the weight gain of newly weaned male rats fed diet A with that of rats fed diet B. To do this she will feed each diet to 10 rats. She has available 10 rats of genetic strain 1 and 10 of strain 2. Strain 1 is more vigorous, so if the 10 rats of strain 1 were fed diet A, the effects of strain and diet would be confounded and the experiment would be biased in favor of diet A.

Label the rats 00, 01, . . ., 19 (and use repeated labels if you wish to). Use Table A to assign 10 rats to diet A. Do this four times using different parts of the table, and write down the four experimental groups you obtained.

Suppose that the strain 1 rats are numbers 00, 02, 04, 06, 08, 10, 12, 14, 16, 18. How many of these rats were in each of the four diet A groups that you generated? What was the average number of strain 1 rats assigned to diet A?

5. Comparison alone does not make a study an experiment. Examples 3 and 4 in Section 1 are observational studies that compare two groups, but are not experiments. Can you clearly describe the difference between a comparative observational study and a comparative experiment? Can you say what advantages comparative experiments have over comparative observational studies?

6. Read the article "The Biggest Public Health Experiment Ever" by Paul Meier in *Statistics: A Guide to the Unknown.* Describe the experimental design used in the Salk vaccine trials. What extraneous factors would have been confounded with the treatment if the "observed control" approach had been used?

7. Makers of competing pain relievers sometimes claim that their pill dissolves faster, and illustrate this claim with pictures of pills dissolving in a glass of water. You are to compare the dissolving time of Anacin and aspirin.

   (a) Give the statistical design of an experiment to make this comparison.
   (b) Discuss any nonstatistical aspects of the experiment that may be important to your conclusion. For example, what do you mean by "aspirin"?
   (c) Do the experiment you designed. Is a clear difference in dissolving time apparent to you? (You may want to give your data to your instructor for a more formal analysis.)

8. Think of a simple question of interest to you that might be settled by an experiment. (See Exercise 7 for an example.) Design and carry out an appropriate experiment and write a report discussing it in detail.

9. The following article by the Associated Press appeared in *The New York Times* of October 16, 1975. Describe in detail how you think the experiment was designed. Does the news report omit any important information about the design? Are there any inconsistencies in the details given?

Marijuana Is Called An Effective Relief In Cancer Therapy

BOSTON, Oct. 15 (AP)—Marijuana is far more effective than any other drug in relieving the vomiting and nausea that plagues thousands of cancer patients undergoing chemical therapy, researchers say.

Clinical trials with cancer patients using a marijuana derivative have been so successful that the drug should be considered seriously as a treatment for the chemical therapy side effects, they add.

In a report to be published tomorrow in the New England Journal of Medicine, Harvard Medical School researchers at the Sidney Farber Cancer Center say they tested the effectiveness of the marijuana drug against a dummy drug in 22 patients with a variety of cancers.

For patients who completed the study, 12 of 15 cases involving marijuana drug treatments resulted in at least a 50 per cent reduction in vomiting and nausea after cancer therapy. And in five of these treatments, the patients suffered no nausea at all, the report added.

There was no decrease in nausea or vomiting in 14 cases in which placebo, or dummy treatment, was used, the researchers said. In the "double-blind" experiment, neither patients nor doctors knew in advance who got the real or dummy drugs.

Dr. Stephen E. Salan said in an interview that about 75 per cent of the thousands of patients getting chemotheraphy for cancer suffered moderate to extreme nausea and vomiting.

And of this group, 90 per cent get no relief from convential antinausea drugs, he added.

Dr. Salan said he and his colleagues in the study, Dr. Norman E. Zinberg and Dr. Emil Frei 30, did not know specifically why marijauna worked to decrease nausea.

---

10. The following Associated Press dispatch appeared in the *Lafayette Journal and Courier* of November 30, 1974.

   (a) What important information about the experiment design is given in the article?
   (b) Is any important information omitted?
   (c) Do you consider the results of the experiment convincing? Why or why not?

Praying to soybeans aids in higher yields

By GEORGE CORNELL

With county officials measuring the results, experimenters on an Ohio farm say they found that portions of a field that had been the object of loving prayers yielded the biggest crop.

The case offered an unusual instance of recent stepped-up interest in psychic phenomena, viewed by many with keen skepticism.

"Somehow God's creative energy of growth can be channeled through us even to plants," says Gus Alexander of Wright State University, who holds a doctorate in communications research and who set up the project.

It was carried out on a soybean field near Jamestown, Ohio, east of Dayton, with daily prayerful attention of a church group focused on six designated plots, but not on six adjoining control plots.

Alexander says the yield of soybeans receiving the special attention was increased by 4 percent over the comparable control plot, even though the experiment had extended over only a third of the growing season.

In checking results of the experiment late in October, the Greene county agent's technical assistant, Donald H. Tate, was on hand to weigh the yields from the six experimental and six control plots.

According to the figures, five of the experimental strips had produced heavier yields than had adjacent control strips, while in the sixth case the control strip had a slightly greater yield.

In the experiment, a group of 10 people at Dayton's Church of the Golden Key, supplied with diagrams of the soybean plots, took on the task of "sending love" to the experimental areas each night at 11:30 p.m. for about 40 days.

Reprinted by permission of The Associated Press.

Section 3

1. In each of the following cases, discuss briefly how far you think the experimental conclusions can be generalized. (We cannot be definite about this question of external validity without expert knowledge, so our answers will be partly guesses.)

   (a) The vitamin C study of Example 7 on p. 64.
   (b) The propaganda study of Example 6 on p. 63.
   (c) The dissolving time study of Exercise 7 on p. 91.

2. Fizz Laboratories, a pharmaceutical company, has developed a new pain relief medication. Sixty patients suffering from arthritis and needing pain relief

are available. Each patient will be treated and asked an hour later "About what percentage of pain relief did you experience?"

(a) Why should Fizz not simply administer the new drug and record the patients' responses?

(b) Design an experiment to compare the drug's effectiveness with that of aspirin and of a placebo.

(c) Should patients be told which drug they are receiving? How would this knowledge probably affect their reaction?

(d) If patients are not told which treatment they are receiving, the experiment is single-blind. Should this experiment be double-blind also? Explain.

3. An experiment that was publicized as showing that a meditation technique lowered the anxiety level of subjects was conducted as follows. The experimenter interviewed the subjects and assessed their level of anxiety. The subjects then learned how to meditate and did so regularly for a month. The experimenter re-interviewed them at the end of the month and assessed whether their anxiety level had decreased or not.

(a) There was no control group in this experiment. Why is this a blunder? What extraneous variables may be confounded with the effect of meditation?

(b) The experimenter who diagnosed the effect of the treatment knew that the subjects had been meditating. Explain how this knowledge could bias the experimental conclusions.

(c) Briefly discuss a proper experimental design, with controls and blind diagnosis, to assess the effect of meditation on anxiety level.

4. Additional randomization will improve the Coke versus Pepsi taste experiment described in Exercise 4 on p. 89. Explain what randomization is needed, and why.

5. Experiments with human subjects that continue over a long period of time face the problem of "dropouts" (subjects who quit the experiment) and "nonadherers" (subjects who stay in, but don't follow the experimental protocol). In his account of the University Group Diabetes Program (Example 8 on p. 66), Dr. Cornfield makes the following statement.

> For this complex problem, the UGDP has followed the generally accepted practice of comparing the mortality experience of the originally randomized groups, and of not eliminating dropouts or nonadherers from the analysis. This practice is conservative in that it dilutes whatever treatment effects, beneficial or adverse, are present.

Explain why not counting dropouts and nonadherers in the final results might exaggerate differences between groups.

Section 4

1. Since 1974, most cars have been equipped with catalytic converters to reduce harmful emissions. The Corning Glass Company is a manufacturer of the ceramic used to make the converters. The ceramic must be baked to a certain hardness. Corning had to decide which of three temperatures (500°F, 750°F, 1000°F) was best. But they also found that it mattered where the converter was placed in the oven (front, middle, back). So there are two experimental factors, temperature and placement.

   (a) Design a completely randomized experiment with 5 units in each group.
   (b) Using Table A, beginning with line 101, do the randomization required by your design.

2. In Exercise 4 of Section 2, a nutritionist had 10 rats of each of two genetic strains. She would certainly use a randomized complete block design with the two strains as blocks, and not the completely randomized design of that exercise.

   Give a randomized complete block design assigning 10 rats to each diet. Use Table A, beginning in line 111, to actually make the assignment.

3. Can aspirin help prevent heart attacks? There are reasons to think it can, and a large clinical trial called AMIS (Aspirin Myocardial Infarction Study) is underway to settle the matter. AMIS involves 4524 patients who have already had a heart attack, and will last four years and cost $17 million. The subjects have been randomly divided into control and experimental groups, with patients in the experimental group receiving 1 gram of aspirin each day.

   Now there appears Philip Majerus of the Washington University Medical School, who has evidence that as little as 180 milligrams (180/1000 of a gram) of aspirin each day has the chemical effect needed to help prevent heart attacks. What is more, says he, 1 gram a day may have other chemical effects that make this amount ineffective for heart attack prevention. Maybe AMIS will have to be done over with a lower dose (and another $17 million).

   Discuss the design of an experiment to study the effect of several different dosages of aspirin on heart attacks. (AMIS is discussed in *Science*, Volume 196 (1977), p. 1075.)

4. Hearing loss is much more common among premature infants than among full-term babies. It has long been thought that this is a physical effect of premature birth. Recently it has been suggested that hearing loss develops in infants who spend long periods in incubators due to the high noise level in standard incubators. (You see that the effect of being premature is confounded with the effect of spending a long period in an incubator because usually only premature babies spend time in incubators.)

   Design an experiment to decide which explanation is true. (Ignore practical and moral problems. You can get more or less information out of a correct experiment here, depending on how elaborate you want to make it.)

5. In the early 1940s, the Tennessee Valley Authority proposed to fertilize the farms in a poor mountain area of Virginia at no cost to the farmers for four years. It was hoped that fertilization of poor soil would improve the health of the people by improving their nutrition and income. Because overall nutrition improved rapidly during these years, such an uncontrolled study would have yielded invalid data. Fortunately, a statistician was asked to redesign the study before it was conducted.

   (a) Describe the independent and dependent variables and the extraneous factors that are confounded with the independent variables.
   (b) Give an experiment that will provide the TVA with valid data. (A discussion of this example, with more detail than given here, is provided by the TVA's statistician in Boyd Harshbarger, "An Example of How a Designed Experiment Saved Research Workers from False Recommendations," *The American Statistician*, Volume 28 (1974), pp. 128–129.)

6. A drug is suspected of affecting the coordination of subjects. The drug can be administered in three ways: orally, by injection under the skin, or by injection into a vein. The potency of the drug probably depends on the method of administration as well as on the dosage administered. A researcher therefore wishes to study the effect of the two factors, dosage at 3 levels and method of administration at the 3 levels mentioned. The response variable is the score of the subjects on a standard test of coordination. Ninety subjects are available.

   (a) Describe an appropriate completely randomized design. (Just give the design—don't do any randomization.)
   (b) The researcher could study the effect of dosage in an experiment comparing three dosage levels for one method of administration. He then could separately study the effect of administration by comparing the three methods for one dosage level. What advantages does the two-factor experiment you designed in (a) have over these two one-factor experiments together?

7. There is good evidence that physical stress, even stroking the leaves of a house plant for a minute each day, inhibits plant growth. Some claim (without good evidence) that speaking kindly to house plants encourages growth.

   (a) Discuss the design of an experiment to assess the effects of physical contact, talking to plants, or both, on growth. You must carefully describe the treatments and other aspects of the protocol.
   (b) Carry out your experiment and write a report describing the results.

Section 5

1. Two reports of social experiments are S. J. Press, "Police Manpower Versus Crime" and F. A. Haight, "Do Speed Limits Reduce Traffic Accidents?" both in *Statistics: A Guide to the Unknown.*

(a) Neither the New York experiment of Press' article nor the Scandinavian experiment discussed by Haight use statistical design to the extent of the New Jersey Income-Maintenance Experiment. What aspects of design (control, randomization, repetition on many units) are present and which are absent in each case?

(b) Describe briefly the practical barriers to social experiments mentioned in these essays. Many potential social experiments remain undone for similar reasons.

2. Another of the experimental trials of the negative income tax was conducted in Gary, Indiana. Unlike the New Jersey experiment, households with both male and female heads were included. (A word of explanation: Government statisticians do not classify married women as heads of households if their husbands are living with them. So a household with a female head rarely has an employable male present. The government has eliminated this somewhat sexist definition, and indeed the entire "head of household" label, effective with the 1980 Census.) The statistical design of the Gary experiment divided families into two blocks, those with male heads and those with female heads, and randomly assigned families to treatments within each block separately.

Explain why blocking was used in this social experiment.

3. Choose an issue of public policy that you feel might be clarified by a social experiment. Briefly discuss the statistical design of the experiment you are recommending. What are the treatments? Should blocking be used?

Section 6

There are no "right" answers to these exercises. Thoughtful persons are found on both sides of the dilemmas presented. I wish mainly to invite you to think about the ethics of experimentation.

1. *(Deception of subjects)* A psychologist conducts the following experiment. A team of subjects plays a game of skill against a computer for money rewards. Unknown to the subjects, one team member is a stooge whose stupidity causes the team to lose regularly. The experimenter observed the subjects through one-way glass. Her intent is to study the behavior of the subjects toward the stupid team member.

This experiment involves no risk to the subjects, and is intended simply to create the kind of situation that might occur in any pick-up basketball game. To create the situation, the subjects are deceived. Is this deception morally objectionable? Explain your position.

2. *(Enticement of subjects)* A psychologist conducted the following experiment. She measured the attitude of subjects toward cheating, then had them play a game rigged so winning without cheating was impossible. Unknown to them, the subjects were watched through one-way glass and a record was kept of who cheated and who did not. Then a second test of attitude was given.

Subjects who cheated tended to change their attitude to find cheating more acceptable. Those who resisted the temptation to cheat tended to condemn cheating more strongly on the second test of attitude. These results confirmed the psychologist's theory.

Unlike the experiment of Exercise 1, this experiment entices subjects to engage in behavior (cheating) that probably contradicts their own standards of behavior. And the subjects are led to believe that they can cheat secretly when in fact they are observed. Is this experiment morally objectionable? Explain your position.

3. *(Morality, good taste, and public money)* In 1976 the House of Representatives deleted from an appropriations bill funding for an experiment to study the effect of marijuana on sexual response. Like all government supported research, the proposed study had been reviewed by a panel of scientists both for scientific value and for risk to the subjects. *Science* (Volume 192 (1976), p. 1086) reported:

> *Dr. Harris B. Rubin and his colleagues at the Southern Illinois Medical School proposed to exhibit pornographic films to people who had smoked marihuana and to measure the response with sensors attached to the penis.*
>
> *Marihuana, sex, pornographic films—all in one package, priced at $120,000. The senators smothered the hot potato with a ketchup of colorful oratory and mixed metaphors.*
>
> *"I am firmly convinced we can do without this combination of red ink, 'blue' movies, and Acapulco 'gold,'" Senator John McClellan of Arkansas opined in a persiflage of purple prose. . . .*
>
> *The research community is up in arms because of political interference with the integrity of the peer review process.*

Several questions arise here.

(a) Assume that no physical or psychological harm can come to the volunteer subjects. I might still object to the experiment on grounds of "decency" or "good taste." If you were a member of a review panel, would you veto the experiment on such grounds? Explain.

(b) Suppose we concede that any legal experiment with volunteer subjects should be permitted in a free society. It is a further step to say that any such experiment is entitled to government funding if the usual review procedure finds it scientifically worthwhile. If you were a member of Congress, would you ever refuse to pay for an experiment on grounds of "decency" or "good taste"?

4. *(Informed consent)* The information given to potential subjects in a clinical trial before asking them to decide whether or not to participate might include:

(a) The basic statement that an experiment is being conducted—that is,

something beyond simply treating your medical problem occurs in
your therapy.

(b) A statement of any potential risks from any of the experimental
treatments.

(c) An explanation that random assignment will be used to decide which
treatment you get.

(d) An explanation that one "treatment" is a placebo and a statement of
the probability that you will receive the placebo.

Do you feel that all of this information is ethically required? Discuss.

5. *(Informed consent)* The subjects in the New Jersey Income-Maintenance
Experiment (Section 5) were given a complete explanation of the purpose
of the study and of the workings of the treatment to which they were
assigned. They were *not* told that there were other treatments that would
have paid them more (or less), and that the luck of randomization had
determined the income they would receive. Do you agree or disagree that
the information given is adequate for informed consent?

6. *(Prison experiments)* The decision to ban medical experiments on Federal
prisoners followed uncovering of experiments in the 1960s that exposed
prisoners to serious harm. But experiments such as the vitamin C test of
Example 7 on p. 64 are also banned from Federal prisons. Is it necessary to
ban experiments in which all treatments appear harmless because of the
difficulty of obtaining truly voluntary consent in a prison? What is your
overall opinion of this ban on experimentation?

7. *(Dependent subjects)* Students in PSY 001 are required to serve as experimental subjects. Students in PSY 002 are not required to serve, but are
given extra credit if they do so. Students in PSY 003 are required either to
sign up as subjects or to write a term paper.

Do you object to any of these policies? Which ones, and why?

8. *(Popular pressure)* The substance Laetrile received abundant publicity in
1977 as a treatment for cancer. Like hundreds of thousands of other chemical compounds, Laetrile had earlier been tested to see if it showed anti-
tumor activity in animals. It didn't. Because no known drug fights cancer in
people but not in animals, the medical community branded Laetrile as
worthless. Advocates of Laetrile wanted the FDA to conduct a clinical trial
on human cancer patients.

It is usually considered unethical to use a drug on people without some
promise based on animal trials that it is safe and effective. What is more,
Laetrile may have toxic side effects. Do the popular interest in Laetrile and
the fervor of its advocates justify a clinical trial?

9. *(Animal welfare)* Some people are concerned about the ethics of experimentation with living animals. Discuss guidelines for animal experimentation. Current practice allows treatments that harm—or even kill—
animals. But it is considered unethical to cause pain to animals beyond the

level essential to the experiment. Do you agree with these practices? Do you distinguish between dogs, laboratory rats, and frogs in what you consider permissible?

(Just as in the case of human subjects, the issues here are more sharply defined in a specific example. If possible, read the article by Nicolas Wade, "Animal Rights: NIH Cat Sex Study Brings Grief to New York Museum," *Science,* Volume 194 (1976), pp. 162–167, and the replies in the letters to the editor in *Science,* Volume 194 (1976), p. 784.)

10. Read the article by Elliot Aronson, "The Rationalizing Animal," *Psychology Today,* May 1973, pp. 46–52. This is an account of a fascinating theory in social psychology (called "cognitive dissonance") and of the studies that led to it. Almost *every* study discussed in the article would be considered un-ethical by some people; a few (those by Davis, Jones, and Glass, p. 49) are quite similar to Milgram's experiment. Yet it is difficult to see how cognitive dissonance could have been understood without at least some of this work.

List the separate research studies mentioned in the article. Taking into account the knowledge they yielded, which do you consider ethically justified?

Chapter 3

Measurement

P rofessor Nous is interested in how much the intelligence of a child is influenced by the environment in which the child is raised. Children raised in the same environment still differ in intelligence because of heredity and other factors, so a comparative study is needed.

Professor Nous daydreams about randomized comparative experiments in which newborn babies are snatched from their mothers and assigned to various environments. Alas, in this instance she must be content with an observational study. A brilliant idea strikes: Why not look at the variation in intelligence between identical twins who for some reason have been raised in separate homes since birth? Because twins have the same heredity, differences in their intelligence must reflect the effect of environment. A careful search turns up 50 pairs of separated twins. Professor Nous feels that her troubles are over.

Not so. Once the units for study (the twins) are chosen, it remains to collect data by measuring the properties of each unit that interest the good professor. In particular, she must measure the intelligence of each child. Because intelligence, unlike sex or age, is not directly observable, Professor Nous is faced with a serious problem.

In Chapters 1 and 2, we thought about designing a study by choosing or assigning the units of study. Professor Nous has successfully completed this task. Now we must think about measurement, for the final step in collecting data is to measure some property of the units. Measurement produces numbers. You always thought that statistics concerns numbers, but I have not allowed them to encroach on you until this chapter. The real point of thinking about measurement is to help you become more comfortable with numbers. We will ask when numbers are meaningful (Section 1), inquire about their accuracy (Section 2), and learn that not all numbers are equally informative (Section 3). All you have learned will be applied in Section 4 to the art of looking at numbers intelligently.

1. First Steps in Measurement: Validity

In Chapters 1 and 2, we defined a *variable* as "a measured characteristic of a unit." Variables result from measuring properties of units. To be useful, a variable must be exactly defined. And to use data intelligently, we must know the definitions of the variables whose values are reported. What, for example, does it mean when the Bureau of Labor Statistics (BLS for short) announces that last month's unemployment rate was 7.3%? We know (see Exercises 6 and 7 for Section 4 of Chapter 1) that this figure comes from the Current Population Survey, a large and carefully conducted sample survey. So its numerical value is quite accurate. In fact, the Bureau's statisticians will happily tell us that

(a) There is a small bias, mainly because the survey can't find perhaps 5% or 6% of the population. We guess that these persons are more likely to be unemployed than the rest of us. Fortunately, this small bias is probably about the same from month to month, so *changes* in the unemployment rate (that's what economists and politicians really watch) have little bias.

(b) The precision of the sampling process is such that 95% of all samples drawn will give an unemployment rate within $\pm 0.2\%$ (that's ± 0.002) of the rate a census would produce.

Fine. That's a review of Chapter 1. But we don't understand the monthly unemployment rate until we know the definition of "unemployed." Is a full-time student who holds no job unemployed? Is a worker on strike unemployed? And when the unemployment rate is 7.3%, that's 7.3% of what group? You can see that changing the definition could change the announced unemployment rate a great deal.

Here is the BLS definition. You are *employed* if you did any paid work in the last week, or worked at least 15 hours in a family business, or were on leave from a regular job. You are *unemployed* if you were not employed last week *and* were available for work and looking for work. If you were not available and looking, you were *not in the labor force*. So a full-time student who chooses not to seek a paying job is neither unemployed nor employed; he is not in the labor force. The unemployment rate is the percent unemployed among civilians over 16 years of age who are in the labor force.

That definition took a paragraph and is still not detailed enough so you or I could say exactly who is unemployed. But it is a great help in assessing the meaning of a 7.3% unemployment rate. In particular, you can appreciate the argument of labor leaders that this announced rate always underestimates the seriousness of unemployment. If you hold a part-time job but want a full-time job and can't find one, you are "employed." If you are without a job and so discouraged that you stop looking for one, you are "out of the labor force" and therefore no longer unemployed! Definitions can accomplish wondrous things.

The interviewers employed by the Current Population Survey are engaged in measuring employment status. They measure the employment status of the

"Unemployed? Not me, I'm out of the labor force."

persons in the sample by asking them questions spelled out on the interview form, then classifying them according to the BLS definitions of employment status. I want to go one step further by insisting that the result of measurement be a number.

> To *measure* a property means to assign numbers to units as a way of representing that property.

Note that we measure properties of things, not the things themselves. You can measure my weight, or my intelligence, or my employment status, but you can't measure me. And note that measurement is always an operation that produces a number. Specifying the details of that operation is as important as specifying the protocol of an experiment. Height can be measured with a tape measure. My height is 182 centimeters; that's the number resulting from measurement. Dr. Nous might decide to measure intelligence by the Wechsler Adult Intelligence Scale, the most common "IQ test." I won't tell you my IQ, but it's a number determined by that specific process. My employment status is measured by classifying me according to the BLS definitions. I'm employed. That's not a number, you say. True enough, but to run my employment status through the computer, we must assign a numerical code to each employment status. Let's use 0 for "not in the labor force," 1 for "unemployed," and 2 for "employed." Now my employment status is 2. Any measurement *must* result in a number. (That's the *definition* of measurement; we too can play the definition game.)

It is possible to talk about "classifying" or "categorizing" separately from measurement because classifying persons by sex or race or employment status does not naturally produce numbers. I prefer to lump classifying in with measurement by insisting that we assign numbers to the classes. As we saw with employment status, that's no hardship. In Chapters 1 and 2, variables could have values such as "agree' or "disagree" (as when an opinion poll asks your reaction to a statement). Now we insist that variables have numerical values.

Statistics deals with variables, that is, with numbers resulting from measurement. Beware of the easy passage from a property of units to a variable that claims to represent the property. The variable must be clearly and exactly defined. The property may be vague, inexact, and not directly observable. In this situation, the variable is rarely a complete representation of the property.

> **Example 1.** The BLS definition of "unemployed" may not agree in detail with your vague idea of what it means to be unemployed. Labor says this variable understates unemployment by insisting that only persons actively seeking work can be unemployed. On the other hand, management argues that the BLS overstates unemployment because some persons who are looking for work may refuse to accept a job unless it is exactly right for them. Many married women and teenagers, secure because the household already has one steady wage-earner, shop around for the right job. By the BLS definition, these persons are unemployed. (I pass over in silence the claim of the National Association of Manufacturers, recorded on the front page of the *Wall Street Journal* on September 13, 1976, that the official employment rate is inflated because "criminal elements" are included in the labor force.)

Though both management and labor would prefer slightly different definitions of "unemployed," neither accuses the BLS of having a completely inappropriate definition. The official unemployment rate is a useful indicator of the state of the economy. That is, the BLS produces a *valid* measure of employment and unemployment.

A variable is a *valid* measure of a property if it is relevant or appropriate as a representation of that property.

Validity of a measurement process is a simple but slippery idea. Does the process measure what you want it to? That is the question of validity. If I measured your height in inches and recorded you as "employed" if your height exceeds 65 inches, that is an invalid measure of your employment status. The BLS uses a valid measure: not a perfect measure of employment (whatever that might mean), not the whole story about employment status, not the only variable that might measure employment status, but an appropriate and relevant variable. The idea of validity in measurement is similar to the idea of validity in designing a study. Indeed, they can be treated together. Valid measurement is part of *internal validity;* do we obtain usable, relevant data for the actual units studied? *External validity* refers to the generalizability of the study results to a larger population.

It is *easy* for persons who are not experienced with numbers to fall into the trap of using an invalid measure. A common case is the use of absolute numbers when rates are appropriate. Here is an example.

> **Example 2.** If customers returned 36 coats to Sears and only 12 to La Boutique Classique next door, this does not mean that Sears' customers were less satisfied. Sears sold 1100 coats that season, while La Boutique sold 200. So Sears' return rate was
>
> $$\frac{36}{1100} = 0.033 \text{ or } 3.3\%$$
>
> while the return rate at La Boutique was
>
> $$\frac{12}{200} = 0.06 \text{ or } 6\%.$$
>
> This return rate, or percentage of coats returned, is a more valid measure of dissatisfaction than the number of returns.

It is easy to decide if a variable is a valid measure of a property when we understand the property well. That's true of physical properties such as length. Employment status and customer satisfaction (Examples 1 and 2) are a bit less clear, but we still have a good idea of what we want to measure. But it sometimes happens that the property to be measured is so fuzzy that reasonable persons can disagree on the validity of a variable as a measure of that property. This situation is not uncommon in the social and behavioral sciences. Psychologists wish to measure such things as intelligence, or authoritarian personality, or mathematical aptitude. The variables are typically scores on a test—an IQ test for intelligence, the mathematics part of the Scholastic Aptitude Test (the "college boards") for mathematical aptitude, and so on. The validity of these variables is exceedingly controversial.

> **Example 3.** Standardized tests such as IQ tests and college board exams have been attacked because persons not in the American cultural mainstream (such as blacks and persons in low income households) score considerably lower on the average than white members of the middle class. This is a question of validity. To discuss the issue sensibly, we must

ask validity *for what purpose* and validity *for what population*. Critics of the SAT's, for example, often complain that these tests measure only cognitive ability, ignoring emotional and physical abilities that are just as important. That is much like criticizing a yardstick for not giving the time of day because the SAT's do not claim to measure such other abilities. But it is also difficult to argue that the SAT's are valid measures of cognitive ability because such "ability" is vague and no doubt includes aspects that cannot be measured by a multiple-choice exam. What can be said is that the SAT's are valid for predicting academic success in college. Success in college is a clear concept and there is an observed connection between high SAT scores and later success in college. That is an answer to "Validity for what?"

There remains the question of "Validity for whom?" The most common criticism of standardized tests is that they are *culturally biased*—that they are valid for the middle class but not for other groups. It is quite plausible that such tests are not equally valid for all persons. An IQ test written in English, for example, is not a valid measure of anything for persons who don't read English. The SAT's, considered as measures not of ability but of future academic success, appear to be innocent of cultural bias. They predict success as well for blacks as for whites, for example. Now the fact that blacks average about 100 points lower than whites on the SAT scale of 200 to 800 is certainly connected with blacks' being outside the cultural mainstream more than whites. But success in college depends in part on exposure to middle class education and habits. The white middle class has an advantage on the SAT's, but it has the same advantage in college. In one sense, the conclusion that the SAT's are not culturally biased as predictors of college success amounts to admitting that the tests and the colleges have the same cultural bias.

Much of the controversy over standardized tests such as the SAT's arises because some users ignore the limitations on the validity of the tests. The SAT's are valid predictors of future academic success, but they are far from perfect predictors. Many factors not measured by such tests also influence a student's success in college. For example, it is not appropriate to base college admissions decisions on test scores alone. It is appropriate to regard low SAT scores as a danger signal, to look for other abilities that will help the student overcome them, or even to plan special compensatory training for such students. Like a sharp knife, a standardized test can be used wisely by the wise or foolishly by the foolish. Those who call for an end to such tests finally base their case on the judgment that the foolish so outnumber the wise that sharp knives ought to be confiscated.

The example of standardized tests illustrates the care needed in discussing the validity of measures of fuzzy concepts. It also illustrates the way social and behavioral scientists often deal with this problem; they try to show a connection between the measuring variable and other variables that ought to be connected with the original fuzzy idea. Persons of high mental ability ought to do better in school than those of low ability. Persons with high IQ or SAT scores do tend to do better in school than those with low scores. The final step is to replace the vague idea with the precise variable that seems to be connected with the same behavior. That is, for statistical purposes *the best way to define a property is to give a rule for measuring it.* The saying that "Intelligence is whatever it is that IQ measures" is an example of such a definition. IQ measures some combination of innate ability, learned knowledge, and exposure to mainstream culture. This is a clearly defined property of people because it is established by the Wechsler Adult Intelligence Scale. It is an interesting variable because it is related to success in school and other interesting dependent variables. But IQ is not necessarily the same as our everyday idea of intelligence. Our old friend Professor Nous should probably decide to study the effect of environment on IQ by using her sample of separated twins. To study "intelligence" is beyond her reach.

Statistics can deal only with measured properties. "Intelligence" and "maturity" cannot be studied statistically, though variables such as IQ can be. Beware of the arrogance that says that everything can be measured, or that only things we can measure are important. The world contains much that is beyond the grasp of statistics.

2. Accuracy In Measurement

Even the most exact laboratory measurements are not perfectly accurate. Physicists and chemists, who make little use of statistical ideas in data collection, use statistics heavily in analyzing errors in their measurements. When a measurement is made as accurately as the instrument allows, repeated measurements do not always give the same result. Try Exercises 1 and 2 to see that for yourself. Accuracy in measurement has two aspects: lack of bias and reliability.

> **A measurement process is *unbiased* if it does not systematically overstate or understate the true value of the variable.**
>
> **A measurement process is *reliable* if repeated measurements on the same unit give the same (or approximately the same) results.**

Lack of bias and reliability in measurement carry the same meanings as do unbiasedness and precision in data collection. (In fact, it is common in the physical sciences and engineering to use the word "precision" instead of "reliability" to describe the repeatability of the results of measurement.) Unbiased means correct on the average; reliable means repeatable. The difference is that these meanings now apply to the process of measuring a property of a unit, not to the process of choosing units to be measured. If an egg scale always weighs 10 grams high, it is biased. If the scale has dust in its pivot and gives widely different weights when the same egg is weighed several times, it is unreliable.

The analogy between repeated measurement and repeated sampling extends further. The results of repeated measurement are *random* in the same sense that the results of repeated sampling are random. That is, individual results vary, but there is a definite *distribution* of results when many trials are made. The average of several measurements is less variable (more reliable) than a single measurement, just as a sample statistic becomes more precise in larger samples. That is why laboratory instructors in physics or chemistry suggest that you repeat your measurements several times and use the average value. It is a pleasing instance of the harmony of thought that measurement error and sampling error can be studied and overcome by the same ideas.

Example 4. If you want to know how much something weighs, you use a scale. If an analytical chemist wants to know how much a specimen weighs, he uses a better scale. His scale is less biased and more reliable than yours, and he calibrates it regularly by weighing a "standard weight" whose mass is accurately known. The mass of standard weights is accurately known because they have been compared with super-standard weights kept by the National Bureau of Standards (NBS) in Washington, D.C. And the mass of *these* weights is known very accurately because they have been compared with The International Prototype Kilogram, which lives in a guarded vault in Paris and indirectly determines all weights in the world.

These National Bureau of Standards mass standards provide the basis for measuring weight in the United States, whether by a laboratory balance or your bathroom scale. [Photo courtesy of Mass and Volume Section, National Bureau of Standards.]

The NBS standard weight called NB 10, for example, weighs 9.999596 grams. (It is supposed to weigh 10 grams, but is light by about the mass of a grain of salt.) Because the NBS knows that the results of repeated measurements are random, it repeatedly weighs standards such as NB 10 to determine the reliability of the weighing process. Then when the analytical chemist sends in his standard weight for calibration, the NBS can tell him the reliability of their answer, just as the Gallup Poll can state the precision of their conclusions. Here are the results of 11 determinations of the mass of NB 10, made in May 1963 with all the care the NBS can apply.[1]

9.9995992	9.9995985
9.9995947	9.9996008
9.9995978	9.9996027
9.9995925	9.9995929
9.9996006	9.9995988
9.9996014	

You see that the 11 measurements do vary. There is no such thing as an absolutely accurate measurement. The average (mean) of these measurements is 9.9995982 grams, which is a more reliable estimate of the true mass than a single measurement. In fact, the NBS says it is 95% confident that this average is within ±0.0000023 gram of the truth. (Compare this with the statement of the precision of the Gallup Poll on page 18.) Such reliability statements also apply to unknown masses such as that of the analytical chemist's standard weight.

I hope that this excursion into the world ruled by the International Prototype Kilogram has reminded you that even physicists and chemists don't get "the right answer" on every measurement. If you have spent part of your youth in laboratories, you need no reminder. I well remember the dark midnight when, after hours of failing to get the same answer twice in an optics lab, I faced the alternative of smashing the wretched interferometer or choosing a major other than physics. Because the interferometer was expensive, I got out of physics.

As usual, things are tougher yet outside the laboratory. Measuring unemployment is also "measurement," and the concepts of bias and reliability apply here just as they do to measuring the mass of NB 10. The sampling process from which the unemployment rate is obtained has a high but not perfect precision, which can be clearly stated because probability sampling is used. The measurement of employment status is also not perfectly repeatable—not perfectly reliable. The BLS checks the reliability of its measurements by having supervisors re-interview about 5% of the sample. This is repeated measurement on the same unit, just as when NB 10 is weighed several times. It turns out that interviewers and supervisors almost always agree on who is not in the labor force and who has a full-time job. These measurements are extremely reliable. But supervisors and interviewers disagree on the status of about 10% of the "unemployed." The distinctions between "unemployed," "temporarily laid off," and "underemployed" are a bit subjective. The measurement of unemployment is therefore somewhat unreliable. To sum up: The precision of sampling refers to the repeatability of sample statistics in *different* samples. The reliability of measurement refers to repeatability of measured values on the *same* units.

Bias has the same meaning in measuring unemployment as in measuring mass: systematic deviation of the measured result from the "true value" that perfect measurement would produce. The "true value" isn't exactly known even for a mass, but the idea of a biased scale that systematically weighs high or low is clear enough. For unemployment, the "true employment status" of a person might be his status by the BLS definitions when classified by the Commissioner of Labor Statistics himself. Other interviewers will sometimes disagree with the commissioner (the reliability of measurement is not perfect), but there is no bias unless, for example, the interviewers systematically call "unemployed" persons the commissioner would say are "not in the labor force." There appears to be little bias in measuring unemployment.

Take note of one detail: If the definition of unemployment from the BLS understates the "unemployment problem," this is not bias in measurement. It is instead a question of the validity of the BLS definition as a measure of unemployment. Bias in a measurement process means that the process gives measurements on a variable that are systematically higher or lower than the true value of that variable. Whether the variable is a valid measure of a property such as intelligence or employment status is a different—and harder—question.

Example 5. As college enrollments approach their peak before an expected decline in the 1980s, deans and other interested persons watch the national enrollment data collected by the federal government's National Center for Education Statistics. The preliminary data for the fall of 1976 showed that the number of first-time students in public universities had grown by 4%. But the questionnaire for collecting preliminary data contained confused wording that led many colleges to include new graduate students in the category of first-time students, a category meant to include only students with no previous higher education. The final figures showed that the number of new students in public institutions was *down* 9%, not up 4% compared with a year earlier.

This is an example of measurement bias. The badly worded form produced values of the variable "number of first-time students" that were systematically higher than the true value.

Reliability of weighings or of employment status classifications is checked by making repeated measurements on the same units. Reliability of IQ tests or the

SAT's cannot be checked this way because subjects taking a test the second time have an advantage over their first try. Even with different but (one hopes) equivalent forms of the test, this learning effect rules out assessing reliability from many repeated measurements. Behavioral scientists must fall back on less direct and more complicated ways of checking reliability, though the basic ideas we have covered still apply. Here is yet another way in which psychology is a more complicated subject than physics.

3.   Scales of Measurement

Measurement of a property means assigning a number to represent it. Having designed our data collection process and stated what measurements are to be made on the units, we can cheerfully amass our data—a pile of numbers resulting from the measurements we made. The next step is usually to find averages or prepare some other summary of these data. Before plunging ahead, it is wise to ask how much information our numbers carry. Consider, for example, my employment status. We agreed to represent this by the variable having value 0 if I'm not in the labor force, value 1 if I'm unemployed, and value 2 if I'm employed. Now 2 is twice as much as 1. And 2 inches is twice as much as 1 inch. But an employment status of 2 is *not* twice an employment status of 1. That's obvious, but sneaky. The numbers used to code employment status are just category labels disguised as numbers. We could have used the labels A, B, and C, except that to include categorization as part of measurement we insisted on numbers. So not all numbers resulting from measurement carry information, such as "twice as much," that we naturally associate with numbers. What we can do with data depends on how much information the numbers carry.

We speak of the kind of information a measurement carries by saying what kind of *scale* the measurement is made in. Here are the kind of scales.

A measurement of a property has a *nominal scale* if the measurement tells only *what class* a unit falls in with respect to the property.

The measurement has an *ordinal scale* if it also tells when one unit has *more of* the property than does another unit.

The measurement has an *interval scale* if it also tells us that one unit *differs by a certain amount* of the property from another unit.

The measurement has a *ratio scale* if it tells us that one unit has *so many times as much* of the property as does another unit.

Measurements in a nominal scale place units in categories, nothing more. Such properties as race, sex, and employment status are measured in a nominal scale. We can code the sex of a subject by

> 0—female
>
> 1—male

or by

> 0—male
>
> 1—female.

Which numbers we assign makes no difference; the value of this variable indicates only what the sex of the subject is.

In an *ordinal scale,* the order of numbers is meaningful. If a committee ranks 10 fellowship candidates from 1 (weakest) to 10 (strongest), the candidate ranked 8 is better than the candidate ranked 6. Not just different (as a nominal scale would tell us), but better. But the usual arithmetic is not meaningful: 8 is not twice as good as 4, and the difference in quality between 8 and 6 need not be the same as between 6 and 4. Only the order of the values is meaningful. Ordinal scales are important when social scientists measure properties such as "authoritarian personality" by giving a test on which a subject can score, (say,) between 0 and 100 points. If the test is valid as a measure of this property, then Esther who scores 80 is more authoritarian than Lydia who scores 60. But if Jane scores 40, we can probably not conclude that Esther is "twice as authoritarian" as Jane. Nor can we say that "the difference in authoritarianism between

Copyright © 1974 United Feature Syndicate, Inc.

Esther and Lydia is the same as between Lydia and Jane" just because their scores differ by 20 in each case. Whether a particular test has an ordinal scale or actually does carry information about differences and ratios we leave for psychologists to discuss. Many tests, including examinations in this course, have ordinal scales.

With *interval and ratio scales* we reach the kind of measurement familiar to us. These are *measurements made on a scale of equal units,* such as height in centimeters, reaction time in seconds, or temperature in degrees centigrade. Arithmetic such as taking differences is meaningful when these scales are used. A cockroach 4 centimeters long is 2 centimeters longer than one 2 centimeters long. There is a rather fine distinction between interval and ratio scales. A cockroach 4 centimeters long is twice as long as one 2 centimeters long; length in centimeters has a ratio scale. But when the temperature is 40°C it is not twice as hot as when it is 20°C. Temperature in degrees centigrade has an interval, not a ratio, scale. Another way of expressing the difference is that ratio scales have a meaningful zero. A length of 0 centimeters is "no length," a time of 0 seconds is "no time." But a temperature of 0°C is just the freezing point of water, not "no heat." (There is a temperature scale, the absolute or Kelvin scale, with 0° at "absolute zero," the temperature at which molecules stop moving and there is literally "no heat." This is a ratio scale.)

We will not pay attention to the distinction between interval and ratio scales. But it is important (and usually easy) to notice whether a variable has a nominal scale (objects are put into categories), an ordinal scale (objects are ordered in some way), or an interval/ratio scale (measurements are made on a scale marked off in units).

One concluding fine point: The scale of a measurement depends mainly on the method of measurement, not on the property measured. The weight of a carton of eggs measured in grams has an interval/ratio scale. But if I label the carton as one of

small,   medium,   large,   extra large.

I have measured the weight in an ordinal scale. If a standard test of authoritarian personality has an ordinal scale, this does not mean that it is impossible to measure authoritarian personality on an interval/ratio scale, only that this test does not do so.

4.   Looking at Data Intelligently

Political rhetoric, advertising claims, debate on public issues—we are assailed daily by numbers employed to prove a point or to buttress an argument. Asking a few preliminary questions of such data will help us to distinguish sense from nonsense.

What is the Source of the Data?

Knowledge of the source helps us decide whether to trust the data. Knowing the source of data also allows us to check whether it was quoted correctly, and to use the knowledge gained in Chapters 1 and 2 to assess the quality of the data. Here are some examples.

> **Example 6.** "A poll by the Lou Harris organization in June 1976 found that if Mr. Reagan were to win the Republican Presidential nomination, almost one-half of the Republicans who favor President Ford would vote for Governor Carter in November." This statement in a newspaper political commentary has its faults; it does not give the details of date, sample size, and precise wording. But the source is indicated, and since the Harris organization is a respected national polling firm, we are inclined to believe the statement. If the issue were important to us, we could obtain details from the Harris organization.

> **Example 7.** "So we went to 21 major cities and asked 550 drinkers to compare white rum with the leading brands of gin and vodka. 24.2% preferred gin. 34.4% preferred vodka. And 41.4% preferred white rum." This statement in a rum advertisement by the Commonwealth of Puerto Rico describes a comparative taste test, but says little about the design of the experiment. Government regulations require that claims such as "More drinkers prefer rum than either gin or vodka" be based on actual studies, and that the details of such studies be available on request. We can write the advertiser if we wish to assess the claim.

> **Example 8.** "Dr. Oilup, director of the bureau's energy task force, estimated that natural gas for residential heating would fall short of current usage by the winter of 1985." Here we have an expert opinion. We cannot sample natural gas supply in 1985, so any conclusion must be based on past data and informed judgment about the future. We must ask ourselves if we trust the expert. Is his statement a careful estimate or a shot in the dark? Is he speaking under political pressure or in support of a pet project? Does his judgment agree with that of other experts? Is it supported by a reasonable reading of past data?

The first two examples involved a sample survey and an experiment. We are well equipped to assess data from these sources, if only we are given the details we need. The third example is based on informed opinion, a common source of data in public issues concerning future trends. Some additional comments are needed here. First, no informed judgment is as reliable as a properly designed survey or experiment. Whenever surveys or experiments are possible, informed judgment is a second-rate source of data. Our earlier considerations of social

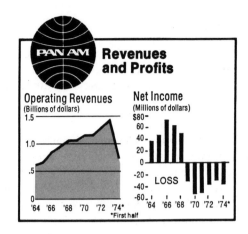

Figure 1. Extrapolation is risky. [Copyright © 1974 by the New York Times Company. Reprinted by permission.]

experiments and of opinion surveys as campaign tools illustrate this point in detail. Second, extrapolation is always dangerous. Extrapolation means projecting the trend of past data to future results. The future can differ from past trends, as we all learned at the gas pump after the 1973 oil embargo. Figure 1 provides another example. The unwary investor looking at Pan Am's net income from 1964 to 1968 might have been rather more optimistic about the future than was justified.

A third comment is that even experts can be corrupted, either by outside pressure or by their own prejudices. A government energy expert of my acquaintance tells of a booklet on U.S. energy supply written in 1975 for a Federal agency by another energy expert. The booklet contains a graph showing U.S. oil production (which has been declining since 1970) increasing for the rest of the century. The author of the booklet, my acquaintance says, refers to it in conversation as "the funny book." But he wrote it, because his bosses wanted it that way. Reaching a clear conclusion in an area where extrapolation is necessary and political and economic special interests are strong is extraordinarily difficult. Unfortunately, crucial issues such as future energy supply fall in this category.

Do the Data Make Sense?

You would not accept verbal nonsense in a discussion. Don't accept numerical nonsense either.

Example 9. "The mayor said that 90% of the police force had never taken a bribe. These honest men should not be tarnished by the misdeeds of a few." That "90%" is a *meaningless number*. The mayor has no idea what percent of the police have never taken a bribe. He wants to say that "a great majority" or "all but a few" have not. We can (and do) ignore his "90%."

Example 10. "True cigarettes have 5 milligrams less tar." This is a *meaningless comparison*. Five milligrams less tar than what?

A more serious aspect of asking whether data make sense is to examine them for *internal consistency*. Do the numbers fit together in a way that makes sense? A little thought here will do wonders. Here is part of an article dealing with a cancer researcher at the Sloan-Kettering Institute who was accused of committing the ultimate scientific sin, falsifying data.[2]

Example 11. One thing he did manage to finish was a summary paper dealing with the Minnesota mouse experiments. . . . That paper, cleared at SKI and accepted by the *Journal of Experimental Medicine,* contains a statistical table that is erroneous in such an elementary way that a bright grammar school pupil could catch the flaw. It lists 6 sets of 20 animals each, with the percentages of successful takes. Although any percentage of 20 has to be a multiple of 5, the percentages that Summerlin recorded were 53, 58, 63, 46, 48, and 67.

In Example 11, lack of internal consistency led to the suspicion that the data were phony. *Too much precision or regularity* can lead to the same suspicion, as when a student's lab report contains data that are exactly as the theory predicts. The laboratory instructor knows that the accuracy of the equipment and the student's laboratory technique are not good enough to give such perfect results. He suspects that the student made them up. Here is another example of phony precision.[3]

Example 12.
Industrialization is good politics in the South and because of that most state governments tend to exaggerate in reporting their industrial progress.

During the last 10 years, probably no state has been more industrious, if not imaginative, in reporting its industrial growth than Gov. George C. Wallace's Alabama.

Mr. Wallace went before a huge meeting of Alabama business and political leaders early this year and announced that the state had just completed its "greatest year" in industrial growth.

"During 1972," he said, "Alabama gained a grand total of 682 new and expanding industries, with a capital investment of $838,390,120, creating 42,878 new jobs – all three figures representing record highs."

• • •

But another, less publicized, source of information casts grave doubt on the accuracy of that figure. The Alabama Department of Industrial Relations, which keeps records of employment in cooperation with the Federal Bureau of Labor Statistics, says that only 8800 more people were working in manufacturing in Alabama this June than in June 1972.

What happened to the other jobs created in Alabama's "greatest year"?

The answer seems to lie in the difference between two state agencies, the Department of Industrial Relations and the Alabama Development Office. The department is an accountant. The development office is a salesman.

• • •

The Development Office has reported the creation of 422,657 new industrial jobs in Alabama in the last 25 years. The records in the Department of Industrial Relations show a gain of 103,000 industrial workers in that time.

Notice that the Development Office tells us that exactly 422,657 new industrial jobs were created in Alabama in the last 25 years. That is spurious (phony) precision. The more careful Department of Industrial Relations indicates the imprecision of such job figures by reporting its data in round thousands as 103,000. Careful statistical writers avoid the appearance of more precision than the data warrant. In nontechnical writing, the degree of precision is indicated by rounding off. We can surmise that the gain of 103,000 industrial workers is precise to about the nearest thousand, and that the annual increase of 8800 workers is precise to about the nearest hundred.

This example is also another reminder of the importance of checking the source of the data. The *Times* article goes on to explain that the Development Office simply adds up company announcements of how many new jobs they plan to create and does not check how many jobs are actually created. There is also a matter of definition of variables. The Office reports the number of "new industrial jobs." It does not subtract the number of jobs eliminated, so the actual number of jobs might even be decreasing. The Department reports the actual change in number of industrial jobs. The latter is clearly a more valid measure of employment trends in Alabama.

The final part of asking if the data make sense is to *ask if they are plausible*. Numbers are easily misquoted, and the result is often wildly too high or too low. A little knowledge and common sense will detect many unbelievable numbers. A national columnist reported in 1975 that New England supplied only 9.1% of its energy needs. Common sense suggests that this is too low. The columnist later confessed that he had mistakenly misquoted a report stating that New England supplied 9.1% of its energy needs with natural gas. The same columnist reported on another occasion that 75,000 Vietnam war veterans had attempted suicide. Common sense suggests that this number is too high. The columnist later admitted this, stating that he had obtained the number from an article in *Penthouse* magazine, which got it from a radical veterans' group, which presumably made it up. Here the problem is not misquotation, but once again an untrustworthy source.

> **Example 13.** A writer in *Science* [Volume 192 (1976), p. 1081] stated that "People over 65, now numbering 10 million, will number 30 million by the year 2000, and will constitute an unprecedented 25 percent of the population." Such explosive growth of the elderly—tripling in a quarter century to become a fourth of the population—would profoundly change any society. But wait. Thirty million is 25% of 120 million, and the U.S. population is already much higher than that. Something is wrong with the writer's figures. Thus alerted, we can check reliable sources such as Census reports to learn the truth. A reader of *Science* did so [letter to the editor, Volume 193 (1976)], and noted that in 1975 there were 22.4 million persons over 65, not 10 million. The projection of 30 million by the year 2000 is correct, but that is only 11% or 12% of the projected population for that year. The explosive growth of the elderly vanishes in the light cast by accurate statistics.

I hope that reading this book will help you form the habit of looking at numbers closely. Your reward will be the reputation for brilliance that accrues to those who point out that a number being honored by everyone else is clearly nonsense.

Are the Data Valid for the Intended Use?

We learned in Section 1 that correct data may be worth little if they are not valid for the purpose at hand. So BurpEze antacid dissolves faster in a glass of water than its competitors—does that mean it's more effective?

A more subtle way of using data in support of dubious conclusions is giving only part of the relevant information. This is perhaps the single most common trick employed by those who use numbers to make an impression rather than to tell the whole truth. Here are some typical examples.

> **Example 14.** A television advertisement by the Investment Company Institute (the mutual fund trade association) said that a $10,000 investment made in 1950 in an average common stock mutual fund would have increased to $113,500 by the end of 1972. That's true. *The Wall Street Journal* (June 7, 1972) pointed out that the ad had omitted the fact that the same investment spread over all the stocks making up the New York

Stock Exchange Composite Index would have grown to $151, 427. That is, mutual funds performed worse than the stock market as a whole.

Example 15. International Paper Company once advertised its commitment to the environment by announcing a $101-million, four-year plan to combat pollution. The Council on Economic Priorities cited this as an example of misleading environmental advertising. They noted that the ad did not place that $101 million in any frame of reference. The Council claimed that Weyerhaeuser, with less than half the pulp production, had already spent $125 million, and Scott, with one quarter the pulp production of International, planned to spend $85 million.[4]

Example 16. A television commercial for Schick Super Chromium razor blades showed a group of barbers shaving with the same blade, one after another. The 12th, 13th, 15th, and 17th men to use the blade were interviewed. All said the shave was satisfactory. Consumers Union repeated this experiment with 18 men. The 17th and 18th to shave with the same blade were satisfied, but the 7th, 8th, 9th, and 10th all said the blade needed changing. Did all 17 users in the commercial get good shaves, or was the interviewing selective? Were the barbers chosen at random? Was their judgment biased by the knowledge that Schick was sponsoring the test and that they might appear on TV?[5]

Examples 14, 15, and 16 illustrate the misleading effect of giving true information out of context. The truth without the *whole* truth can lie.

Even complete and accurate data may mislead us if we are not aware of changes in the process of measuring and collecting the data. This too is part of the background information needed to interpret data intelligently. The reported size of a university's faculty changed when postdoctoral researchers, who had been listed as faculty members, were dropped from the list. This is a change of definition. The number of petty larcenies reported in Chicago more than doubled between 1959 and 1960 because a new police commissioner had introduced an improved reporting system. The new system gave a much better count of crimes committed, so the number of crimes reported rose. This is a change in data collection procedure. Almost all series of numbers covering many years are affected by changing definitions and collection methods. Often these changes are pointed to by sudden jumps in the series of numbers (lack of internal consistency) but not always. Alertness and care are needed to avoid false conclusions.

Example 17. Data collected by the General Electric Company once showed that a component of a major appliance was failing at ever higher rates as the appliance became older. Preparations began for the manufacture of a more reliable component. Then a statistician noted that the rate of failure was roughly constant for the first year of service, turned sharply up

"Sure your patients have 50% fewer cavities. That's because they have 50% fewer teeth!"

at exactly 12 months, was roughly constant at this higher rate during the second year of service, and turned up again at exactly 24 months. No appliances in the sample had been in service more than 29 months.

Alerted by this suspicious regularity, the statistician checked into the source of the data. For the first 12 months, all appliances were sampled because all had a one-year warranty. Data for the second 12 months referred only to appliances whose owners had bought a service contract for the second year. Data beyond 24 months were collected only for appliances on a renewed service contract. Because a service contract provides free service, such appliances are serviced more often. And owners of troublesome appliances are more likely to buy and renew a service contract. So the higher failure rates in the second and third years were not representative of the entire population of appliances. GE did not have to develop a new component. I hope they paid part of the savings to their statistician.[6]

Is the Arithmetic Crooked?

Conclusions that are wrong or just incomprehensible are often due to a plain old-fashioned blunder. Rates and percentages are the most common causes of crooked arithmetic. Sometimes the matter can be straightened out by some numerical detective work. Here is an example.

Example 18. The BLS report on employment and unemployment for August 1977 noted that the unemployment rate was 6.1% for whites and 14.5% for blacks. *The New York Times* (September 3, 1977) included the following paragraph in its article on this report.

"The bureau also reported that the ratio of black to white jobless rates 'continued its recent updrift to the unusually high level of 2.4 to 1 in August,' meaning that 2.4 black workers were without jobs for every unemployed white worker."

Now 14.5% is 2.4 times as great as 6.1%, so the BLS is correct in stating that the ratio of black to white jobless rates was 2.4 to 1. But the *Times'* interpretation is completely wrong. Because blacks make up only a small part of the labor force, there are fewer jobless blacks than whites even though the percent of blacks who are unemployed is higher than the percent of whites who are without jobs. The *Times* confused percent unemployed with actual counts of the number of unemployed workers.

I concede that percents are a bit mysterious, but if you are going to write on statistical subjects you will have to get such things straight. Most subjects these days are statistical subjects.

NOTES

1. These data appear in Harry H. Ku, "Statistical Concepts in Metrology," in Harry H. Ku, ed., *Precision Measurement and Calibration* (National Bureau of Standards Special Publication 300, 1969), p. 319.
2. Quoted from Barbara Yuncker, "The Strange Case of the Painted Mice," *Saturday Review/World,* November 30, 1974, p. 53.
3. From Roy Reed, "Statistics on Rise in Jobs are Disputed in Alabama," *The New York Times,* August 20, 1973.
4. Reported in *The New York Times* of November 5, 1971.
5. *Consumer Reports,* October 1971, pp. 584–586.
6. This example appears in Wayne B. Nelson, "Data Analysis with Simple Plots," General Electric Technical Information Series, April 1975.

Exercises

Section 1

1. One of the preliminary problems in the negative income tax social experiments (Section 5 of Chapter 2) was to give a definition of the income of a family. This was important because the welfare "negative tax" payments decrease as income rises. Write an exact definition of "income" for this purpose. A short essay may be needed. For example, will you include non-

money income, such as the value of food stamps or of subsidized housing? Will you allow deductions for the cost of child care needed to permit the parent to work?

2. The essay by Brian J. L. Berry, "Measuring Racial Integration Potentials," in *Statistics: A Guide to the Unknown* describes an attempt to define a variable that measures a complex and somewhat vague concept. Read the essay and explain clearly what was to be measured.

3. The number of persons killed in bicycle accidents rose from about 600 in 1967 to over 1100 in 1973. Does this indicate that bicycle riding is becoming less safe? Let us put this question more specifically.

   (a) Is this total number of fatalities per year a valid measure of the danger of bicycle riding? Why or why not?

   (b) If you question the validity of total deaths as a measure of danger, suggest a variable that is a more valid measure. Explain your suggestion.

4. Congress wants the medical establishment to show that progress is being made in fighting cancer. Some variables that might be used are

   (a) Death rates—what percent of all Americans die from cancer of various kinds? (These death rates are rising steadily.)

   (b) Survival rates among cancer patients—what percent of cancer patients survive for five years from the time it was discovered that they had the disease? (These rates are rising slowly for all cancer, though the survival rate has improved greatly for a few kinds of cancer.)

Discuss the validity of each of these variables as a measure of the effectiveness of cancer treatment.

5. Properties that cannot be directly observed can be very difficult to measure. What variables would you examine to estimate the number of heroin addicts in New York City? (Start with the number of deaths from heroin overdose). None of these variables allows an accurate estimate of the number of addicts. But they are valuable because changes in such variables may help us to discover whether addiction is increasing or decreasing, and how rapidly.

6. You wish to study the effect of watching violent television programs on antisocial behavior in children.

   (a) Define (that is, tell how to measure) the independent and dependent variables. You have many possible choices of variables—just be sure that the ones you choose are valid and clearly defined.

   (b) Do you think that an experiment is practically and morally possible? If so, briefly describe the design of an experiment for this study.

   (c) If you were unable or unwilling to do an experiment, briefly discuss the design of a sample study. Will confounding with other variables threaten the validity of your conclusions about the effect of TV violence on child behavior?

7. "Standardized tests" are so called because a certain score—say 500 on the SAT verbal test—represents the same level of ability independent of whether it was measured in 1963 or 1983. The 1963 test form cannot be used in 1983, for by then the questions would have leaked out and students could prepare for them. To see how tests are kept standardized, read William H. Angoff, "Calibrating College Board Scores," in *Statistics: A Guide to the Unknown*. Discuss briefly the "equating" of scores on different forms of a standardized test.

Section 2

1. Use a ruler to mark off a piece of stiff paper in inches about as shown here. (Mark only full inches—no fractions.)

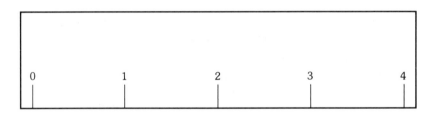

Measure the line below with your instrument, recording your answer to a hundredth of an inch (such as 2.23 inches or 2.39 inches):

To make this measurement, you must estimate what portion of the distance between the 2- and 3-inch marks the line extends. Careful measurements usually involve an uncertainty such as this; we have only magnified it by using an instrument divided into inches only.

(a) What is the result of your first measurement?
(b) Measure the line 5 times and record your results. What margin of error do you think a measurement with your instrument has? (That is, how reliable is it?)
(c) Suppose that someone measures the line by placing its left end at the end of the instrument, instead of at the 0 mark. This causes bias. Explain why. Is the reliability of the measurement also affected, or not?

Comment: Your work in part (b) may not be a good indication of variability in measurement because your trials are not independent. You remember the answer you gave in part (a), and this may affect your later measurements. A better picture of the degree of reliability here is obtained by collecting the answers of the entire class to part (a). Doing this will produce a graph similar to Figure 1 in Chapter 1.

2. Take a 1-foot ruler and measure the length of one wall of a room to the nearest inch. Do this 5 times, recording your answers in feet and inches. What is your average result? If possible, now use a tape measure at least as long as the wall to get a more accurate measurement. Did your ruler measurements show bias? (For example, were they almost all too long?)

3. A news article reported a study of pre-employment job performance tests and subsequent job performance for 1400 government technicians. Such tests are often accused of being biased against minority groups. A psychologist for the Educational Testing Service commenting on the results of the study said "Six years later, we found that belief wrong, if you define bias as meaning the scores are unrealistically low in relation to performance on the job." (*The New York Times*, July 27, 1973.)

   Is "bias" in the everyday sense used in this news article the same as "measurement bias" in the technical sense of this chapter? Why or why not?

4. Give an example of a measurement process that is valid but has large bias. Then give an example of a measurement process that is invalid but highly reliable.

Section 3

1. Identify the scale of each of the following variables as nominal, ordinal, or interval/ratio.

   (a) The concentration of DDT in a sample of milk, in milligrams per liter.
   (b) The species of each insect found in a sample plot of cropland.
   (c) The reaction time of a subject, in milliseconds after exposure to a stimulus.
   (d) A subject's response to the following personality test question: "It is natural for people of one race to want to live away from people of other races.

   > Strongly agree
   > Agree
   > Undecided
   > Disagree
   > Strongly disagree"

   (e) The zip code of a respondent to a mail questionnaire.
   (f) The position of the New York Mets in the National League Eastern Division standings (1st, 2nd, 3rd, 4th, 5th, or 6th).
   (g) The pressure in pounds per square inch required to crack a specimen of copper tubing.

2. Here is an article from *The New York Times* of July 8, 1976.

    (a) What type of scale was used to measure the personal enthusiasm of a voter toward a candidate? Explain your answer.

    (b) On page 23 in Chapter 1 is a list of questions for which any account of a sample survey should give answers. Find answers to these questions in the article, or state that the article does not give the answer. What is the most serious omission in the article?

Candidates Stir Voter Less Now Than in Recent Past, Poll Finds

None of the three leading Presidential candidates today engenders the personal enthusiasm of voters that other leading contenders for the office since 1960 did, the Gallup Poll reported yesterday.

In the current survey, the expected Democratic candidate, Jimmy Carter, was given a "highly favorable" rating by 25 percent of voters nationwide, while President Ford and Ronald Reagan each received a "highly favorable" rating by 2 percent.

By comparison, Gen. Dwight D. Eisenhower was rated "highly favorable" by 47 percent and 65 percent of voters in his successful Presidential campaigns in 1952 and 1956. John J. Kennedy had a 41 percent high rating in 1960; President Johnson had a 59 percent high rating in 1964; Richard M. Nixon had 28 and 40 percent high rating in 1968 and 1972, respectively.

In all of those election years, their challengers scored better than the current candidates, with the exception of Barry Goldwater, who had a high rating of 15 percent in 1964. George McGovern had a high raitng of 23 in 1972.

The polling organization says that while the current ratings fall below most of the leading Presidential candidates of the past elections, the ratings of the candidates tend to improve following the nominating conventions.

The results reported yesterday are based on personal interviews with 1,543 adults, 18 years of age and older, in more than 300 scientifically selected localities during the period of May 21 to 24.

To measure the personality factor, respondents are asked to indicate on a 10-point scale how highly they regard a candidate. These ratings are measurements of the appeal of a candidate as a person, the Gallup group noted, and should not be confused with hypothetical election results.

3.   **(a)** What type of scale is illustrated by the numbers on the shirts of a basketball team?

    (b) What type of scale is illustrated by house address numbers along a typical city street?

Section 4

1. The following quotation appears in a book review in *Science,* Volume 189 (1975), p. 373. ". . . a set of 20 studies with 57 percent reporting significant results, of which 42 percent agree on one conclusion while the remaining 15 percent favor another conclusion, often the opposite one."

   Do the numbers given in this quotation make sense? Can you decide how many of the 20 studies agreed on "one conclusion," how many favored another conclusion, and how many did not report significant results?

2. The following graph and excerpts are from a United Press International dispatch that appeared in *The Times Herald Record* (Middletown, NY) of June 7, 1975.

   (a) Is the source of the data given, and is that source trustworthy?
   (b) Because of suspicious regularity, I do not believe that 21.8% of manufacturing workers were unemployed, as the graph claims. Explain why I'm suspicious and how you think this apparent error came about.

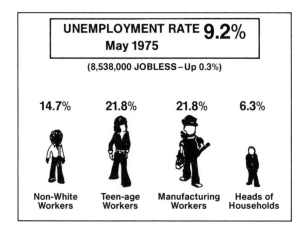

UNEMPLOYMENT RATE 9.2%
May 1975

(8,538,000 JOBLESS – Up 0.3%)

| 14.7% | 21.8% | 21.8% | 6.3% |
| Non-White Workers | Teen-age Workers | Manufacturing Workers | Heads of Households |

Unemployment hit a 34-year high of 9.2 percent in May, the government reported Friday, but a labor analyst insisted there are new signs the recession may be over.

The Bureau of Labor Statistics said the number of unemployed rose 362,000 in May to a total of 8,538,000 – 9.2 percent of the labor force compared to 8.9 percent in April.

It was the first time the rate exceeded 9 percent since the final Depression year of 1941 when the 12-month average was 9.9 percent.

• • •

The report showed unemployment in construction trades hit an all-time high of 21.8 percent in May.

Reprinted with permission of U.P.I.

3. The late English psychologist Cyril Burt is famous for studies of the IQ scores of identical twins who were raised apart. The high correlation be-

tween the IQ's of separated twins in Burt's studies pointed to heredity as a major factor in IQ. ("Correlation" is a measure of the connection or association between two variables. We will become acquainted with it in Chapter 5.) In 1955, Burt reported a correlation of 0.771 for 21 pairs of twins. In 1958 he had collected "over 30" pairs, and the correlation was 0.771. A final report in 1966 had 53 pairs of twins, with correlation 0.771 between the IQ scores of the twins. What is suspicious here? (Burt's data are now considered unusable, and perhaps fraudulent. A full account appears in Nicholas Wade, "IQ and Heredity: Suspicion of Fraud Beclouds Classic Experiment," *Science,* Volume 194 (1976), pp. 916–919.)

4. A series of measurements of weights in grams is recorded as

| 11.25 | 13.75 | 12.00 | 13.25 | 10.75 |
| 12.50 | 12.25 | 11.00 | 13.25 | 11.75 |

Because two decimal places are given, we might conclude that the measurements are precise to two decimal places, that is, to about ±0.01 grams. A closer look at the data suggests that they are much less precise than this. How precise do you think these data are? Why?

5. Here are some citations containing numbers that may not be plausible. In each case, identify the data which seem implausible. Try to decide if the numbers are actually right. (Not all of them are wrong!)

   (a) From *The New York Times,* May 8, 1976, p. 25: "Altogether, in some 30 associations and groups of independents, there are almost 80 million Baptists in the nation. They are outnumbered only by the Roman Catholics."

   (b) From *Audubon,* May 1976, p. 28, writing of Alaska: "Throughout the state each year, hunters harvest upward of 10,000 moose, skin them out, pack them out, and dress them out—five, six million pounds of meat in their freezers. . . ."

   (c) *The Statistical Abstract of the United States,* 1973 edition, p. 83 reports that on December 31, 1971 there were 82,294 narcotics addicts in the United States.

6. An advertisement for the pain reliever Tylenol was headlined "Why Doctors Recommend Tylenol More Than All Leading Aspirin Brands Combined." A counteradvertisement by the Bayer Aspirin, headlined "Makers of Tylenol, Shame On You!", accused Tylenol of misleading by giving the truth but not the whole truth. You be the detective again: How is Tylenol's claim misleading even if true?

7. A commercial states that "Recent studies show that 9 out of 10 doctors prescribe the ingredients in Zappit for minor inflammation." Discuss this statement as to possible omission of important information.

8. Find in a magazine or newspaper, or on radio or television, an example of *one* of the following. Describe your example in detail.

> Meaningless comparison
> Spurious precision
> Risky extrapolation
> Lack of internal consistency
> Omission of essential information
> Implausible numbers

9. Example 14 in the text contains a well-hidden internal inconsistency. Can you find it? Exercise 9 for Section 2 of Chapter 2 contains a less elusive internal inconsistency. Find it too.

10. The question-and-answer column of the Purdue campus newspaper was asked what percent of the campus was Greek. The answer given was "the figures for the fall semester are approximately 13 percent for the girls and 15–18 percent for the guys, which produces a 'Greek' figure of approximately 28–31 percent of the undergraduates at Purdue." (*The Purdue Exponent,* September 21, 1977). Discuss the campus newspaper's arithmetic.

11. A newspaper story on housing costs (*Lafayette Journal and Courier,* September 21, 1977.) noted that in 1975 the median price of a new house was $39,300 and the median family income was $13,991. (The median income is the amount such that half of all families earn less than this, and half earn more. We become acquainted with the median in Chapter 5.) The writer then claimed that "the ratio of housing prices to income is much lower today than it was in 1900 (2.8 percent in 1975 vs. 9.8 percent in 1900)."

   I do wish that I could buy a new house for 2.8% of my income. Where did that 2.8 come from? What is the correct expression for $39,300 as a percent of $13,991?

"Tonight, we're going to let the statistics speak for themselves."

Part II

Organizing Data

Data, like words, speak clearly only when they are organized. Also like words, data speak more effectively when well organized than when poorly organized. Again like words, data can obscure a subject by their quantity, requiring a brief summary to highlight essential facts. The second of statistics' three domains is the organizing, summarizing, and presenting of data.

Data are usually organized and presented in the form of tables and graphs. These are the subject of Chapter 4. Data are summarized most often by giving a few statistics to sum up the meaning of the whole. In Chapter 5 we will meet means, variances, correlations, and other such summary statistics. Chapter 6 presents ways of summarizing data that are regularly collected over time, and focuses on understanding some of the economic and social statistics that attract such attention in difficult times.

Summarizing and presenting a large body of facts offers to ignorance or malice ample opportunity for distortion. This is no less (but also no more) the case when the facts to be summarized are numbers rather than words. We will therefore take due note of the traps that the ignorant fall into and the tools of duplicity that the malicious use. Those who picture statistics as primarily a piece of the liar's art concentrate on the part of statistics that deals with summarizing and presenting data. I claim that misleading summaries and selective presentations go back to that after-the-apple conversation between Adam, Eve, and God. Don't blame statistics. But do remember the saying, "Figures don't lie, but liars figure," and beware.

Chapter 4

Tables, Graphs, and Distributions

W hat mental picture does the word "statistics" call to mind in most people? Very likely a picture of tables crowded with numbers. And close behind tables come graphs, zigging up or zagging down. Now tables do lack sex appeal, and you may have exhausted your interest in graphs when you mastered pie charts in grade school. But tables remain the first step in organizing data, and data are most vividly presented in graphs. I promise to be brief in presenting tables and graphs, and not to mention pie charts again.

Yet there is an art to presenting complex data clearly, an art best learned by example. One of the best ways to decide how to make a table or graph of a set of data is to look for similar examples in the *Statistical Abstract of the United States*. This yearly compilation of data contains tables of every sort, and many graphs as well, that are models of clear presentation. Any library will have copies of the *Statistical Abstract*. Two principles apply to all tables and graphs: First, always *label* the graph or table clearly; second, always give the *source* of the data. These principles, some educated common sense, and the *Statistical Abstract* will carry you most of the way through these subjects. Sections 1 and 2 of this chapter will educate your common sense.

It is no accident that we met our first table and an accompanying graph in discussing the sampling distribution of statistics computed from a SRS in Chapter 1. Sampling distributions are central to statistical inference. They therefore receive VIP treatment in Section 3.

1. Frequency Tables

One of our first acts in organizing a set of data is usually to count how often each value occurs. After completing a sample survey of 1537 students that included

Table 1

FARMS BY SIZE (1969)

Size of farm (acres)	Number of farms (thousands)	Percent of farms
Under 10	162	5.9
10–49	473	17.3
50–99	460	16.8
100–179	542	19.9
180–259	307	11.2
260–499	419	15.3
500–999	216	7.9
1000–1999	91	3.3
2000 and over	60	2.2
Total	2,730	99.8

SOURCE: *Statistical Abstract of the United States*, 1976, Table 1070.
From the 1969 U.S. Census of Agriculture.

the question "Do you agree or disagree that possession of small amounts of marijuana should not be a crime?" we are eager to tabulate the answers and learn that 928 agreed, 543 disagreed, and 66 had no opinion. (Check that 928 + 543 + 66 = 1537, so all the answers are accounted for. That's a check for internal consistency.) Because rates or proportions are often more useful than totals, we go on to compute that

$$\frac{928}{1537} = 0.60 \text{ or } 60\% \text{ agreed}$$

$$\frac{543}{1537} = 0.35 \text{ or } 35\% \text{ disagreed}$$

$$\frac{66}{1537} = 0.04 \text{ or } 4\% \text{ had no opinion.}$$

Again you should check for internal consistency. There should be 100% in all. We got 60% + 35% + 4% = 99%. What happened? The arithmetic is right, but when we rounded the fractions off to two decimal places a little precision was lost and the results do not quite add up to 100%. Such *roundoff errors* will be with us from now on as we do more arithmetic.

Totals and percentages of this kind occur so often that they deserve formal names.

The *frequency* of any value of a variable is the number of times that value occurs in the data. That is, a frequency is a count.

The *relative frequency* of any value is the proportion or fraction or percent of all observations that have that value.

In the sample survey, the frequency of students in the sample who agreed that marijuana possession should be legalized was 928. The relative frequency was 0.60. Relative frequencies are usually expressed in this decimal form, but we can just as correctly say that the relative frequency was 60%. Remember that 1% is 1/100 or 0.01. A number in decimal form can be changed to a percent by moving the decimal point two places to the right. So 0.60 is 60%.

Frequencies and relative frequencies are a common way of summarizing data when a nominal scale is used. Even when an interval/ratio scale is used and the variable has numerous possible values, we often summarize data by giving frequencies or relative frequencies for groups of values. Such a summary is conveniently presented in a table. Table 1 is an example. From this table we can learn much about the size of American farms. For example, the most common size category in 1969 was 100–179 acres. There were 542,000 farms in that size range. (Did you read the heading carefully enough to see that the number of farms is given in *thousands*?) This was 19.9% of all U.S. farms. The "number" column gives frequencies, while the "percent" column gives relative frequencies; it is good practice to follow the *Statistical Abstract* in *not* using the technical terms so the table is easier for untrained persons to read. Finally, it is important that the source is given. Remembering how essential it is to know the definitions of variables, we should ask what the definition of a "farm" is. Without knowing

"5.9% of American farms are under 10 acres."

what makes a piece of land a farm, we don't know what is being counted in Table 1. The source cited gives the exact definition: A farm is any place from which $250 or more of agricultural products are normally sold in a year, or any place of 10 acres or more from which $50 or more of agricultural products are normally sold in a year.

Frequency tables become more interesting when more than one variable is measured on each unit. We have already noted many examples in which several variables are measured, sometimes as independent and dependent variables when causation is at issue, and sometimes just for descriptive purposes. It is time to learn the proper vocabulary here.

> Data are *univariate* when only one variable is measured on each unit.
>
> Data are *bivariate* when two variables are measured on each unit.
>
> Data are *multivariate* when more than one variable is measured on each unit.

If both the height and weight of each pupil in a schoolroom are measured, we have a set of bivariate data. These data carry much more information than do the two sets of univariate data (heights alone and weights alone). Knowing which height and weight go together (come from the same pupil), lets us study the connection or association between height and weight.

To see how much information bivariate data contain, look at Table 2, a *bivariate frequency table.* The entries are numbers of earned degrees, categorized by two nominal variables, the level of the degree and the sex of the recipient. For example, 7803 doctorate degrees were earned by women in 1976. Here are some questions we might ask of this table.

1. What fraction of all degrees were doctorates earned by women?
2. What fraction of all doctorate degrees were earned by women?
3. What fraction of all degrees earned by women were doctorates?

Table 2

EARNED DEGREES, BY LEVEL AND SEX (1976)

	Bachelor's	Master's	Doctorates
Male	508,549	167,745	26,273
Female	425,894	145,256	7,803
Totals	934,443	313,001	34,076

SOURCE: National Center for Education Statistics.

These questions sound alike, but are not. Recognizing which question we want to ask in a given situation and learning how to answer all of them from the table is part of developing statistical skill. Each question asks for the relative frequency of doctor's degrees earned by women. In a bivariate frequency table, an entry has *three* relative frequencies, which differ in the total of which the table entry is a fraction. Question 1 asks the relative frequency of doctorates earned by women among all degrees. The table does not give the total number of degrees awarded, so we must compute it by adding the totals for each level:

$$934{,}443 + 313{,}001 + 34{,}076 = 1{,}281{,}520.$$

So the answer to Question 1 is

$$\frac{\text{entry}}{\text{table total}} = \frac{7803}{1{,}281{,}520} = 0.006.$$

Only six-tenths of 1% of degrees awarded fell in this category.

Question 2 says: Look only at the "Doctorates" column in the table. What is the relative frequency of women among the degrees in this column? The answer is

$$\frac{\text{entry}}{\text{column total}} = \frac{7803}{34{,}076} = 0.229.$$

About 22.9% of all doctorate degrees were earned by women. This is sometimes called a *conditional* relative frequency because it is the relative frequency of female degree earners given the condition that only doctorate degrees are considered.

Question 3 says: Look only at the "Female" row in the table and find the relative frequency of doctorates among the degrees in this row. The table does not give the total number of degrees earned by women. This row total is

$$425{,}894 + 145{,}256 + 7803 = 578{,}953.$$

The answer to Question 3 is then

$$\frac{\text{entry}}{\text{row total}} = \frac{7803}{578{,}953} = 0.0134.$$

About 1.3% of all degrees earned by women were doctorates. This is another conditional relative frequency. Now the given condition is that only degrees earned by women are considered.

Answering these questions was mainly a matter of straight thinking, complicated a bit because the table did not give all of the totals we needed. We might well have begun the study of these data by putting the row totals at the right of

Table 3

EARNED DEGREES, BY LEVEL AND SEX (1976)

	Bachelor's	Master's	Doctorates	Total
Male	508,549	167,745	26,273	702,567
Female	425,894	145,256	7,803	578,953
Totals	934,443	313,001	34,076	1,281,520

SOURCE: National Center For Education Statistics.

the table, and the grand total of all degrees in the lower right corner. Table 2 then becomes Table 3. The column totals (bottom row) are a univariate frequency table of degrees by level. The row totals (right column) are a univariate frequency table of degrees by sex of the recipient. Both of these univariate tables can be obtained from the bivariate table (the 6 entries in the box), but the bivariate table *cannot* be obtained from the two univariate tables. The entries in these univariate tables are sometimes called *marginal* frequencies because they appear at the margins of the table.*

2.   Graphs

The purpose of a graph is to give a visual summary of data. A good graph frequently reveals facts about the data that would require careful study to detect in a table. We will look at the use and abuse of several common types of graphs.

Line graphs show the trend of a variable over time. Time is marked off on the horizontal axis, and the variable being watched is on the vertical axis. Figure 1 is an example. From this line graph, we can see at once:

- That the number of civil disturbances each year is greatest in the summer months and least in the winter. (This is called a *seasonal effect.*)

- That the number of civil disturbances was generally decreasing during these years. (This is a long-term *trend.*)

It would be difficult to draw these conclusions from a column of numbers; this is a vivid example of how a graph can make clear what the data are saying.

Just because graphs speak so strongly, they can mislead the unwary. The intelligent reader of a line graph looks closely at the *scales* marked off on both

---

*A note for connoisseurs: I condensed Table 2 from a *trivariate* frequency table of degrees awarded categorized by level, sex, and area of study. Look in the education section of the *Statistical Abstract* to find the full table and to learn how to organize and label a trivariate frequency table.

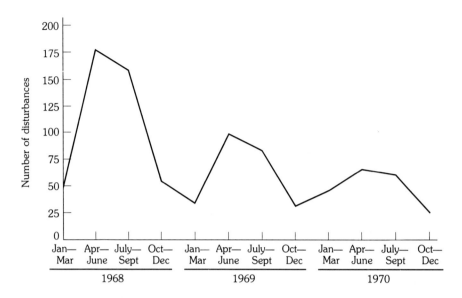

Figure 1. Civil disturbances, 1968 to 1970. [From *Statistical Abstract of the United States,* 1971, p. 139.]

axes. In Figure 2, one can transform the left-hand graph into the right-hand graph by stretching the vertical axis, compressing the horizontal axis, and cutting off the vertical axis at a value above zero. Now you know the trick of giving an exaggerated impression with a line graph. Because there is no one "right" scale for a line graph, perfectly honest sources can give somewhat different impressions by their choices of scale. Figure 3 contains line graphs of the same data that appeared on the same day in the nation's two leading financial newspapers. *The New York Times* drew a larger vertical scale than did the *Wall Street Journal,* cut it off at 125 instead of 90, and used a shorter time period on the horizontal scale. As a result, the *Times'* graph suggests a steeper rise than does the *Journal's.* Moral: Look at the scales.

Once in awhile you may encounter a more barbarous line graph. Figure 4 is the least civilized I have seen. Note first that time is on the vertical axis. So when the graph goes straight up (1940–1946), this means that taxes were not increasing at all. And when the graph is quite flat (1965–1972), this means that taxes were thundering upward. The graph gives an impression exactly the reverse of the truth. That's why time always belongs on the horizontal axis. Second, the time scale does not have equal units; equal lengths on the vertical axis represent first 2 years, then 4 years, then 2 years again, then whatever the interval between 1962 and 1964–1965 is, and so on. So the rise in taxes in different time periods cannot be compared by looking at the steepness of the graph; the graph is stretched and squeezed haphazardly by the changing time scale. These barbarisms were perpetrated by the Associated Press (not by the Census Bureau, which was only the source of the data). The newspaper then provided the

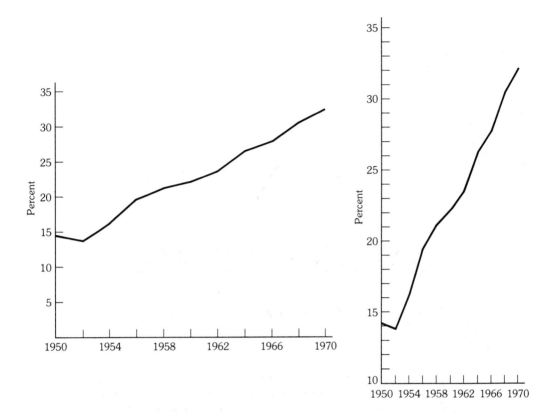

Figure 2. Two line graphs of the same data. Enrollment in higher education as percent of population 18–24 years old. [From *Historical Statistics of the United States, Colonial Times to 1970*, Part I, p. 383.]

caption below the chart, which no doubt refers to the "12 years" from 1940 to 1972.

Bar graphs compare the values of several variables. Often the values compared are frequencies or relative frequencies of outcomes of a nominal variable. For example, Figure 5 is a bar graph of the data in Table 2. This is actually three bar graphs drawn together, showing the number of degrees awarded to men and women separately for each of the three types of degree.

The bars in a bar chart may be vertical (as in Figure 5) or horizontal. They may touch each other (as in Figure 5) or be separated. But all bars must have the same width, for our eyes respond to the *area* of the bars. When the bars have the same width, and a height that varies with the variable being graphed, then the area (height times width) also varies with the variable and our eyes receive the correct impression. The most common abuse of bar graphs is to replace the bars by pictures, and to change both the width and height of the picture as the

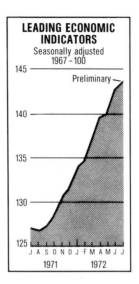

**LEADING ECONOMIC
INDICATORS**

Seasonally adjusted
1967 – 100

COMPOSITE of key indicators of future economic activity rose in July to 143.6% of the 1967 average from a revised 142.6% in June, the Commerce Department reports.

Figure 3. Two line graphs of the same data. [Graph on left from *The Wall Street Journal*, August 29, 1972. Reprinted with permission of The Wall Street Journal. Copyright © Dow Jones & Company, Inc. 1972. All rights reserved. Right graph from *The New York Times*, August 29, 1972. Copyright © 1972 by The New York Times Company. Reprinted by permission.]

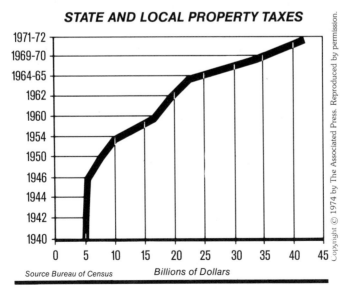

STATE AND LOCAL PROPERTY TAXES

Source Bureau of Census   *Billions of Dollars*

Chart indicates rise in state and local property taxes over 12 years

Figure 4

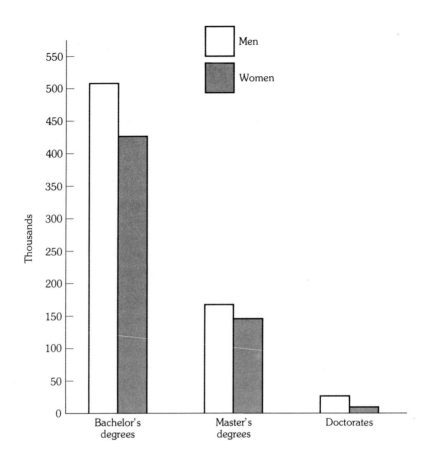

Figure 5. Earned degrees, 1976. [From National Center for Education Statistics.]

variable graphed changes. Figure 6, an advertisement placed by *Time* magazine in the commercial section of *The New York Times,* illustrates this. *Time* enjoys a lead of less than two-to-one over *Newsweek* in dollar value of consumer services advertising. (The dollar amounts appear over the pictures.) But because *both* the height and width of the pen representing *Time* are almost double those of *Newsweek's* pen, the area of *Time's* pen is almost four times that of *Newsweek's.* Our eyes receive the misleading impression that *Time* has a four-to-one rather than a two-to-one edge.

In case you are wondering if graphic attractiveness always must be sacrificed to accuracy, I present Figure 7. This is another *Time* ad making the same point as Figure 6, and it is at least as attractive as Figure 6. Unlike Figure 6, the graph in Figure 7 is accurate. Congratulations to the designer who managed to combine accuracy with graphic impact.

Scatterplots graph bivariate data when both variables are measured in an

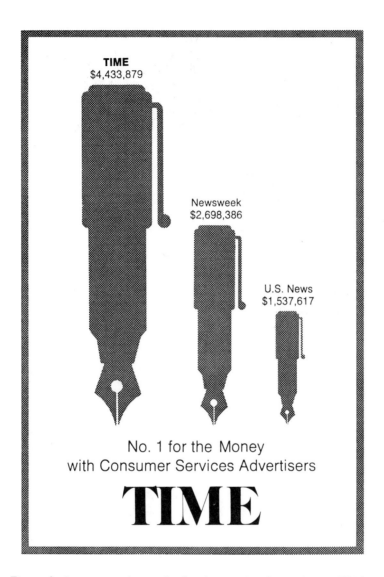

TIME
$4,433,879

Newsweek
$2,698,386

U.S. News
$1,537,617

No. 1 for the Money
with Consumer Services Advertisers

TIME

Figure 6. An attractive but misleading bar graph. [Copyright © 1971 by Time, Inc. Reproduced by permission.]

interval/ratio or ordinal scale. Units for one variable are marked on the horizontal axis and units for the other variable on the vertical axis. The independent variable should always go on the horizontal axis when one of the variables is an independent and one a dependent variable. Each bivariate observation is represented by a point with a horizontal coordinate equal to the value of the first variable and a vertical coordinate equal to the value of the second.

Figure 7. An attractive and accurate bar graph. [Copyright © 1972 by Time, Inc. Reproduced by permission.]

Figure 8 is a scatterplot of data from an agricultural experiment. The independent variable was planting rate for corn (in thousands of plants per acre) and the dependent variable was yield (in bushels per acre). The scatterplot shows 13 observations. One plot received 12,000 plants per acre and yielded 130.5 bushels per acre. This is indicated by the circled dot on the scatterplot at 12 on the horizontal scale and 130.5 on the vertical scale. The association between

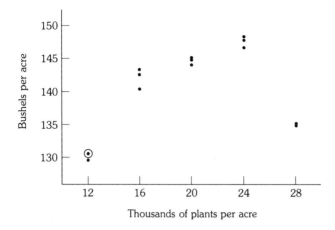

Figure 8. Corn planting rate versus yield, a scatterplot.

planting rate and yield is clear from Figure 8; yield increases with planting rate until about 24,000 plants per acre are planted, then drops off. (This was irrigated corn. The conclusions may differ if irrigation is not used.)

Frequency histograms are the most important type of graph for our progress toward statistical inference. When the data are values of a variable measured in an interval/ratio scale, a table of the frequency in each of several classes of values shows in tabular form the distribution of values of the variable. Table 1 is such a table. Such a distribution of values can be displayed graphically in a frequency histogram. Figure 9 is a histogram of 1977 American League baseball batting averages. The averages are divided into classes 20 points wide. Each bar covers such a class, and the height of the bar is the frequency (count) of players with averages in that class. A frequency table containing this information is below the graph. The histogram is a lot more vivid.

Histograms look like bar graphs. They differ from bar graphs in several respects. First, the bars in a histogram are always vertical, and the base scale is marked off in equal units. There is no base scale in a bar graph. Second, the width of the bars in a histogram has meaning: The base of each bar covers a class of values of the variable, and the height is the frequency for that class of values. The width of the bars in a bar graph has no meaning. Third, the bars in a histogram touch each other (unless some class has frequency zero) because their bases must cover the whole range of values of a variable, with no gaps. Even when the possible values of a variable have gaps between them, we extend the bases of the bars to meet halfway between two adjacent possible values.

Just as with bar graphs, our eye responds to the *area* of the bars in a histogram. To avoid false impressions, the widths of the bars must all be the same if the heights are frequencies. So in dividing a set of data into classes to draw a frequency histogram, choose classes of equal width. We did not make a histogram of the farm acreage data in Table 1 because the classes are of unequal

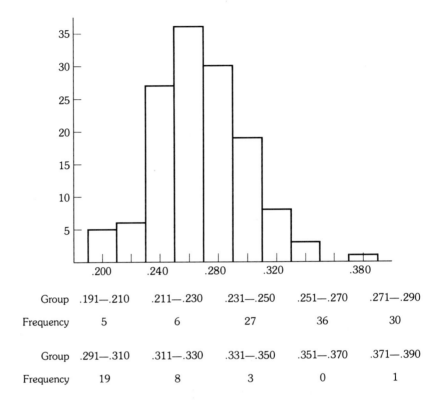

Group	.191—.210	.211—.230	.231—.250	.251—.270	.271—.290
Frequency	5	6	27	36	30

Group	.291—.310	.311—.330	.331—.350	.351—.370	.371—.390
Frequency	19	8	3	0	1

Figure 9. American League batting averages, 1977. Official batting averages for the 135 American League baseball players having 250 or more at bats. [Associated Press.]

width (0–10 acres, 10–49 acres, and so on). Making an accurate graph of frequencies in such a case is a more complicated affair than I want to deal with.

As another example of dividing data into classes and drawing a frequency histogram, consider Figure 10. The data are 1975–1976 academic year salaries for all faculty members in six humanities departments in a Big Ten university. There were 272 salaries in all. I chose to use classes $2000 wide, resulting in 14 classes. There is no one right choice of class width. Our goal is to display the frequency distribution effectively. Avoid either cramming all the observations into a few big classes or sprinkling one or two observations into each of many tiny classes.

A frequency histogram displays the overall shape of the frequency distribution of a set of data. The salary distribution of Figure 10 is *skewed to the right.* That is, the right tail extends farther than the left. Half the salaries fall in or below the $16,000–17,999 class, so that is the midpoint of the distribution. Because no salaries are below $10,000, the lower tail extends only three classes below the midpoint. But the upper tail has observations as far as ten classes above the midpoint. The distribution of batting averages, Figure 9, is somewhat skewed to

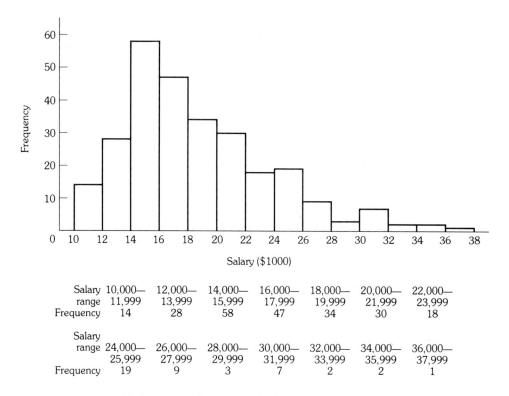

Salary range	10,000– 11,999	12,000– 13,999	14,000– 15,999	16,000– 17,999	18,000– 19,999	20,000– 21,999	22,000– 23,999
Frequency	14	28	58	47	34	30	18

Salary range	24,000– 25,999	26,000– 27,999	28,000– 29,999	30,000– 31,999	32,000– 33,999	34,000– 35,999	36,000– 37,999
Frequency	19	9	3	7	2	2	1

Figure 10. Frequency histogram of salaries of 272 university faculty members.

the right, but much less than the salary data. A frequency histogram is *symmetric* if the two sides of the histogram are mirror images of each other. A symmetric histogram is skewed neither to the right nor to the left. The shape of a frequency distribution is often characteristic of the variable measured. Distributions of incomes such as Figure 10 (whether for persons, firms, or nations) are usually skewed to the right. There are typically many moderate incomes near the midpoint and a few large incomes far out in the right tail.

Because the height of the bars in a frequency histogram grows with the size of a data set, it is not always easy to compare the shapes of two data sets of different size. The histogram for the larger set towers over that of the smaller. This distortion can be avoided by drawing a histogram of *relative frequency* rather than frequency. Just relabel the vertical scale to read in relative frequencies (that is, in fractions of the number of observations). Now the vertical scale extends from 0 to 1 no matter how many observations are involved. Because relative frequency histograms show only what fraction of the data falls in each class, two different relative frequency histograms are easy to compare. But a frequency histogram is the more informative way to picture a single set of data because it shows how many observations fell in each class.

Example 1. As an example of the conversion of frequencies into relative frequencies, look again at Figure 10. There are 272 salaries recorded in that frequency histogram because 272 is the sum of the frequencies (counts) in all the classes. So in this case,

$$\text{relative frequency} = \frac{\text{frequency}}{272}.$$

The relative frequency of salaries in the $22,000–23,999 range, for example, is

$$\frac{18}{272} = 0.066 \text{ or } 6.6\%$$

To convert Figure 10 to a relative frequency histogram, just mark off the vertical scale from 0 to 1, perhaps placing scale marks at 0.1, 0.2, 0.3, and so on. Then redraw the bars to have as heights the relative frequencies of their classes. The new histogram has the same shape as Figure 10; it differs only in the vertical scale.

3. Sampling Distributions and the Normal Curves

Frequency and relative frequency histograms display the shape of any set of data measured in an interval or ratio scale. Whether the data represent a sample or (as in Figure 9) an entire population is immaterial. But we first encountered histograms in another setting. Figure 1 of Chapter 1 showed the distribution of the sample proportion $\hat{p}$ in 200 SRS's drawn independently from the same population. The frequency distribution of a sample statistic in repeated sampling from the same population is the *sampling distribution* of the statistic. Its shape is characteristic of the sampling method and helps to evaluate the precision of the statistic as an estimate of the corresponding population parameter.

Figure 11 redraws the results of these 200 SRS's in terms of relative frequencies. These are the dashed bars. They are identical to Figure 1 of Chapter 1 except for the vertical scale. Now in a strict sense, the sampling distribution of the statistic $\hat{p}$ is not a specific observed distribution but the ideal distribution that is approached as ever more samples are taken. This distribution can be found by long experiments, or much more quickly by mathematics. The solid bars in Figure 11 are a relative frequency histogram of this theoretical sampling distribution of $\hat{p}$ in the bead-sampling experiment of Chapter 1. The sampling distribution is similar to the distribution observed in 200 trials, but it differs in several respects. In particular, the sampling distribution is more symmetric than the observed distribution. Some of the deviation between the observed and theoretical distributions is caused by the chance outcome of the particular 200 trials I

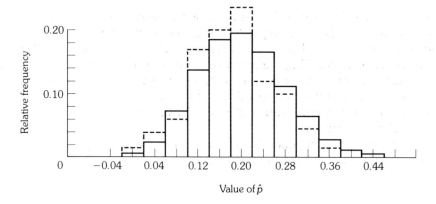

Figure 11. Sampling distribution for a sample proportion, observed (broken bars) and theoretical (solid bars).

made. But some of the deviation is also because the theoretical sampling distribution describes truly random sampling, while my scoop gave only approximately random samples of beads. If we use a table of random digits to select the samples, the observed distribution of values of $\hat{p}$ will always approach the sampling distribution as more and more samples are drawn.

The shape of the sampling distribution in Figure 11 depends on three facts about the bead-sampling experiment. First, that simple random sampling was employed. Second, that the sample size was 25. And third, that the population contained 20% dark beads. This characteristic shape appears even more clearly in Figure 12. The curve in that figure was drawn by placing a dot in the center of the top of each bar in the histogram of the sampling distribution, then drawing straight lines between the dots.

It is a remarkable fact that the sampling distribution of $\hat{p}$ from random sampling can always be approximated by a smooth curve of a certain kind. The top

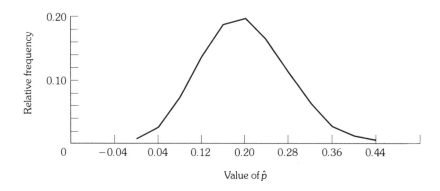

Figure 12

curve in Figure 13 is a *normal curve* that would coincide closely with Figure 12 if it were laid over that sampling distribution. The bottom curve in Figure 13 is another normal curve. There is an entire family of normal curves, but all share several characteristics. They are symmetric. Their tails drop off quickly. They are bell-shaped. I want to stress that not all bell-shaped curves are normal. Normal curves have an exact mathematical description that I will leave to those who concern themselves with mathematics. In Chapter 5 we learn more about the shape of normal curves.

Normal curves are important in statistics because the sampling distributions of many sample statistics can be described quite well by these curves. The bottom

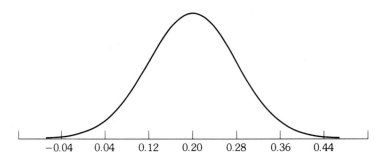

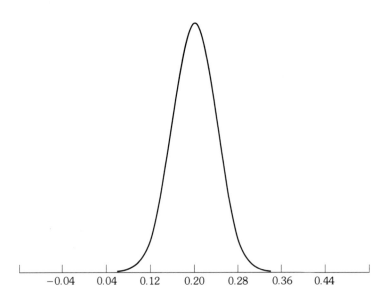

Figure 13. Two normal distribution curves.

curve in Figure 13, for example, describes the sampling distribution of $\hat{p}$ in samples of size 100 from the population of beads used in the experiment of Chapter 1. The characteristic normal shape is present in both curves in Figure 13, while the differences between the two show the effect of increasing the sample size from 25 to 100. Notice first that both normal curves are symmetric with 0.20 as their center. Because the curves are just dressed-up histograms, this means that values of the sample proportion $\hat{p}$ are as likely to fall below 0.20 as above it. Remember that 0.20 was the true proportion of dark beads in the population. We have just reencountered a favorite idea—unbiasedness of a sample statistic from a SRS. When the sampling distribution of a statistic is normal, unbiasedness means that the true value of the population parameter is the point about which the curve is symmetric.

So the sampling distribution of $\hat{p}$ is normal because a SRS was used. The normal curve is centered at 0.20 because that is the population proportion p, of which $\hat{p}$ is an unbiased estimate. The third influence on the sampling distribution is the sample size. The bottom curve in Figure 13 reflects the greater precision of sample size 100. It is more concentrated about its center than is the top curve (sample size 25). So the values of $\hat{p}$ in repeated sampling fall closer together when the larger sample size is employed. Always remember when trying to interpret a distribution curve that it is simply a histogram with its fancy dress on. If you understand histograms, you should understand distribution curves.

Now any histogram, not just histograms of sampling distributions, can be described by drawing a smooth curve through the tops of the bars. This is not a good way to describe a data set unless you have many observations. It is too easy to draw quite different smooth curves through the same histogram. But curves are a useful way to describe the general shape of large sets of data. And many types of data have frequency distributions whose shape is approximately described by a normal curve. You should ponder again the harmony of creation, that distributions derived from a mathematical study of random sampling also should be useful in describing populations occurring in the real world.

One kind of data that are often normal are physical measurements of many members of a biological population. As an example, Figure 14 presents 2000 Hungarian skulls. The results of repeated careful measurements of the same quantity also tend to follow a normal distribution. (Recall that the results of repeated sampling and measurement were said in Chapter 3 to have similar properties!) This tendency was discovered by the great mathematician Carl Friedrich Gauss (1777–1855), who used normal curves to study errors in astronomical measurements. You will sometimes see these curves called "Gaussian" in his honor. That's a small honor for a man who made major contributions to astronomy, surveying, and several fields of physics in addition to being one of the greatest mathematicians. Finally, it can be proved mathematically that any variable which is the sum of many small independent effects will have a distribution of values that is close to normal. So scores on long multiple-choice examinations such as the college boards come close to following a normal curve.

HOWEVER, . . . even though many sets of data follow a normal curve, many

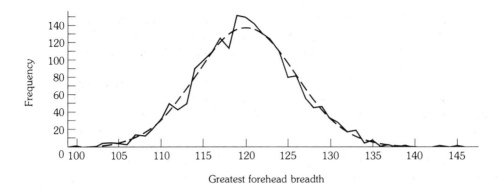

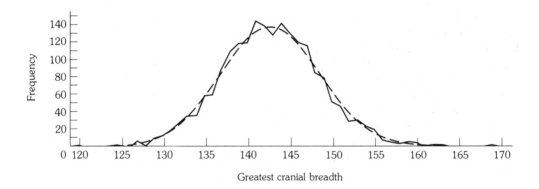

Figure 14. 2000 Hungarian skulls. The distribution of each of two measurements on a large sample of male skulls is approximately normal. The solid line is the actual frequency curve, and the broken line is a normal curve that approximates the distribution [From Karl Pearson, "Craniological notes," *Biometrika*, June 1903, p. 344. Reproduced by permission of the Biometrika Trustees.]

do not. The income distribution of Figure 10 is skewed to the right, and hence is not normal. Nonnormal data, like nonnormal people, meet us quite often and are sometimes more interesting than their normal counterparts.

Exercises

Section 1

1. Answer the following questions from Table 1 (p. 132).

    (a) What percent of all American farms in 1969 were at least 500 acres in size?

(b) How many farms were there in 1969? About how precise is this figure (nearest 1, nearest 100, or nearest 1000)?

(c) Why do the percents in the last column sum to 99.8% rather than to 100%?

2. The Department of Health, Education, and Welfare has among its jobs the investigation of possible sex discrimination in university hiring. The Department wants to know if women are hired for the faculty in the same proportion as their availability in the pool of potential employees. If new university faculty in 1976 were recruited almost entirely from new doctorate degree recipients, which of the three questions following Table 2 is useful to the Department? Why?

3. From Table 2 (p. 134), find the percent of degrees at each level (bachelor's, master's, doctorate) earned by women. What do you conclude about the relative educational patterns of men and women in 1976?

4. Here are the marginal entries of a bivariate frequency table with two rows and two columns.

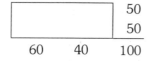

Find *two different* sets of entries in the body of the table that give these same marginal totals. This shows that the bivariate frequencies cannot be obtained from the univariate (marginal) frequencies alone.

5. Look up the table of earned degrees conferred in any recent *Statistical Abstract*. From that table, make a properly labeled frequency table of earned degrees *in mathematical subjects,* categorized by the level of the degree and the sex of the recipient.

6. Here is a bivariate frequency table.

MILLIONAIRES, BY AGE AND SEX
(1972, in thousands)

	Under 50 years	50–64 years	65 and over
Male	24	34	31
Female	39	26	25

SOURCE: *Statistical Abstract of the United States,* 1976, Table 691.

Answer the following questions from this table.

(a) How many millionaires were there in the United States in 1972?

(b) What percent of these millionaires were women?

(c) What percent of these millionaires were under 50 years of age?

(d) Of all female millionaires, what percent were under 50 years of age?

(e) Of all millionaires under 50 years of age, what percent were females?

7. Here is a pleasant little bivariate frequency table

SUICIDES, BY SEX AND METHOD
(1969)

	Male	Female
Poison	3064	3054
Hanging	2317	841
Firearms	9393	1911
Other	1083	701

SOURCE: *Statistical Abstract of the United States*, 1973, Table 235.

Answer the following questions from this table.

(a) How many suicides were recorded in 1969?

(b) What was the method most commonly used, and what percent of all suicides were committed by this method?

(c) What percent of all women who committed suicide used poison?

(d) Describe in words the chief differences between men and women in their choice of suicide methods, referring to the table to support your statement.

Section 2

1. The rate of deaths from cancer in the United States has increased as follows since 1925.

CANCER DEATHS PER 100,000 POPULATION

Year	1925	1930	1935	1940	1945	1950	1955	1960	1965	1970
Death Rate	92.0	97.4	108.2	120.3	134.0	139.8	146.5	149.2	153.5	162.8

SOURCE: *Historical Statistics of the United States*, Part I, p. 58.

(a) Draw a line graph of these data designed to emphasize the rise in the cancer death rates. (Imagine you are trying to persuade Congress to appropriate more money to fight cancer.)

(b) Draw another line graph of the same data designed to show only a moderate increase in the death rate.

2. Use Figure 4 to make an approximate table of the total amount of state and local property taxes in the years 1940, 1942, 1944, 1946, 1950, 1954, 1960, 1962, 1964, 1969, and 1971. Then draw a line graph from your table to see what a correct version of Figure 4 would look like.

3. Figure 15 shows a graph that appeared in the Lexington, Kentucky *Herald-Leader* of October 5, 1975. Discuss the correctness of this graph.

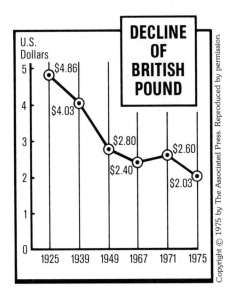

Figure 15

4. The table below shows the trend of U.S. imports of crude oil (in millions of barrels) over the decade from 1965 to 1975. These data appear in Table 910 of the 1976 *Statistical Abstract.* Present them in a clear, well-labeled graph.

Year	1965	1968	1969	1970	1971	1972	1973	1974	1975
Oil Imports	452	472	514	483	613	811	1184	1269	1498

5. Here are data on the percent of females among doctorates earned in 1975 in several fields of study, taken from Table 959 of the 1976 *Statistical Abstract.* Present these data in a well-labeled bar graph.

All fields	21.9%
Psychology	31.8%
Biological sciences	23.7%
Social sciences	20.4%
Physical sciences	8.3%
Engineering	1.7%

6. In Exercise 2 of Section 4 in Chapter 3 there is a newspaper graph of unemployment rates for several groups of workers. Comment on the correctness of the graph as a presentation of the numbers given. (We already saw that some of those numbers are probably incorrect.)

7. Figure 16 is a full-page advertisement for *Fortune* magazine. It contains eight separate graphic presentations of data. Comment briefly on the correctness of each one.

We asked America's top businessmen about business magazines. This is what they said.

Which one contains the best writing?

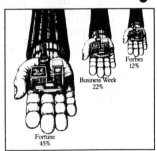

Which one has the most persuasive advertising?

Which one is easiest to read?

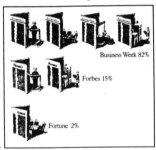

Which one best keeps its readers up to date on business events?

Which one carries the most interesting advertising?

Which one is least accurate?

In which one would you like to see a major story on your company?

Erdos and Morgan recently asked officers of the top one thousand companies—chairmen, presidents, vice presidents, treasurers, secretaries and controllers—for their opinions of Business Week, Forbes and Fortune. 999 executives responded.

You can see the results for yourself. In nearly every instance, Fortune was the winner. Not just by a hair—but overwhelmingly.

Most authoritative? Best writing? Where would they most like to see their company story? Of course they named Fortune. You'd expect them to.

But why did they see the advertising in Fortune as more persuasive and more interesting—when the same advertising often runs in all three magazines?

Obviously, the Fortune climate makes something happen to advertising that doesn't happen anyplace else. It's a valuable edge.

Business leaders get more involved with Fortune, so they get more involved with the advertising. They respond to Fortune, so they respond to the advertising. The survey proves it.

The conclusion is clear and simple: dollar for dollar, your advertising investment gets more impact in Fortune.

You get more than mere advertising exposure in Fortune. You get real communication with the people who can *act* on your business or consumer message. Isn't that what advertising is all about?

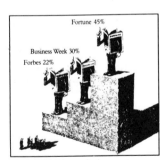

Which one is the most authoritative?

FORTUNE
Nobody takes you to the top like Fortune.

Figure 16

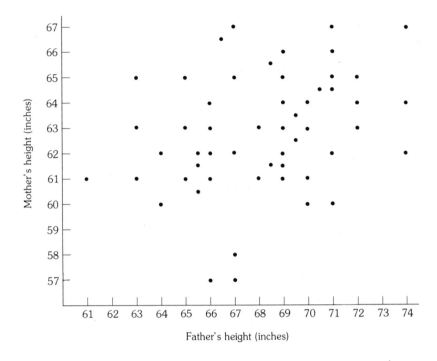

Figure 17. Data for a SRS of 53 pairs of parents from a group of 1079 pairs whose heights are recorded in Table XIII of Karl Pearson and Alice Lee, "On the laws of inheritance in man," *Biometrika,* November 1903, p. 408.

8. Figure 17 is a scatterplot of the heights of the mothers and the fathers in a sample of parents. Answer the following questions from this graph.

   (a) What is the smallest height of any mother in the sample? How many women had that particular height? What were the heights of the husbands of these women?

   (b) What is the greatest height of any father in the sample? How many men had that height, and what were the heights of their wives?

   (c) Does the scatterplot show any connection between the heights of mothers and fathers? (For example, do tall women tend to marry short men?)

9. A homeowner is interested in how demand for heating in cold weather affects the amount of natural gas his home consumes. Demand for heating is often measured in "degree days." (To find the number of degree days for a certain day, record the high and low temperature on that day and find the temperature midway between the high and low. If this temperature is less than 65°F, there is one degree day for every degree below 65°F.)

   The homeowner recorded his natural gas consumption in cubic feet per day, and also the average number of degree days per day, for nine consecutive months. Here are the data.

Degree days per day	15.6	26.8	37.8	36.4	35.5	18.6	15.3	7.9	0
Cubic feet of gas per day	5.2	6.1	8.7	8.5	8.8	4.9	4.5	2.5	1.1

(a) Make a scatterplot of these data. (Which is the independent variable?)

(b) From the scatterplot, give a rough estimate of gas consumption on a day with 20 degree days.

10. A study of bacterial contamination in milk counted the number of coliform organisms (fecal bacteria) per milliliter in 100 specimens of milk purchased in East Coast groceries. The U.S. Public Health Service recommends no more than 10 coliform bacteria per milliliter. Here are the data.

```
5 8 6 7 8   3 2 4 7 8 6 4 4 8 8 8 6 10 6 5
6 6 6 6 4   3 7 7 5 7 4 5 6 7 4 4 4   3 5 7
7 5 8 3 9   7 3 4 6 6 8 7 4 8 5 7 9   4 4 7
8 8 7 5 4 10 7 6 6 7 8 6 6 6 0 4 5 10 4 5
7 9 8 9 5   6 3 6 3 7 1 6 9 6 8 5 2   8 5 3
```

(a) Make a table of the frequencies of each of the values 0 to 10 in this set of 100 observations.

(b) Draw a frequency histogram of these data. Graph paper makes this easier.

(c) On the histogram you have drawn, put a second vertical scale labeled in relative frequency rather than frequency. Because there are 100 observations, relative frequency = frequency/100. Your histogram is now a relative frequency histogram.

(d) Describe the shape of your histogram. Are the data symmetric? If so, approximately where is the center about which they are symmetric? Are the data strongly skewed? If so, in which direction?

11. Agronomists have developed varieties of corn that are higher in the essential amino acid lysine than normal corn. This high-lysine corn has better protein quality than normal corn, and may be quite valuable in areas of the world where corn is a major part of the diet. In a test of the protein quality of this corn, an experimental group of 20 one-day-old male chicks was fed a corn–soybean ration containing high-lysine corn. A control group of another 20 chicks was fed the same diet except that normal corn was used. The weight gains (in grams) after 21 days are recorded below.

Control group				Experimental group			
380	321	366	356	361	447	401	375
283	349	402	462	434	403	393	426
356	410	329	399	406	318	467	407
350	384	316	272	427	420	477	392
345	455	360	431	430	339	410	326

(a) This experiment was designed by using the principles of Chapter 2. Briefly discuss the proper design.

(b) Make two separate frequency tables for the weight gains in experimental and control groups. Use the classes:

270–299 300–329 330–359 360–389 390–419 420–449 450–479

(c) Draw a frequency histogram for the experimental group and another for the control group. For easy comparison, draw them one above the other with the scales on the horizontal axes lined up with one another.

(d) How do the two histograms show the effect of high-lysine corn on weight gain?

12. Draw a histogram skewed to the *left.*

Section 3

1. Return to the coliform counts in Exercise 10 of Section 2. Make a graph of the distribution similar to Figure 12 by connecting the centers of the tops of the bars in the histogram for these data.

   Do coliform counts in this sample appear to be approximately normally distributed? If not, in what way does the curve differ from a normal curve?

2. Below is a frequency table of average income per person in 1975 for the 50 states and the District of Columbia, from Table 644 of the 1976 *Statistical Abstract.*

Income class	Frequency
4000–4499	3
4500–4999	13
5000–5499	6
5500–5999	14
6000–6499	6
6500–6999	7
7000–7499	0
7500–7999	1
8000–8499	0
8500–8999	1

Make a relative frequency histogram for these data. (Here relative frequency = frequency/51 because there are 51 observations.) Is this distribution approximately normal? If not, in what way does it differ from a normal distribution?

3. The normal curve at the top in Figure 13 represents the sampling distribution of the sample proportion $\hat{p}$ of dark beads in a SRS of size 25 drawn from a

population with population proportion $p = 0.20$ of dark beads. Suppose that a SRS of size 25 were drawn from a population containing 50% ($p = 0.50$) dark beads.

Illustrate the effect of the population parameter p on the sampling distribution of $\hat{p}$ by drawing both sampling distributions (for $p = 0.20$ and $p = 0.50$) on the same horizontal axis.

4. The entries in the table of random digits have the property that each value 0, 1, 2, 3, 4, 5, 6, 7, 8, 9 occurs equally often in the long run.

   (a) Make a frequency table and draw a frequency histogram for the entries in the first three rows of Table A (120 digits in all).
   (b) Is this distribution approximately normal? How does it deviate from normality?
   (c) Is this distribution approximately symmetric?
   (d) Draw a curve representing the distribution of values in a large number of observations from a table of random digits.

5. As Exercise 4 demonstrates, the entries in Table A are not normally distributed. But the sampling distribution of the average of samples from this population is approximately normal. To see this, do the following.

   (a) Find the sum of each of 50 groups of 10 successive digits in Table A (that uses 500 digits or 12½ rows in all).
   (b) Divide each sum by 10 (just put in a decimal point one place to the left) to get 50 averages.
   (c) Make a frequency table and draw a frequency histogram of these values. Use classes:

   -0.50 to 0.49, 0.50 to 1.49, 1.50 to 2.49, . . . , 8.50 to 9.49.

   This gives 10 classes of equal width centered on 0, 1, 2, . . . , 9. Averages of samples of size larger than 10 have sampling distributions much closer to normality. But even in these small samples, you can see the characteristic normal shape beginning to emerge.

Chapter 5

Descriptive Statistics: Few Numbers in Place of Many

T ables organize data, and graphs present a vivid overall picture. But more specific aspects of data such as their average and their variability are most succinctly summarized by a few well-chosen numbers. We often read or hear that "HEW Secretary Califano denounced the proposed tax credit for college tuition, pointing out that the median income of $22,000 for families with dependents in college far exceeds the $14,500 median income of all American families," or "Professor McIntosh reported that student ratings and peer ratings of faculty teaching effectiveness had a correlation of over 0.8." Medians and correlations are among the numerical measures called *descriptive statistics* that summarize specific features of a set of data. Descriptive statistics are as important in your statistical vocabulary as histograms and random samples. We have already met counts (frequencies) and rates or proportions (relative frequencies). This chapter lengthens the list of descriptive statistics we can claim as acquaintances, if not as friends.

1. Measuring Center or Average

Almost any presentation of data uses averages—average gas mileage, average income, average score on the exam, average absolutely refractory period of the tibial nerves of rats fed DDT. (I am quoting that last one from a report on the effects of persistent pesticides—don't blame me for it.) Everyone has heard that statistics features the mean, median, and mode. Those are in fact the three "averages" we will study. But do remember that you absorbed four solid chapters of statistics before meeting this famous trio. Our subject has other (and more interesting) parts, but to be statistically literate we must add the mean, the median, and the mode to our vocabulary. Here are brief definitions, followed in turn by a discussion of each measure of center.

> The *mean* of a set of *n* observations is the arithmetic *average*; it is the sum of the observations divided by the number of observations, *n*.
>
> The *median* is the *typical value*; it is the midpoint of the observations when they are arranged in increasing order.
>
> The *mode* is the *most frequent value*; it is any value having the highest frequency among the observations

The *mean* is the usual arithmetic average: Add the observations and divide by the number of them. The mean of the 10 observations

$$4, 6, 10, 3, 7, 6, 6, 8, 5, 9$$

is

$$\frac{4 + 6 + 10 + 3 + 7 + 6 + 6 + 8 + 5 + 9}{10} = \frac{64}{10} = 6.4.$$

When someone says "average" it is usually the mean that is intended. Now that we know the proper vocabulary, be sure to say "mean" and not "average." Means are so common that a compact notation is useful. Remember the idea from algebra of letting letters stand for numbers so recipes applicable to any set of numbers can be given? We will do this. A set of *n* observations is denoted by

$$x_1, x_2, \ldots, x_n$$

and the mean of this set of observations is

$$\bar{x} = \frac{x_1 + x_2 + \ldots + x_n}{n}.$$

That is read "x bar" and is such common notation that in reading literature in psychology, sociology, biology, and other fields you can assume that an $\bar{x}$ or $\bar{y}$ or $\bar{z}$ used without explanation is a mean.

The *median* is the midpoint of the observations when they are arranged in increasing order of magnitude. To find the median of the numbers

$$8, 4, 9, 1, 3$$

arrange them in increasing order as

$$1, 3, 4, 8, 9.$$

The median is 4, because it is the midpoint. Two observations fall below 4 and two fall above it. Whenever the number of observations is odd, the middle observation is the median. If the number of observations is even, there is no one middle observation. But there is a middle pair, and we take the median to be the mean of this middle pair, the point halfway between them. So the median of

$$8, 4, 1, 9, 1, 3$$

is found by arranging these numbers in increasing order

$$1, 1, 3, 4, 8, 9$$

$$\text{median} = \frac{3 + 4}{2} = 3.5.$$

Note that three observations fall below 3.5 and three fall above.

Several words to the wise about finding medians are needed. First, never fail to arrange the observations in increasing order; the middle value in the haphazard order in which the numbers come to you is not the median. Second, never fail to write down all the observations, even if some have the same value. The median of

$$4, 5, 5, 6, 6, 6, 8, 9$$

is 6 because both of the middle pair of numbers have the value 6. Third, a recipe can save you from trying to locate the middle one of 471 observations or the middle pair of 232 observations by counting in from both ends. Here it is.

> **If there are n observations in all, find the number $(n + 1)/2$. Arrange the observations from smallest to largest, and count $(n + 1)/2$ observations up from the bottom. This gives the *location* of the median in the list of observations.**

Returning to the examples, the set of data 1, 3, 4, 8, 9 has $n = 5$ observations. Because $(n + 1)/2 = (5 + 1)/2 = 3$, the median is the third number in the list, which is 4. The data set 4, 5, 5, 6, 6, 6, 8, 9 has $n = 8$ observations. So $(n + 1)/2 = (8 + 1)/2 = 4.5$. This means that the median has location "four and a half," or midway between the fourth and fifth numbers in the list. (Note that 4.5 is not the median but merely its location in the list.) The median of a set of 232 numbers has location $(232 + 1)/2 = 116.5$, or midway between the 116th and 117th numbers when arranged from smallest to largest. The median of 471 observations is the 236th in order of magnitude because

$$\frac{471 + 1}{2} = \frac{472}{2} = 236.$$

The *mode* is any value occurring most frequently in the set of observations. It is convenient to arrange observations in increasing order as an aid to seeing how often each value occurs. The mode of

$$4, 5, 5, 6, 6, 6, 8, 9$$

is 6 because this value occurs three times and no other value appears more than twice. What about

$$1, 4, 5, 5, 5, 6, 8, 9, 9, 9, 12?$$

Both 5 and 9 are modes because both are "most frequent" in this data set. Such a data set is called *bimodal.* When no value occurs more than once, we could say that all are modes; that's not very helpful, so we prefer to say that such a set of data has no mode.

Having made the acquaintance of mean, median, and mode, we now ought to inquire how they do their job of describing a set of observations. Certainly "most frequent value," "midpoint," and "arithmetic average" are quite different notions with different uses. Here is a survey of their use.

The *mode* is little used because it records only the most frequent value, and this may be far from the center of the distribution of values. We have also seen that there may be several modes, or none. The chief advantage of the mode is that, of our three measures, it alone makes sense for variables measured in a nominal scale. It is nonsense to speak of the median sex or mean race of United States ambassadors, but the most frequent (modal) sex is male and the modal race is white.

The *median* uses only order information in the data. (How many observations are above a point? How many are below?) The median therefore makes sense for ordinal variables as well as for interval/ratio variables. The median does not employ the actual numerical value of the observations; it is not affected by how far above or below it the observations fall, but only requires that equal numbers of observations fall above and below. The *mean* alone of our measures of center does use the actual numerical values of the observations. Thus the mean utilizes more of the information in the data than either the mode or median. For this reason, the mean is the most common measure of center. In a strict sense, the mean makes sense only for interval/ratio data because it requires adding the observations. But in practice means are frequently computed for ordinal variables as well.

Some occasions when the median is a better description of the center of a distribution of values than is the mean are determined by the fact that the median does *not* respond to actual numerical values. An example will show how this insensitivity can be a virtue.

> **Example 1.** A certain professional basketball team has 5 players earning $30,000 per year, 5 who earn $100,000, and a superstar who earns $780,000. The mean salary for the 11 players on this team is therefore

$$\frac{(5)(30,000) + (5)(100,000) + 780,000}{11} = \frac{1,430,000}{11} = \$130,000.$$

You see that the superstar's salary has pulled the mean well above the amount paid to any other player. The mean is quite sensitive to a few extreme observations. The median, though, is $100,000 and does not change even if the superstar earns $3 million; his salary is just one number falling above the mid-point. Because income data often have a few extremely high observations, descriptions of income distributions usually use the median—"half earned more than this, and half earned less." Medians are prominent in the income data in the *Statistical Abstract,* for example. This is not to say that the median always should

"Should we scare the opposition by announcing our mean height or lull them by announcing our median height?"

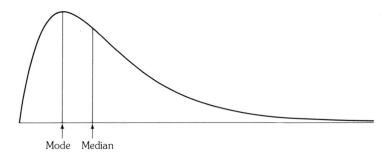

Mode   Median

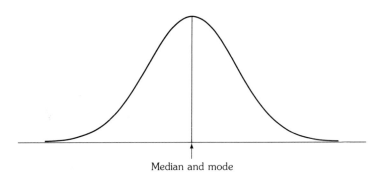

Median and mode

Figure 1. The mode and median of a frequency distribution. The mode is the point at which the frequency curve attains its highest value. The median is the point that divides the area under the curve into two equal parts to the left and the right of it. The median is the center point of any symmetric frequency curve. This normal curve is highest at the center, so that the center point is also the mode.

be used for data containing extreme observations. If you were interested in the total income of a group, the median income would be uninformative while the mean would tell you what you want to know because it is computed from the sum of the incomes. Always ask which of "most frequent value," "midpoint," or "arithmetic average" best represents the data for your intended use.

The different response of the mean and the median to extreme values can be pictured by using the frequency curve for a set of data. The mode is the value where the curve peaks. The median is the value such that half the area under the curve lies below and half above it. These facts are true because the frequency curve is a smooth version of the frequency histogram. So it is highest at the most frequent value, or mode. And because areas in a histogram represent frequencies, equal areas lie above and below the median. Figure 1 illustrates these facts.

It is not so clear where to place the mean on a frequency curve or histogram. But these are the facts: If we think of the curve as cut out of solid material, the mean is the point where the shape would balance. Figure 2 illustrates this.

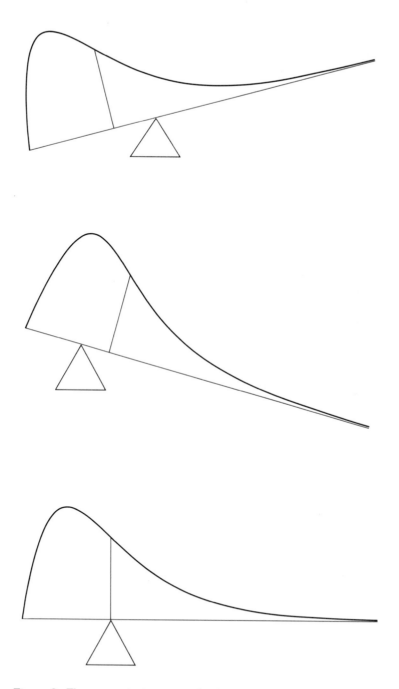

Figure 2. The mean of a frequency distribution. The mean is the center of gravity of the frequency curve, the point about which the curve would balance on a pivot placed beneath it.

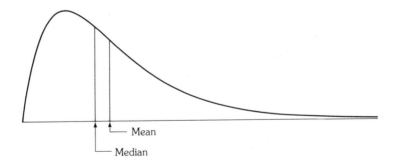

Figure 3. The mean and median of a skewed distribution. The mean is located farther toward the long tail of a skewed frequency curve than is the median.

Now if a frequency curve is symmetric, the "balance point" and the "equal areas" point are the same. The mean and median are the same for symmetric distributions. This is one reason that mean scores are often reported for standardized tests even though the scores have an ordinal scale. The distribution of such scores is often roughly normal, and therefore symmetric, so the mean and median will fall close together. If one tail of a frequency curve is stretched to correspond to a few extreme observations on one side, the frequency curve becomes skewed. A little weight far out in one direction moves the balance point quite a bit in that direction. So the mean moves farther toward the long tail than does the median. We saw a numerical example earlier, and Figure 3 gives a pictorial view.

Now you are an expert on mean, median, and mode. I hope they have lived up to your expectations. Be warned, however, that averages of all kinds can play tricks if you are not alert. Some examples of these tricks appear in the exercises. Arithmetic is never a substitute for understanding.

2.   Measuring Spread or Variability

Useful as the measures of center are, they are usually incomplete and often misleading without some accompanying indication of how spread out or dispersed the data are. That the median medical costs for an American family of four in 1969 were $260 seems less reassuring when we learn that 5% of such families had medical costs in excess of $2600. The distribution of medical costs is skewed to the right and very spread out. Knowing the median alone gives us an inadequate description of the distribution of medical costs. Similarly, the mean potency of a drug may be exactly what the doctor ordered, but if the potency of the lot varies too much, many doses will be ineffective owing to low potency or perhaps dangerous owing to high potency. The simplest adequate summary of a univariate distribution usually requires both a measure of center and a measure of variability.

Beware of falling prey to partial information in the form of an average without a measure of variability. Has the press overstated the harm done by rising food prices? In 1973, Secretary of Agriculture Earl Butz thought so, and gave an argument based on an average.

> *In his speech, Dr. Butz said that food costs were now under 16 percent of Americans' spendable personal income, indicating he felt that the press gave too little attention to this figure.*
>
> *However, many economic experts believe that that figure is itself misleading.*
>
> *"Whenever they use it like this, it makes us shudder," one official said. "The trouble is, it lumps the Rockefellers in with the welfare cases."* [1]

That's the weakness of an average alone: It lumps the Rockefellers in with the welfare cases.

When the median is used to measure center, the variability or spread is often indicated by giving several percentiles.

The pth **percentile of a set of numbers is a value such that p percent of the numbers fall below it, and the rest fall above.**

The median is the 50th percentile. We saw that $2600 was the 95th percentile of family medical costs in 1969, because 95% of all families had medical costs less than this figure, while 5% had higher costs. Percentiles are familiar to victims of College Board or Graduate Record Examinations. Your performance on these tests is reported both as a score and as a percentile which tells you how you did relative to other test-takers. Some percentiles are important enough to have individual names.

The 25th percentile is called the *first quartile*.

The 75th percentile is called the *third quartile*.

A convenient way of indicating the spread of a data set is to give the first and third quartiles along with the median, which is the second quartile. If the quartiles for scores on a statistics exam are 66, 75, and 83, you know that the top quarter of the class had scores above 83, while the bottom quarter had scores below 66. Because the first and third quartiles are about the same distance above and below the median (75), the distribution of scores seems to be roughly symmetric. I will not give detailed rules for computing percentiles other than the median but will be satisfied with approximate answers. For example, to find the 30th percentile of a set of 111 observations, note that 30% of 111 is

$$(0.30) \ (111) = 33.3.$$

Now arrange the observations in increasing order and count up from the bottom of the list. We will accept as the 30th percentile any value between the 33rd and 34th observations up from the bottom. It's simplest to use the 33rd observation itself.

The most common measures of spread or variability are the variance and the standard deviation. These should be used only when center is measured by the mean, as they are specifically measures of spread about the mean as center.

> The *variance* is the mean of the squares of the deviations of the observations from their mean.

> The *standard deviation* is the positive square root of the variance.

These definitions require an example to see what they say, and then some commentary to see why they say it. Here is the example.

Example 2. Find the variance and standard deviation of the 5 observations

$$6, 7, 5, 3, 4.$$

(a) First compute the mean

$$\bar{x} = (6 + 7 + 5 + 3 + 4)/5 = 25/5 = 5.$$

(b) The deviation of any observation x from the mean is the difference $x - \bar{x}$, which may be either positive or negative. Use this arrangement to compute the variance:

Observation x	Deviation $x - \bar{x}$	Squared deviation $(x - x)^2$
6	$6 - 5 = 1$	$(1)^2 = 1$
7	$7 - 5 = 2$	$(2)^2 = 4$
5	$5 - 5 = 0$	$(0)^2 = 0$
3	$3 - 5 = -2$	$(-2)^2 = 4$
4	$4 - 5 = -1$	$(-1)^2 = 1$
		Sum $= 10$

The sum of the squares of the deviations from the mean is 10. The variance is therefore

$$\text{variance} = \frac{\text{sum of squared deviations}}{\text{number of observations}} = \frac{10}{5} = 2.$$

(c) The standard deviation is the square root of the variance, $\sqrt{2} = 1.4$. Table B at the back of the book is a table of square roots.

In the language of algebra, the recipe for the variance is as follows.

Observations $\qquad x_1, x_2, \ldots, x_n$

Mean $\qquad \bar{x} = \dfrac{x_1 + x_2 + \ldots + x_n}{n}$

Variance $\qquad s^2 = \dfrac{(x_1 - \bar{x})^2 + (x_2 - x)^2 + \ldots + (x_n - \bar{x})^2}{n}$

If you have difficulty following this algebraic recipe, look back at the example for guidance. Because the standard deviation is the square root of the variance, it is denoted by s. *

Some comments on variance and standard deviation will help you to interpret them.

1. The variance is always zero or positive because it is a mean of squared deviations. It can be zero only if all the squared deviations are zero, which means that every observation x_i has the same value as $\bar{x}$, and so all observations x_i are the same. *Variance zero means no spread at all; otherwise the variance is positive.*

2. The variance makes sense as a measure of spread or variability. To understand this, note that if the observations are spread out, they will tend to be far from their mean, both above and below. Some deviations will be large positive numbers, and some will be large negative numbers. But the squared deviations will all be large and positive, so the variance will be large when data are spread out. And the variance will be small when all the data are close together. Notice that spread about the mean is being measured. (The deviations from the mean will always be both positive and negative and always have sum zero. This helps you check your arithmetic. Look back at the example to check that the sum of the "Deviation" column is zero. Remember that the square of a negative number is positive, so squared deviations are never negative.)

3. When the observations x_i are measured in some units (seconds, centimeters, grams), their variance s^2 is measured in the square of those units. If, for example, the times required for 5 subjects to complete a test of dexterity are (in seconds)

$$81, 93, 106, 74, 87$$

---

*There is a complication that you should be aware of if you study more statistics. When the observations form a SRS of size n, the variance is usually found by dividing the sum of the squared deviations by $n - 1$, not by n. This is also the recipe programmed into calculators having a push-button variance. There is a reason for using $n - 1$ instead of n. The sample variance so defined is an unbiased estimator of the variance of the entire population, while the variance as we defined it is biased; on the average it underestimates the variance of the population. The bias is quite small when n is of moderate size, so we use n for simplicity.

then the mean is $\bar{x}$ = 88.2 seconds. The mean has the same units as the observations. The deviations from the mean are also measured in seconds. But the squared deviations are measured in square seconds, so the variance is

$$s^2 = 118.96 \text{ (seconds)}^2.$$

This is annoying. And this is one reason for using the standard deviation. Taking the square root brings us back to the original units,

$$s = \sqrt{118.96} = 10.9 \text{ seconds.}$$

The standard deviation has the same units as the observations. Because the standard deviation shares properties 1 and 2 of the variance and has more convenient units, it is used more often than is the variance. Another reason why the standard deviation is usually used instead of the variance appears in Section 3.

4. When direct comparisons are involved, interpreting the variance or standard deviation is easy. If machine A makes ball bearings having diameters with $\bar{x}$ = 2 centimeters and s = 0.002 centimeters, while machine B produces bearings with $\bar{x}$ = 2 centimeters and s = 0.001 centimeters, then B's bearings show less variability than A's. But in other circumstances, simply seeing which standard deviation is larger is not always a meaningful comparison of variability. What about comparing the variability of B's bearings with the variability of turbine shafts having $\bar{x}$ = 40 centimeters and s = 0.002 centimeters? The standard deviation of the shafts is twice as large as that of the bearings. But as a fraction of the mean diameter, the standard deviation of the shafts is

$$\frac{s}{\bar{x}} = \frac{0.002}{40} = 0.00005$$

and for the bearings

$$\frac{s}{\bar{x}} = \frac{0.001}{2} = 0.0005.$$

So relative to the size of the objects, the shafts are only one-tenth as variable. Comparison of variability therefore requires some care.

3.   More on the Normal Distributions

When a set of data has a distribution described by one of the normal curves, the mean can be spotted easily on the curve. Because normal distributions are symmetric, the mean and median lie together at the midpoint of the curve. The normal curves reach their highest point at the center, so the mode is also at the midpoint. For normal curves, the mean, the median, and the mode are all equal.

The standard deviation of a normal distribution also can be located on the normal curve. Notice that near its center, a normal curve falls ever more steeply as we move away from the center, like this:

But in either tail, the curve falls ever less steeply as we move away from the center, like this:

The points at which the curvature changes from the first type illustrated to the second are located one standard deviation on either side of the mean. With a bit of practice, you can learn to find these points by running a pencil along the curve and feeling where the curvature changes. So both the mean and the standard deviation (but not the variance) of a normal frequency distribution are visible on the normal curve. Because normal curves are common, here is another reason why the standard deviation is often preferred to the variance.

Figure 4 reproduces the two normal curves from Figure 13 of Chapter 4, now with the means and standard deviations marked. Study those curves. The shape of a normal curve is completely determined by its mean and standard deviation; there is only one normal curve with mean 0.2 and standard deviation 0.08, for example, and it appears in Figure 4(a). The mean fixes the center of the curve, while the standard deviation determines its shape. Changing the mean of a normal distribution does not change its shape, only its location on the axis. Changing the standard deviation does change the shape of a normal curve, as Figure 4 illustrates. The distribution with the smaller standard deviation is less spread out and more peaked. But in both cases the frequency curve is about six standard deviations wide. This is true of any normal curve, no matter what mean and standard deviation it has.

Many sample statistics (especially sample proportions and sample means) have approximately normal sampling distributions when probability sampling is employed. The spread or dispersion of a normal curve is completely described by its standard deviation. So when the sampling distribution is normal, *the precision of a sample statistic can be described by giving the standard deviation of its sampling distribution.* The smaller the standard deviation, the greater the precision. You already know that the bias of a sample statistic can be described by comparing the mean of its sampling distribution with the value of the population parameter being estimated. Now we see that when the sampling distribution is normal, the mean and standard deviation together describe both bias and

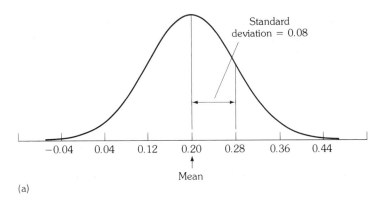

(a)

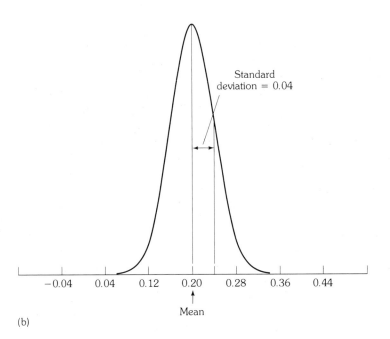

(b)

Figure 4. Two normal distribution curves.

precision. This is our final recycling of those ideas. News releases of sample results usually give precision in the "95% confidence of a margin of error of ± 3 points" form we met in Chapter 1. Accounts in professional publications more often give the standard deviation (sometimes called the "standard error" in this context) of the sample statistic.

To show the connection between these two ways of stating precision, here are some facts about the way the mean and standard deviation describe any normal distribution.

1. In any normal distribution, half of the observations fall above the mean and half fall below.

2. In any normal distribution, **68%** of the observations fall within one standard deviation of the mean. Half of these (**34%**) fall within one standard deviation above the mean, and the other **34%** within one standard deviation below the mean.

3. Another 27% of the observations fall between one and two standard deviations away from the mean. So 95% (68% plus 27%) fall within two standard deviations of the mean.

4. In all, **99.7%** of the observations fall within three standard deviations of the mean.

The fourth fact makes precise the earlier comment that any normal curve is about six standard deviations wide. The third fact states that when a statistic with a normal sampling distribution has no bias, 95% of all samples will give values of the statistic falling within two standard deviations of the true parameter value. The sample proportion from a SRS, for example, has a normal sampling distribution and is an unbiased estimate of the true proportion in the population. So

The sample proportion has a standard error of 1.5 points.

implies our former statement of precision:

In repeated sampling, 95% of all samples have sample proportions falling within 3 points (two standard deviations) of the true parameter value.

Facts 2, 3, and 4 are illustrated in Figure 5. Let's call them the "68-95-99.7

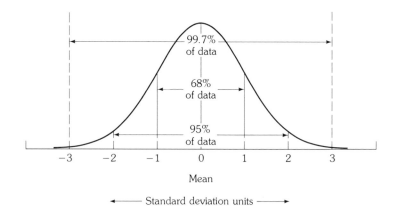

Figure 5. The 68-95-99.7 rule for normal distributions.

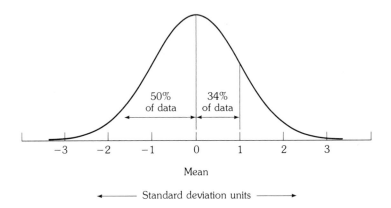

Figure 6. The 84th percentile of a normal distribution lies one standard deviation above the mean.

rule." This rule describes the shape of normal curves more exactly than the description "bell-shaped" used in Chapter 4. When using the normal curves to describe the shape of data sets, remember that no set of data is exactly described by a normal curve. The 68-95-99.7 rule will be only approximately true for SAT scores or the forehead breadth of 2000 male Hungarian skulls.

The 68-95-99.7 rule shows just how the standard deviation measures the spread or variability for normal distributions. Because any normal distribution satisfies the rule, the point one standard deviation above the mean is always the 84th percentile (because 50% of the observations fall below the mean and another 34% within one standard deviation above the mean, as Figure 6 shows). Similarly, one standard deviation below the mean is always the 16th percentile, and the point two standard deviations above the mean is the 97.5th percentile.

The standard deviation is therefore the natural unit of measurement for normally distributed data. Observations from different normal distributions can be compared by expressing them in "standard deviation units above or below the mean." Here is an example.

Example 3. Elanor scores 700 on the mathematics part of the Scholastic Aptitude Test (SAT). Scores on the SAT follow a normal distribution with mean 500 and standard deviation 100.* Gerald takes the American College Testing Program test of mathematical ability, which has approximately

*This is an oversimplification that is true only for a standardization population used to set up the original scale of SAT scores. The group of students who took the same form of the test as did Elanor may have had a mean score higher or lower than 500 depending on their ability. For an account of how the tests are calibrated so that reported scores have the same meaning no matter when the test was taken, see William H. Angoff, "Calibrating College Board Scores" in *Statistics: A Guide to the Unknown*. Notice the normal curves on p. 242 of that essay.

mean 18 and standard deviation 6. He scores 24. If both tests measure the same kind of ability, which student ranks higher?

Elanor scored two standard deviations above the mean, while Gerald's score was one standard deviation above the mean. In terms of percentiles, Elanor stands at about the 97th percentile in mathematical ability, while Gerald's score is at the 84th percentile. Elanor's score is higher than Gerald's.

Observations expressed in standard deviation units about the mean are called *standard scores*. The recipe is

$$\text{standard score} = \frac{\text{observation} - \text{mean}}{\text{standard deviation}}.$$

Thus Gerald's score of 24 on a test having mean 18 and standard deviation 6 translates into a standard score of

$$\frac{24 - 18}{6} = \frac{6}{6} = 1.$$

A standard score of 1 is always the 84th percentile, as Figure 6 shows. In fact, *every* standard score translates into a specific percentile, which is the same no matter what the mean and standard deviation of the original normal distribution are. Table 1 lists the percentile corresponding to various standard scores. This table enables us to convert observations from a normal distribution into percentiles, after first converting them into standard scores. For example, a score of 450 on the SAT mathematics test (mean 500, standard deviation 100) translates into a standard score of

$$\frac{450 - 500}{100} = \frac{-50}{100} = -0.5$$

or one-half standard deviation below the mean score. Table 1 translates this into the 30.85th percentile. That is, 30.85% of the scores fall below 450, and the rest are higher. For most purposes we would round off the table value and state that a score of 450 falls at the 31st percentile. Your own SAT scores were probably reported to you in just that fashion.

Because a standard score translates into the same percentile for all normal distributions, standard scores allow direct comparison of scores from different normal distributions. Do remember that standard scores can be used to compare observations from different distributions only when both distributions are approximately normal. This condition is not always fulfilled.

Table 1

THE STANDARD NORMAL DISTRIBUTION

Standard score	Percentile	Standard score	Percentile	Standard score	Percentile
− 3.0	0.13	− 1.0	15.87	1.0	84.13
− 2.9	0.19	− 0.9	18.41	1.1	86.43
− 2.8	0.26	− 0.8	21.19	1.2	88.49
− 2.7	0.35	− 0.7	24.20	1.3	90.32
− 2.6	0.47	− 0.6	27.42	1.4	91.92
− 2.5	0.62	− 0.5	30.85	1.5	93.32
− 2.4	0.82	− 0.4	34.46	1.6	94.52
− 2.3	1.07	− 0.3	38.21	1.7	95.54
− 2.2	1.39	− 0.2	42.07	1.8	96.41
− 2.1	1.79	− 0.1	46.02	1.9	97.13
− 2.0	2.27	0.0	50.00	2.0	97.73
− 1.9	2.87	0.1	53.98	2.1	98.21
− 1.8	3.59	0.2	57.93	2.2	98.61
− 1.7	4.46	0.3	61.79	2.3	98.93
− 1.6	5.48	0.4	65.54	2.4	99.18
− 1.5	6.68	0.5	69.15	2.5	99.38
− 1.4	8.08	0.6	72.58	2.6	99.53
− 1.3	9.68	0.7	75.80	2.7	99.65
− 1.2	11.51	0.8	58.81	2.8	99.74
− 1.1	13.57	0.9	81.59	2.9	99.81
				3.0	99.87

NOTE: The table gives the percentile corresponding to each standard score for the normal distributions. The percentile corresponding to any observation from a normal distribution can be found by converting the observation to a standard score and then looking in the table.

4.   Measuring Association

A set of univariate data can be summarized by a measure of center and a measure of spread. Such a summary is far from a complete description of the data, but does provide basic information. In contrast, even the briefest summary of bivariate data requires more than measures of center and spread for each of the two variables. We are usually interested also in the connection between the variables. Do they tend to increase together, as height and weight of people do? Do they tend to move in opposite directions, as do number of cigarettes smoked per day and the life expectancy of the smoker? Such a connection, or association, may well be the motive for studying both variables together. As our study of bivarate frequency tables in Chapter 4 made clear, this association cannot be spied out from the marginal distributions alone. A measure of association, unlike measures of center and spread, will include both variables jointly. Let us make our language more exact.

> **Association** in bivariate data means a systematic connection between changes in one variable and changes in the other.
>
> When an increase in one variable tends to be accompanied by an increase in the other, the variables are *positively associated.*
>
> When an increase in one variable tends to be accompanied by a decrease in the other, the variables are *negatively associated.*

Association in a data set must be measured "on the average." Height and weight of people are positively associated—someone 75 inches tall is usually heavier than someone 60 inches tall. But not always. There is a systematic connection between height and weight on the average over most groups of people, but not an ironclad connection always forcing taller people to be heavier. Statistics is more concerned with "on the average" associations such as that between height and weight or that between smoking and lung cancer than

"He says we've ruined his positive association between height and weight."

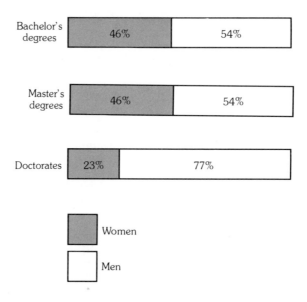

Figure 7.   Earned degrees by sex, 1976. [Data from Table 2, p. 134.]

with ironclad connections such as that between the temperature and pressure of a fixed volume of a gas.

Association makes sense for variables measured in any type of scale. For example, Figure 7 shows an association between sex and level for earned academic degrees; women received 46% of the bachelor's and master's degrees awarded, but only half that share of the doctorates. But association can be described as positive or negative only when both variables have ordinal or interval/ratio scales, so that "increase" and "decrease" make sense. We will give only one measure of association, the *correlation coefficient*. By a strict interpretation of the theory of scales of measurement, this measure requires that both variables have an interval/ratio scale. Just as with the mean and standard deviation, however, the correlation coefficient is often used with ordinal scales as well. Correlation is almost as common as mean and standard deviation in summaries of data.

The correlation coefficient is the algebraic high point of this book. Be of good courage: In mastering this, you have passed the worst. The notation of algebra is essential for a brief definition of correlation. Here is the definition.

Given n bivariate observations on variables x and y,

$$x_1, x_2, \ldots, x_n$$

$$y_1, y_2, \ldots, y_n$$

compute the correlation coefficient as follows.

(1) **Find the mean** $\bar{x}$ **and standard deviation** s_x **of the values** $x_1, x_2, \ldots,$ x_n **of the first variable.**

(2) **Find the mean** $\bar{y}$ **and standard deviation** s_y **of the values** $y_1, y_2, \ldots,$ y_n **of the second variable.**

(3) **The** *correlation coefficient* **is**

$$r = \frac{\dfrac{1}{n}\,[(x_1 - \bar{x})\,(y_1 - \bar{y}) + \ldots + (x_n - \bar{x})\,(y_n - \bar{y})]}{s_x s_y}$$

This definition deserves a short explanation, then an example to show what it says, and then a commentary on what exactly *r* measures. First, the explanation of the definition. The data are bivariate, so x_1 goes with y_1 ("my height and my weight"), and x_2 goes with y_2 ("your height and your weight"), and so on. The numerator in *r* is the mean of the products of the deviations of each *x* and the corresponding *y* from their means. The denominator in *r* is the product of the standard deviation of the *x*'s alone and the standard deviation of the *y*'s alone. Because both numerator and denominator are built up from deviations from the mean, there is a convenient arrangement for putting the definition into practice. The following example illustrates the arithmetic.

Example 4. Suppose that the data are

x	6	2	2	-2
y	5	5	-3	-3

A scatterplot (Figure 8) shows positive association as a trend from lower left (both *x* and *y* small) to upper right (both *x* and *y* large). The means are

$$\bar{x} = (6 + 2 + 2 - 2)/4 = 8/4 = 2$$
$$\bar{y} = (5 + 5 - 3 - 3)/4 = 4/4 = 1$$

Now make the following table:

(1)	(2)	(3)	(4)	(5)	(6)	(7)
x	y	$x - \bar{x}$	$y - \bar{y}$	$(x - \bar{x})(y - \bar{y})$	$(x - \bar{x})^2$	$(y - \bar{y})^2$
6	5	4	4	16	16	16
2	5	0	4	0	0	16
2	-3	0	-4	0	0	16
-2	-3	-4	-4	16	16	16
		0	0	32	32	64

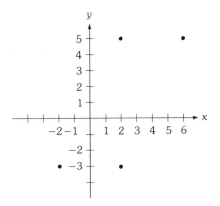

Figure 8

Columns (3) and (4) are the deviations from the mean for the x's and y's obtained from columns (1) and (2) by subtracting the proper mean. Note that the sum of each set of deviations is 0, as is always the case. Columns (6) and (7) are the squares of these deviations. If we divide the sums of these columns by the number of observations, 4, the variances of x and y are

$$s_x^2 = 32/4 = 8$$
$$s_y^2 = 64/4 = 16$$

and the standard deviations are

$$s_x = \sqrt{8} = 2.8$$
$$s_y = \sqrt{16} = 4.$$

Column (5) contains the products of each entry in column (3) with the corresponding entry in column (4). Be careful of the signs here! Both positive and negative products may occur. The sum of the entries in column (5) is the sum in the numerator of r. We need only divide by the number of observations $n = 4$ (*not* $n = 8$ because n is the number of *bivariate* observations). So finally

$$r = \frac{32/4}{(2.8)\,(4)} = \frac{8}{(2.8)\,(4)} = \frac{2}{2.8} = 0.71.$$

The primary purpose of Example 4 is not to show you how to calculate r. You will not have to do such calculations often in this course, and if you must do them elsewhere no doubt you will use a calculator or a computer. Rather, we have shown by example what the recipe for the correlation coefficient r says. Be sure that you now understand the definition of r. I won't blame you if the thought of computing the correlation of IQ and grade index for 1200 college freshmen makes you a bit ill. Let a machine do that. But when the result is $r = 0.38$, we need to know what this means. And to know that, we first must know what r is. Now we know, so let's relax and interpret r. There are five points to be made.

1. *The correlation coefficient r makes sense as a measure of association; it is positive when the association is positive, and negative when the association is negative.* To understand how r measures association, look at the sum of products of deviations in the numerator of r. When x and y are positively associated, above-average values of x tend to go with above-average values of y, and below-average values of both variables also tend to occur together. So the deviations $x - \overline{x}$ and $y - \overline{y}$ are usually both positive or both negative. In either case, the product $(x - x)(y - y)$ is positive, and is large whenever both x and y are far from their means in the same direction. So "on the average" for all observations (that's what the numerator of r does) we get a large positive result when the association is strong. If, though, the association between x and y is negative, corresponding values of x and y tend to be on opposite sides of their means; when one is large, the other is small. The numerator of r is then negative, and more negative if large x's go with small y's and vice versa. So the numerator of r does seem to measure association. What about the denominator of r, which we have been ignoring? That brings us to the second point.

2. *The correlation coefficient r always has a value between -1 and $+1$.* It turns out that the standard deviations in the denominator standardize r in this way. That's why they are there. Can you see that the units in both numerator and denominator of r are the same? If x is height in centimeters and y is weight in grams, both numerator and denominator have the units "centimeters times grams." Therefore r itself has no units; it is a "pure number" between -1 and 1. And r does not depend on the choice of units for x and y. If x were measured in inches (not centimeters) and y in ounces (not grams), the correlation between height and weight would be unchanged so long as the same set of objects were being measured.

3. *The extreme values $r = -1$ and $r = +1$ indicate perfect straight-line association.* In particular, $r = -1$ means that all of the data points fall exactly on a straight line having negative slope. (That is, when x increases, y decreases.) And $r = +1$ means that all of the data points fall exactly on a straight line with positive slope (as x increases, y also increases).

4. *The correlation coefficient r measures how tightly the points on a scatterplot cluster about a straight line.* That is, r does not measure association in general, but only straight-line association. Correlations near either $+1$ or -1 indicate that the points fall close to a straight line. When $r > 0$, the scatterplot shows a trend from lower left to upper right, and the line about which the points cluster has positive slope. For $r < 0$, the trend is from upper left to lower right and the slope is negative. The scatterplots in Figure 9 illustrate how r measures

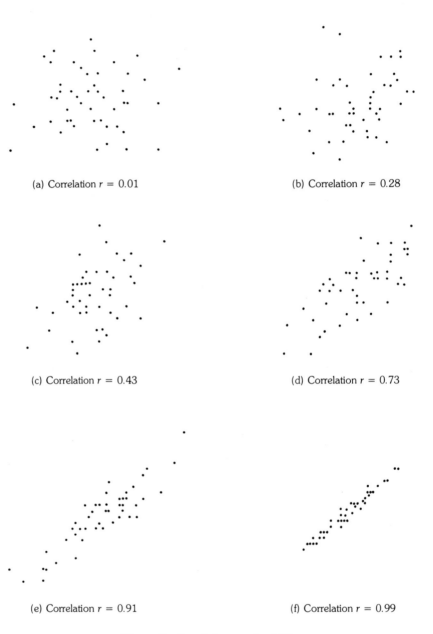

(a) Correlation r = 0.01

(b) Correlation r = 0.28

(c) Correlation r = 0.43

(d) Correlation r = 0.73

(e) Correlation r = 0.91

(f) Correlation r = 0.99

Figure 9. Correlation made visible.

straight-line association. Study them carefully. (These scatterplots are arranged so the two variables have the same standard deviation in all six cases. It is not as easy to guess r from a scatterplot as these examples suggest, because changing the standard deviations can change the appearance of the scatterplot quite a bit.)

5. There is a specific way in which r measures straight-line association. *The*

square r^2 of the correlation coefficient is the proportion of the variance of one variable that can be explained by straight-line dependence on the other variable. Notice that r^2 always falls between 0 and 1, so it can be interpreted as a proportion. To understand the meaning of the italicized fact, think about a case of perfect straight-line association with $r = -1$, such as Figure 10(a). The variable y

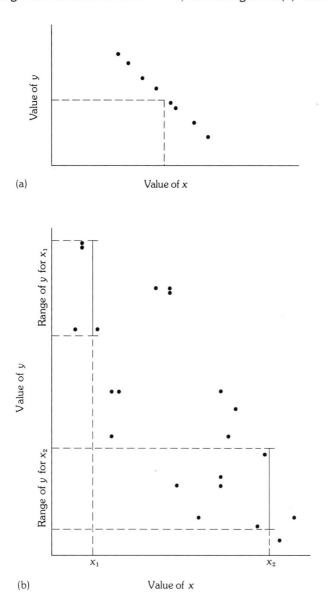

Figure 10. (a) Correlation $r = -1$. For a given x, there is no variation in y, hence y is perfectly predictable from x. (b) Correlation $r = -0.7$. For a given x, y takes on a range of values, hence y is only approximately predictable from x. Because the range of values of y does change with x (compare x_1 and x_2), x is of some use in predicting y.

is completely tied to x; when x changes, y moves so the point (x, y) moves along the line. Now the eight values of y in Figure 10(a) have a fairly large variance. But that variance is entirely due to different x values occurring bringing with them different y values. For a fixed x, there is *no* variation in y because the data points all fall on the line. Straight-line dependence on x accounts for *all* of the variability in y, and $r^2 = 1$. The y values in Figure 10(b) also show a large variance. Some of this variance can be explained again by the fact that changing x brings with it (on the average) a change in y. This is shown by the quite different values of y that accompany the two different x values in Figure 10(b). But in this case r is not ± 1, and the association between x and y explains only part of the variability in y. Even when x remains fixed, y still varies. It is possible by mathematics to separate out the part of the variance of y that is explained by straight-line dependence on x. This is the fraction r^2 of the variance of the y values. In Figure 10(b), for example, $r = -0.7$ and so $r^2 = 0.49$. The straight-line dependence of the y's on the x's accounts for 49% of the variance of the y's in that figure. Because r^2 has this specific interpretation, it is used almost as much as is r itself. Of course, r^2 only measures the *strength* of the association, not whether it is positive or negative.

It has been, you no doubt feel, a long, dry journey through the desert from $\bar{x}$ to r^2. True enough, but we have managed to mine some valuable resources on the way. In the Introduction, I mentioned a study of political science journals as an example of the invasion of new fields by statistics. That study also lists the numerical measures most often used in a sample of 576 articles in political science journals.[2] They are, in order of use,

1. Relative frequency
2. Frequency
3. Mean
4. Correlation coefficient r
5. Index numbers
6. r^2
7. Standard deviation and variance.

We have encountered six of these top seven statistics already, and the other (index numbers) will be treated in Chapter 6. You now can deal with much of the statistics you will meet in discussions of public policy and in many academic areas. That knowledge is worth the effort you put into gaining it.

5.   Association, Prediction, and Causation

Many of the most heated controversies in which statistical evidence plays a role center on the interpretation of association. Here are two examples.

MEN (age 45—64)

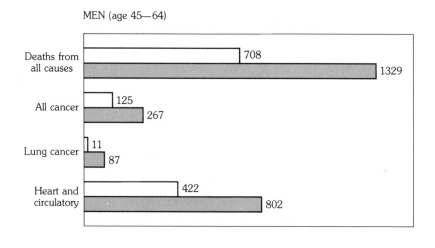

WOMEN (age 45—64)

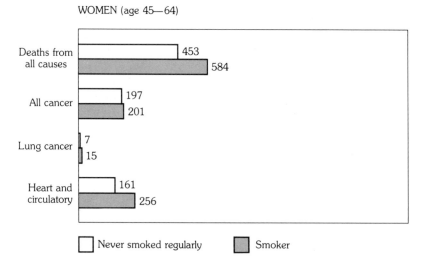

Death rates for smokers and nonsmokers (deaths per year per 100,000 persons). These death rates were obtained from studies involving more than one million persons. Although death rates vary greatly with sex and other variables, they are almost always higher for smokers than for nonsmokers. [From *Chart Book on Smoking, Tobacco and Health,* U.S. Department of Health, Education and Welfare, 1972.]

- A strong association exists between how much people smoke and their chances of contracting lung cancer and many other unpleasant maladies. Does this mean that smoking causes lung cancer?*

*See Byron W. Brown, Jr., "Statistics, Scientific Method, and Smoking," in *Statistics: A Guide to the Unknown.* This is one of the best essays in that book.

- A moderate correlation (about $r = 0.5$) exists between the IQ of parents and that of their offspring. Does this mean that IQ is mainly inherited? In IQ tests of American children, the scores of white children have a mean of about 100 with a standard deviation of 15; scores of black children have a mean of about 85 with a standard deviation of 14. Does this association mean that IQ is heavily influenced by race?[3]

The interpretation of association in the questions of smoking and health and race and intelligence is controversial in part because explaining an observed association is often extremely difficult. These examples ask whether a specific association is due to changes in one variable (lung cancer, IQ) being *caused* by changes in another (smoking, race). Tain't necessarily so.

To illustrate some circumstances other than cause-and-effect that may give rise to a strong association, here are two examples.

Example 5. A moderate correlation exists between the Scholastic Aptitude Test (SAT) scores of high school students and their grade index later as freshmen in college. Surely high SAT scores do not cause high freshman grades. Rather, the same combination of ability and knowledge shows itself in both high SAT scores and high grades. Both of the observed variables are responding to the same unobserved variable, and this is the reason for the correlation between them. Figure 11(b) illustrates this type of relationship.

Example 6. A study once showed a *negative* association between the starting salary of persons with a degree in economics and the level of the degree. That is, persons with a master's degree earned less on the average than those with a bachelor's degree, and Ph.D.'s earned less than holders of a master's. So much for the rewards of learning. But wait. Further detective work revealed that there was a *positive* association between starting salary and degree level among economists who went to work for private industry. There was also a positive association among economists working in government. And if only economists who took teaching jobs were considered, there was again a positive association between salary and degree level. So within *every* class of job, holders of higher degrees were better paid.

What happened? Teaching salaries were much lower than those in government and industry. Few holders of bachelor's degrees in economics chose teaching, but many holders of advanced degrees did. So average salaries for advanced degree holders were lower, even though each employer paid them more than B.A. employees. The negative association between salary and level of degree did not mean that more education depressed salaries; it was due to the effect of another variable (type of employer) on salaries. This third variable was confounded with the degree held. Figure 11(c) displays this relationship schematically.

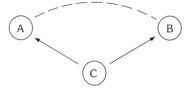

CAUSATION—Changes in A cause changes in B

COMMON RESPONSE—Changes in both A and B are caused
by changes in a third variable C.

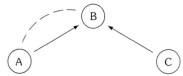

CONFOUNDING—Changes in B are caused both by changes
in A and by changes in a third variable C.

Figure 11. Some causes of association. Variables *A* and *B* show a strong association, indicated by the broken line. This association may result from any of several types of causal relationships, indicated by solid arrows.

Because an association can be due to (in the language of Figure 11) either *common response* or *confounding* as well as *causation,* be cautious in drawing conclusions. For example, the association between smoking and poor health might be an instance of common response. Perhaps heavy smokers are more likely than others to overeat, overdrink, underexercise, and in general be careless about their health. Then smoking and poor health both would be reflections of a careless style of life, and would be positively associated even if smoking had no direct effect on health. As for race and IQ, the great differences (on the average) between black and white Americans in nutrition, quality of schooling, and social environment all contribute to the difference in mean IQ scores. The effects of these variables are confounded with the effects of race, leaving any causal connection between race and IQ very dubious.

I have only three words of wisdom to offer on the question of causation. First, *causation is not a simple idea.* Rarely is A "the cause" of B. Smoking is at best only a *contributory cause* of lung cancer. It is one of many circumstances that make lung cancer more likely but not certain. Breathing polluted air and working in an asbestos factory may be other contributory causes of lung cancer.

Second, as I stressed in Chapter 2, *properly designed experiments are the best means of settling questions of causation.* But as I also stressed there, such experiments are often practically and morally impossible. You can imagine experiments that would settle the smoking and health and race and IQ disputes. Even the heritability of IQ could be studied by randomly assigning identical twins to different environments immediately after birth. These experiments must remain imaginary.

Third, *to conclude that association is due to causation requires evidence and judgment beyond what statistics can provide.* The case for causation is strengthened if

- the association is repeated in different circumstances, thus reducing the chance that it is due to confounding;
- a plausible explanation is available showing how one variable could cause changes in the other.
- no equally plausible third factors could cause changes in both variables together.

The case for the conclusion that smoking is a contributory cause of lung cancer meets these criteria. The association has been observed in studies of many different groups of people in many places and over long periods of time. For example, as smoking among women has increased, lung cancer among women (once rare) also has increased. Though we cannot be certain without randomized experiments, unusually good evidence suggests that the association between smoking and lung cancer is not due to confounding or other defects in collecting the data. Second, cigarette smoke contains substances that, in high concentration, cause lesions in the skin of laboratory animals. So it is plausible that over many years these substances, in low concentrations, could cause lesions in human lungs. Finally, the suggested third factors that might contribute to both tobacco addiction and lung cancer (such as differences between the lifestyles of smokers and nonsmokers) are only hypothetical and have not been clearly found in studies of smokers versus nonsmokers. The evidence that smoking is a cause of lung cancer is about as convincing as nonexperimental evidence can be. And so it is that we read

---

Warning: The Surgeon General Has Determined That Cigarette Smoking Is Dangerous to Your Health.

What about association that is not simply the result of the direct influence of one of the observed variables on the other? When confounding with the effects of other variables is present, association can be quite misleading, as Example 6 illustrates.* If the confounding cannot be eliminated by a properly designed

---

*Another illustration appears in Lincoln E. Moses and Frederick Mosteller, "Safety of Anesthetics," in *Statistics: A Guide to the Unknown.* There a strong association between the death rate of surgery patients, and the anesthetic used was misleading because some anesthetics were more commonly used in serious operations.

experiment, it can be difficult to ferret out the true relationship between the variables. Association owing to common response, on the other hand, is often extremely useful. SAT scores and freshmen grades in Example 5 are both responses to characteristics that cannot be directly observed. Because SAT scores for next year's college freshmen are available this year, they can be used to *predict* future academic performance.

Correlation and prediction are closely connected. Suppose that an independent variable x (say pounds of nitrogen fertilizer per acre) and a dependent variable y (corn yield in bushels per acre) have an r^2 near 1. This means that a set of observations on x and y fell close to a straight line. The scatterplot might look like Figure 9(e) or (f). If we drew a line through the scatterplot, we could use it to predict y from x. If I tell you how much nitrogen I plan to use and ask you to predict my corn yield, you could give a prediction by guessing that the bivariate observation will fall on the line. Figure 12 illustrates this. When r^2 is smaller, the prediction is less precise because the points do not fall as close to the line and y varies more for a fixed x, as in Figure 12(b).

What line shall we use for doing prediction from a scatterplot? Here is the idea behind the *regression line* commonly employed for this purpose. For each observation x_i on the independent variable (pounds per acre of nitrogen) we have the corresponding observed value y_i of the dependent variable (bushels per acre of corn). Now any line drawn through the scatterplot gives a value $\hat{y}_i$ corresponding to x_i, as Figure 13 shows. The difference $y_i - \hat{y}_i$ between the observed and predicted value is the error that particular line made in predicting y for the value x_i of the independent variable.

> The *regression line* for predicting y from x based on bivariate observations
>
> $$x_1, x_2, \ldots, x_n$$
> $$y_1, y_2, \ldots, y_n$$
>
> is the line that makes the sum of the squares of the errors in the y direction
>
> $$(y_1 - \hat{y}_1)^2 + (y_2 - \hat{y}_2)^2 + \ldots + (y_n - \hat{y}_n)^2$$
>
> as small as possible.

I will not ask you to calculate the regression line from the x_i's and y_i's. Any computer and many portable calculators are programmed to do this arithmetic for you. But here are a few facts about regression lines.

- The regression line for predicting y from x makes the errors in the y direction small. It is not the same as the regression line for predicting x from y, which makes the errors in the x direction small. In regression (unlike correlation) it

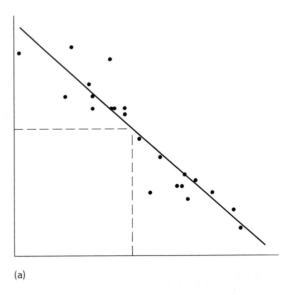

(a)

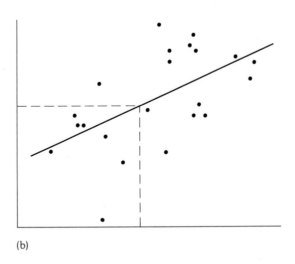

(b)

Figure 12. Predicting y from x with a regression line. (a) Correlation $r = -0.93$. The predicted value $\hat{y}$ of the dependent variable for the given value x of the independent variable is quite precise. A second sample would probably give nearly the same prediction. (b) Correlation $r = 0.56$. The predicted value $\hat{y}$ for the given x is less precise. Repeated samples would give somewhat different predictions.

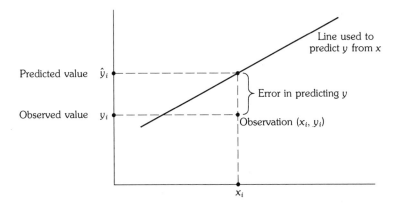

Figure 13. Using a line to predict y from x. For any x, the predicted value of y is the $\hat{y}$ such that $(x, \hat{y})$ falls on the line. The actual observations (x_i, y_i) do not fall exactly on the line. A good prediction line makes the predictions $\hat{y}_i$ close to the observed values y_i. The regression line for predicting y from x makes the sum of the squares of the errors $\hat{y}_i - y_i$ as small as possible.

is important to distinguish the independent variable x from the dependent or response variable y.

- Attention, experts in geometry. The regression line for predicting y from x can be exactly described in terms of the means $\bar{x}$, $\bar{y}$ and standard deviations s_x, s_y of the two variables and the correlation r between them. It is the line passing through the point $(\bar{x}, \bar{y})$ and having slope rs_y/s_x. (If you are not an expert in geometry, fear not. I said you could leave this to a computer.)

- When the data from which the regression line is computed are a random sample from the population of interest, the resulting predictions have the same properties we met in other conclusions based on random samples. When many predictions are made, they will be correct on the average; the prediction process has no bias. The precision of the prediction increases as r^2 increases because r^2 measures the strength of the straight-line association on which the prediction is based.

You will discover that how large an r^2 you can expect depends on the variables you are interested in. In many fields outside the physical sciences, high correlations are rare. We would like very much to be able to predict how well a high school senior will do next year if admitted to the university. Yet it would be unusual to find a correlation coefficient as high as $r = 0.4$ between any one independent variable measured on high school seniors and their grade indices as university freshmen. Because such a correlation means that only 16% of the variance in grade indices is accounted for, this is discouraging. The remedy is to use more than one independent variable. Throw anything available—high school grades, College Board scores, the performance of past students from that high school—into the hopper. Fortunately, there are ways of computing a *multiple correlation coefficient* (also called r) between a dependent variable and several independent variables at once. More fortunately, we won't discuss how to compute this statistic or the *multiple regression* used to predict a dependent variable from several independent variables. But most fortunately, the square r^2 of the multiple correlation coefficient r has exactly the same interpretation as in the one-independent-variable case. It is the proportion of the variance of the dependent variable accounted for by straight-line dependence on all of the independent variables taken together.

Many independent variables sometimes result in a value of r^2 close to 1. This means that changes in the dependent variable are closely associated with changes in the independent variables. And this means that multiple regression can quite accurately predict the value of the dependent variable from the values of the independent variables. If you understand this, you can see the beginnings of some unpleasant science fiction stories. I will tell only one pleasant nonfiction story.

One program at Purdue wishes to predict the grades of incoming freshmen in core courses such as mathematics. The story is pleasant because the goal is to offer special tutoring to students for whom academic trouble is predicted. (I will not go into the use of multiple correlation and prediction by medical school and

"How did I get into this business? Well, I couldn't understand multiple regression and correlation in college, so I settled for this instead."

law school admissions offices!) The set of independent variables is large, and the multiple correlation in the test study reached almost $r^2 = 0.90$. By contrast, the strongest simple correlation of freshman grades with a single independent variable was about $r^2 = 0.20$. This illustrates the power of using many variables. To obtain so large an r^2, scores on special tests given when the students arrive on campus must be among the independent variables. That largest simple r^2 belongs to one such test, a test of anxiety about academic performance. The correlation of anxiety with grade index is *negative*, $r = -0.45$. Students who worry about their grades seem to know the truth about themselves, and tend to get low grades. So whatever you do, don't worry about your statistics grade.

I hope our tour of association, causation, and prediction has left you with that slightly winded feeling that follows a good workout. Overconfidence in interpreting association is the root of many a statistical sin. Most users of statistics have learned that "correlation does not imply causation." Some go to the other extreme, and label all correlations not due to causation as "nonsense correlations." That label is inspired by examples such as the alleged strong positive correlation between teachers' salaries and liquor sales, both of which have steadily increased over time as a result of general prosperity. But this correlation is perfectly real and not at all nonsensical; what is nonsense is the interpretation that teachers are spending their salaries on booze. With sufficient skill and enough information, most associations can be usefully interpreted, even though (as in Example 6) the obvious interpretation may be seriously misleading.

NOTES

1. From an article by William Robbins in *The New York Times* of February 23, 1973.

2. James L. Hutter, "Statistics and Political Science," *Journal of the American Statistical Association*, Volume 67 (1972), p. 741.

3. The information cited appears on pages 92 and 128 of John C. Loehlin, Gardner Lindzey, and James N. Spuhler, *Race Differences in Intelligence* (San Francisco: W. H. Freeman and Company, 1975). This judicious discussion of a heated issue was prepared under the auspices of the Social Science Research Council.

Exercises

Section 1

1. Compute the mean, the median, and the mode for each of the following sets of numbers.

   (a) 4, 15, 2, 8, 4, 6, 10
   (b) 4, 2, 2, 6, 4, 4, 15, 8, 2, 17, 10, 4, 2, 6
   (c) 6, −3, 0, −11, 7, 120, −3

2. Return to the sample of 100 counts of coliform bacteria in milk given in Exercise 10, Section 2 of Chapter 4. You drew a frequency histogram for these data as part of that exercise.

(a) Compute the mean and the median of these data.
(b) Explain in terms of the shape of the frequency distribution why these measures of center fall as they do (close together or apart).

3. Here is a sample of 100 reaction times of a subject to a stimulus, in milliseconds.

10, 14, 11, 15, 7, 7, 20, 10, 14, 9, 8, 6, 12, 12, 10, 14, 11, 13, 9, 12

13, 11, 12, 10, 8, 9, 14, 18, 12, 10, 10, 11, 7, 17, 12, 9, 9, 11, 7, 10

14, 12, 12, 10, 9, 7, 11, 9, 18, 6, 12, 12, 10, 8, 14, 15, 12, 11, 9, 9

11, 8, 11, 10, 13, 8, 11, 11, 13, 20, 6, 13, 13, 8, 9, 16, 15, 11, 10, 11

20, 8, 17, 12, 19, 14, 17, 12, 18, 16, 15, 16, 10, 20, 11, 19, 20, 13, 11, 20

(a) Compute the mean and the median of these data.
(b) Find the frequency of each outcome 6, 7, 8, ... , 20 and draw a frequency histogram for these data.
(c) Explain in terms of the shape of the frequency distribution why these measures of center fall as they do (close together or apart).

4. Identify which measure of center (mean, median, or mode) is the appropriate "average" in each of the following situations.

(a) Someone declares "The average American is a Caucasian female."
(b) Middletown is considering imposing an income tax on its citizens. The city government wants to know the average income of citizens so it can estimate the total tax base.
(c) In an attempt to study the standard of living of typical families in Middletown, a sociologist estimates the average family income in that city.

5. As part of its twenty-fifth reunion celebration, the Class of '54 of Central New Jersey University mails a questionnaire to its members. One of the questions asks the respondent to give his or her total income last year. Of the 820 members of the Class of '54, the university alumni office has addresses for 583. Of these, 421 return the questionnaire. The reunion committee computes the mean income given in the responses and announces, "The members of '54 have enjoyed resounding success. The average income of class members is $60,000!"

This result exaggerates the income of the members of the Class of '54 for (at least) three reasons. What are these reasons?

6. According to the Bureau of the Census Construction Report C25, *New One-Family Houses Sold and for Sale,* for April 1977, the mean and median prices of new homes sold in that month were $48,900 and $55,100. Which of these numbers is the mean, and which is the median? Explain your answer.

7. The mean age of 5 persons in a room is 30 years. A 36-year-old person walks in. What is now the mean age of the persons in the room?

8. You wish to measure the average speed of vehicles on the interstate highway on which you are driving. So you adjust your speed until the number of vehicles passing you equals the number you are passing. Have you found the mean speed, the median speed or the modal speed of vehicles on the highway?

9. Figure 14 presents three frequency curves, each with several points marked on them. At which of these points on each curve do the mean, the median, and the mode fall? (More than one measure of center may fall at one point.)

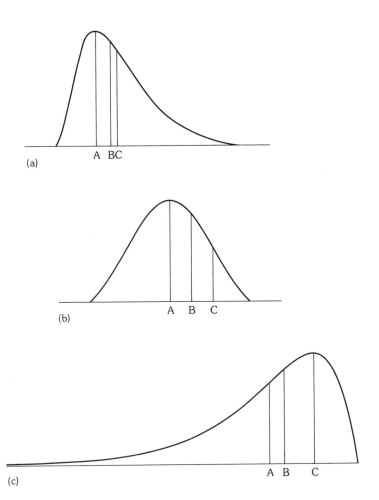

Figure 14

10. Make up a list of numbers of which only 10% are "above the average" (that is, above the mean). What percent of the numbers in your list fall above the median?

11. Which of the mean, median, and mode of a list of numbers must always appear as one of the numbers in the list?

12. In computing the median income of any group, Federal agencies omit all members of the group who had zero income. Give an example to show how the median income of a group (as reported by the Federal government) can go *down* when the group becomes better off economically.

13. The mean age of members of the class of '14 at their fiftieth reunion was 71.9 years. At their fifty-first reunion the next year, the mean age was 71.5 years. How can the mean age decrease when all the class members are a year older?

14. You drive 5 miles at 30 miles per hour, then 5 more miles at 50 miles per hour. Have you driven at an average speed of 40 miles per hour? (Your average speed is total miles driven divided by the time you took to drive it.)

15. It has been argued that equal opportunity can do little to reduce income inequality. One piece of evidence for this comes from a sample survey taken in 1968. A random sample of adult men was taken and the differences in income between all pairs of men in the sample were calculated. The median difference in income was $6200. Then a random sample of brothers was taken, and the median difference in the income of two brothers was $5700. Because brothers certainly have equal opportunity (the same home environment, school quality, etc.), it appears that income inequality can be decreased very little by equal opportunity programs.

    Is there another way to interpret these data? Consider the following two pairs of brothers:

    Pair 1.   N. Rocks—income $1,000,000
              L. Rocks—income $1,011,000
              Difference in income is $11,000.

    Pair 2.   A. Grubb—income $4000
              B. Grubb—income $4400
              Difference in income is $400.

    Show that the median income difference for these pairs is $5700. Then comment on the conclusion, based on median differences, that equal opportunity has little effect on income inequality.

Section 2

1. Calculate the mean, the variance, and the standard deviation of each of the following sets of numbers.

(a) 4, 0, 1, 4, 3, 6

(b) 5, 3, 1, 3, 4, 2

Which of the sets is more spread out? Draw a histogram of each of set (a) and set (b) to see how the set with the larger variance is more spread out.

2. Suppose that we add 2 to each of the numbers in the first set in Exercise 1. That gives us

$$6, 2, 3, 6, 5, 8.$$

(a) Find the mean and standard deviation of this set of numbers.

(b) Compare your answers with those for set (a) in Exercise 1. How did adding 2 to each number change the mean? How did it change the standard deviation?

(c) Can you guess without doing the arithmetic what will happen to the mean and standard deviation of set (a) in Exercise 1 if we add 10 to each number in that set?

This exercise should help you see that the standard deviation (or variance) measures only spread about the mean and ignores changes in where the data are centered.

3. This is a variance contest. You must give a list of 6 numbers chosen from the whole numbers 0, 1, 2, 3, 4, 5, 6, 7, 8, 9 with repeats allowed.

(a) Give a list of 6 numbers with the largest variance such a list can possibly have.

(b) Give a list of 6 numbers with the smallest variance such a list can possibly have.

(c) Do either of parts (a) or (b) have more than one correct answer?

4. Scores on the Stanford–Binet IQ test are approximately normally distributed with mean 100 and standard deviation 15. What is the variance of scores on this test?

5. (a) Find the first and third quartiles of the coliform bacteria counts in Exercise 10, Section 2 of Chapter 4.

(b) Find the 10th percentile and the 90th percentile for these data.

6. (a) Find the first and third quartiles of the reaction times in Exercise 3, Section 1.

(b) Find the 10th percentile and the 90th percentile for these data.

(c) Explain in terms of the shape of the frequency distribution why the 90th percentile is farther from the median than the 10th percentile. How does this compare with the location of these percentiles for the coliform counts of Exercise 5?

7. If two distributions have exactly the same mean and standard deviation, must their frequency curves look exactly alike? Explain.

8. Another measure of the spread of a set of data is the *range*, which is the difference between the largest and smallest observations.

    (a) Find the range of the reaction times in Exercise 3 of Section 1.

    (b) The range is rarely used for any but very small samples. Can you explain why?

    (c) Can you give an example in which the range is the most appropriate measure of spread?

Section 3

1. Figure 15 is a normal frequency curve. What are the mean and standard deviation of this distribution?

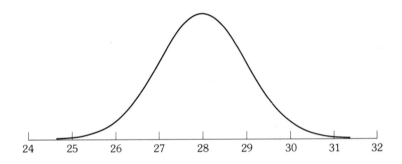

Figure 15

2. Figure 14 in Chapter 4 records two frequency distributions for measurements on 2000 Hungarian skulls. Both are approximately normal. Estimate the mean and standard deviation of each set of data.

3. Return once more to the coliform counts of Exercise 10, Section 2 of Chapter 4. You found the mean of these data in Exercise 2 of Section 1 in this chapter. The standard deviation can be calculated to be 2.02. What percent of the observations fall within one, two, and three standard deviations of the mean? Do you still feel that the distribution of coliform counts is approximately normal?

4. Explain, by using curves like those in Figures 5 and 6, why the point one standard deviation below the mean in a normal distribution is always the 16th percentile. Explain why the point two standard deviations above the mean is the 97.5th percentile.

5. Scores on the Wechsler Intelligence Scale for Children are (within each age group) approximately normally distributed with mean 100 and standard deviation 15. Draw a frequency curve for the distribution of these scores, with the scale on the horizontal axis correctly marked.

6. Scores on the Wechsler Adult Intelligence Scale for the 20–34 age group are approximately normally distributed with mean 110 and standard deviation 25. About what percent of people in this age group have scores

   (a) above 110?
   (b) above 160?
   (c) below 85?

7. Scores on the Scholastic Aptitude Test (Verbal) among applicants to a university are approximately normally distributed with mean 580 and standard deviation 100.

   (a) About what percent of applicants have scores above 680?
   (b) The middle 95% of applicants have scores falling between what two numbers?

8. Scores on the Wechsler Adult Intelligence Scale for the 60–64 age group are approximately normally distributed with mean 90 and standard deviation 25.

   (a) Sarah, who is 30, scores 135 on this test. Use the information of Exercise 6 to restate this score as a standard score.
   (b) Sarah's mother, who is 60, also takes the test, and scores 120. Express this as a standard score by using the information given in this exercise.
   (c) Who scored higher relative to her age group, Sarah or her mother? Who has the higher absolute level of the variable measured by the test?

9. Scores on the Wechsler Adult Intelligence Scale for Air Force flyers aged 20–34 are approximately normal with mean 122 and standard deviation 7. The mean and standard deviation for this group are quite different from those given in Exercise 6 for all Americans in this age group. Can you give a plausible reason for the difference?

10. Here is an excerpt from Robert L. Jacobson, "Standardized Testing and Cultural Bias," in *The Chronicle of Higher Education* of July 25, 1977.

    According to Mr. Angoff, if the College Board's data were released by race, they probably would show the average scores of blacks on various tests to be about 100 points lower, on a scale of 200 to 800, than the average for whites.

    Statistically speaking, the difference of 100 points would approximate one "standard deviation" and would mean that about _____ percent of the whites had scored above the average for blacks.

    Use your knowledge of normal distributions to fill in the blank. (The interpretation of race differences in standardized test scores was discussed in detail in Example 3 on page 104.)

11. Example 4 on page 107 reported 11 measurements of the mass standard

NB10 conducted by the National Bureau of Standards (NBS). I said there that the NBS is 95% confident that the mean of these measurements is within 0.0000023 of the true mass of NB10. Actually, the NBS gave the standard error of the mean measurement, from which I got this statement of precision by assuming (as is roughly true) that the sample mean has a normal distribution. What value of the standard error did the NBS give?

The following exercises, unlike the preceding ones, require Table 1 (p. 176).

12. The IQ scores on the Wechsler Adult Intelligence Scale for the 20–34 age group are approximately normal with mean 110 and standard deviation 25.

   (a) What percent of persons 20–34 have IQ's below 100? What percent have IQ's 100 or above?
   (b) What percent of persons 20–34 have IQ's above 150?
   (c) If only 1% of persons 20–34 have IQ's higher than Elanor's, what is Elanor's IQ? [Use the entry in Table 1 that comes closest to the point with 1% of the observations above it.]

13. SAT scores are approximately normal with mean 500 and standard deviation 100. Scores of 800 or higher are reported as 800. (So a SAT score of 800 does not, as you may have thought, imply a perfect performance.) What percent of scores are 800 or higher?

14. Table 1 shows that a standard score of -2 falls at the 2.27th percentile, while a standard score of $+2$ falls at the 97.73 percentile. Note that 2.27% + 97.73% = 100%. Draw a picture of a normal curve with the standard scores -2 and $+2$ marked on it. Then use the symmetry of the normal curve to explain why the sum of the percentiles for -2 and $+2$ must be 100. (There is nothing special about ± 2. The percentiles for $-b$ and $+b$ have sum 100 for any number b.)

Section 4

1. For each of the following sets of data

   • Draw a scatterplot.
   • Compute the mean, variance, and standard deviation of each variable x and y separately.
   • Compute the correlation coefficient r, and also r^2.

   For your own instruction, compare the values of r^2 and the closeness of the points in the scatterplots to a line.

(a)	x	4	4	-4	-4	
	y	-4	4	4	-4	
(b)	x	4	3	0	-3	-4
	y	-4	-2	0	2	4

(c) | x | 4 | 2 | −2 | −4 |
| y | 4 | −2 | 2 | −4 |

2. Make a scatterplot of the following data

x	−5	−3	0	3	5
y	0	4	5	4	0

Show that the correlation coefficient is zero. (You can do this by showing that the *numerator* of r is zero. You need not compute any standard deviations.) The scatterplot shows a tight connection between x and y. Explain how it can happen that r =0 in this case.

3. Figure 16 shows four scatterplots. Which (if any) of these have the same r? Which (if any) have the same r²?

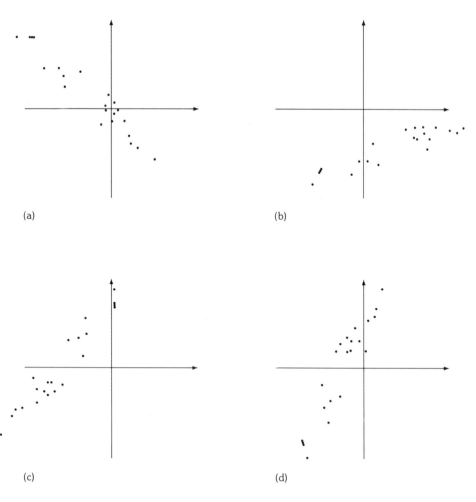

(a)

(b)

(c)

(d)

Figure 16. Recognizing r and r².

4. Make a scatterplot of the following data

x	1	2	3	4	10	10
y	1	3	3	5	1	11

Show that the correlation is about 0.5. What feature of the data is responsible for reducing the correlation to this value despite a strong straight-line association between x and y in most of the observations?

5. Figure 17 contains five scatterplots. Match each to the r below that best describes it. (Some r's will be left over.)

$$r = -0.9 \qquad r = 0 \qquad r = 0.9$$
$$r = -0.7 \qquad r = 0.3$$
$$r = -0.3 \qquad r = 0.7$$

6. Your data consist of bivariate observations on the age of the subject (measured in years) and the reaction time of the subject (measured in seconds). In what units are each of the following descriptive statistics measured?

(a) The mean age of the subjects.
(b) The variance of the subjects' reaction times.
(c) The standard deviation of the subjects' reaction times.
(d) The correlation coefficient between age and reaction time.
(e) The median age of the subjects.

7. A psychologist speaking to a meeting of the American Association of University Professors recently said, "The evidence suggests that there is nearly correlation zero between teaching ability of a faculty member and his or her research productivity." The student newspaper reported this as "Professor McDaniel said that good teachers tend to be poor researchers and good researchers tend to be poor teachers."

Explain what (if anything) is wrong with the newspaper's report. If the report is not accurate write your own plain-language account of what the speaker meant.

8. Measurements in large samples show that the correlation

(a) between father's height and son's adult height is about _____.
(b) between husband's height and wife's height is about _____.
(c) between a male's height at age 4 and his height at age 18 is about

_____.

The answers (in scrambled order) are

$$r = 0.25, r = 0.5, r = 0.8.$$

Match the answers to the statements and explain your choice.

9. If women always married men who were 2 years older than themselves, what would be the correlation between the ages of husband and wife?

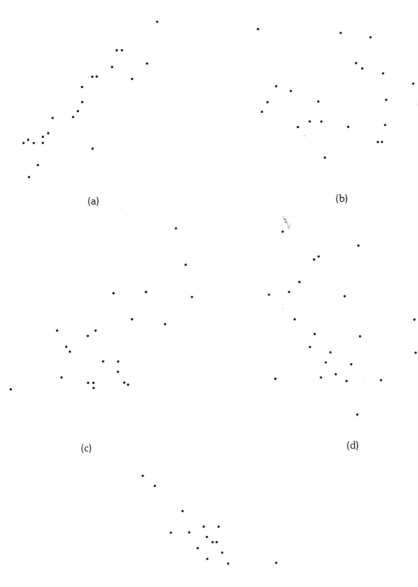

(a)

(b)

(c)

(d)

(e)

Figure 17. Match the correlation.

(*Hint:* Draw a scatterplot for the ages of husband and wife when the wife is 20, 30, 40, and 50 years old.)

10. For each of the following pairs of variables, would you expect a substantial negative correlation, a substantial positive correlation, or a small correlation?

    (a) The age of a second-hand car and its price.
    (b) The weight of a new car and its overall miles-per-gallon rating.
    (c) The height and weight of a person.
    (d) The height of a person and the height of his or her father.
    (c) The height and IQ of a person.

Section 5

Each of Exercises 1–6 reports an observed association. In each case, discuss possible explanations for the association. Note that more than one explanation may contribute to a single association.

1. A study of grade school children, aged 6 to 11 years, found a high positive correlation between reading ability and shoe size.

2. There is a negative correlation between the number of flu cases reported each week through the year and the amount of ice cream sold that week. Perhaps eating ice cream prevents flu.

3. There is a strong positive correlation between years of schooling completed and lifetime earnings for American men. One possible reason for this association is that more education leads to higher paying jobs.

4. A public health survey of 7000 California males found little correlation between alcohol consumption and chance of dying during the 5½ years of the study. In fact, men who did not drink at all during these years had a slightly higher death rate than did light drinkers. This lack of correlation was somewhat surprising.

5. Another public health study using statistics from 41 states found a positive correlation between per capita beer consumption and death rates from cancer of the large intestine and rectum. The states with the highest rectal cancer death rates were Rhode Island and New York. The beer consumption in those states was 80 quarts per capita. South Carolina, Alabama, and Arkansas drank only 26 quarts of beer per capita and had rectal cancer death rates less than one-third of those in Rhode Island and New York. (This study was reported in a Gannett News Service dispatch appearing in the *Lafayette Journal and Courier* of November 20, 1974).

    List some variables possibly influencing state cancer death rates that appear to be confounded with beer consumption. For a clue, look at the high and low consumption states given above.

6. A study of London double-decker bus drivers and conductors found that drivers had twice the death rate from heart disease as conductors. Because drivers sit while conductors climb up and down stairs all day, it was first thought that this association reflected the effect of type of job on heart disease. Then a look at bus company records showed that drivers were issued consistently larger-size uniforms when hired than were conductors. This fact suggested an alternative explanation of the observed association between job type and deaths. What is it?

7. In Exercise 9, Section 2 of Chapter 4 I presented data on natural gas consumption versus heating degree days. Figure 18 is a scatterplot of these data with the regression line for predicting gas consumption from degree days. Using this regression line, estimate gas consumption on a day that has 20 degree days. Estimate gas consumption on a day with 35 degree days.

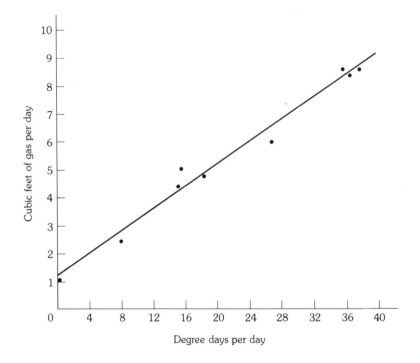

Figure 18

8. Suppose that Figure 19 represents data on slices of pizza consumed by pledges at a fraternity party (the independent variable x) and number of laps around the block the pledges could run immediately afterward (the dependent variable y). The line on the scatterplot is the regression line computed from these points and used to predict y from x.

    (a) At the next party, a pledge eats 6 slices of pizza before running. How many laps do you predict he will complete?

(b) Another pledge eats 9 pieces of pizza. Predict how many laps he will complete.

(c) A third pledge shows off by eating 25 pieces of pizza. You should refuse to predict his performance from the scatterplot and regression line. Explain why.

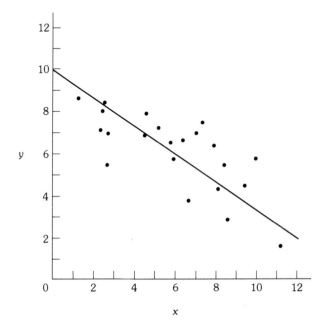

Figure 19

9. "When $r = 0.7$, this means that y can be predicted from x for 70% of the individuals in the sample." Is this statement true or false? Would it be true if $r^2 = 0.7$? Explain your answers.

10. Attention, experts in geometry. On page 191 I gave the exact description of the regression line for predicting y from x. Example 4 on page 179 contains the calculations of means, standard deviations, and correlation for a set of four observations.

   (a) Find the slope of the regression line for predicting y from x. Make a scatterplot like Figure 8 and draw the regression line on the scatterplot.

   (b) By interchanging the roles of x and y, find the slope of the regression line for predicting x from y. Draw this line on the same scatterplot.

Chapter 6

The Consumer Price Index and Its Neighbors

C oncern over the state of the economy rises as economic health declines, but such concern is never far from the front pages of the newspapers. Much of the news that arouses comment and expressions of official concern is veiled in the language of statistics. "The Consumer Price Index rose 0.6% in August. . . ." "Senator Bean called for increased stimulation of the economy, pointing out that the Composite Index of Leading Indicators had leveled off following six months of growth. . . ." "In his speech, the President expressed satisfaction that the Producer Price Index had increased at only a 4% annual rate during the past quarter. . . ." The data that alarm or soothe the politicians are collected by sample surveys. We are therefore well equipped to understand their basic trustworthiness, as well as the occasional comment that last month's rise of 0.1% in the unemployment rate should not be taken seriously since such a change is within the margin of sampling error. In some cases, such as the measurement of unemployment, we have looked at these government economic statistics in more detail. But what is meant by the Consumer Price *Index,* the *index* of leading indicators, the Producer Price *Index*? These are *index numbers,* the only one of the top seven statistics (page 184) that we have not yet met. This chapter introduces index numbers and their uses (Section 1), looks in more detail at the most famous index, the Consumer Price Index (Section 2), then gives a brief overview of the government's economic indicators and the proposal that official social indicators also be compiled (Section 3).

1. Index Numbers

An index number measures the value of a variable relative to its value at a base period. Thus the essential idea of an index number is to give a picture of changes in a variable much like that drawn by saying "The price of gasoline rose 60% in

"Yes sir, I know that we have to know where the economy is going. But do we have to publish the statistics so that everyone else does too?"

1973." Such a statement measures change without giving the actual numerical values of the variable. The recipe for an index number is

$$\text{index number} = \frac{\text{value}}{\text{base value}} \times 100.$$

Here is an example.

> **Example 1.** An apple that cost 10 cents in 1970 cost 14 cents in 1975. The apple price index in 1975 with 1970 as base was
>
> $$\frac{14}{10} \times 100 = 140.$$
>
> The apple price index for the base period, 1970, was

$$\frac{10}{10} \times 100 = 100.$$

Example 1 illustrates some important points. The choice of base is a crucial part of any index number and must always be stated. The index number for the base period is always 100, so it is usual to identify the base period as 1970 by writing "1970 = 100." You will notice in press articles concerning the Consumer Price Index the notation "1967 = 100." This mysterious equation simply means that 1967 is the base period for the index.

Example 2. A Mercedes automobile that cost $10,000 in 1970 cost $14,000 in 1975. The corresponding index number (1970 = 100) for 1975 was

$$\frac{14,000}{10,000} \times 100 = 140.$$

Comparing Examples 1 and 2 makes it clear that an index number measures only change relative to the base value. The apple price index and the Mercedes price index for 1975 were both 140. That the apple rose from 10 cents to 14 cents and the Mercedes from $10,000 to $14,000 is irrelevant. Both rose by 40% of the base value, so both index numbers are 140.

Index numbers can be interpreted in plain terms as giving the value of a variable as a percent of the base value. An index of 140 means 140% of the base value, or a 40% increase from the base value. An index of 80 means that the current value is 80% of the base, a 20% decrease. Be sure to notice that index numbers can be read as percents only relative to the base value. Do not confuse an increase of so many *points* with an increase of so many *percent* in news accounts of an index.

Example 3. The Consumer Price Index increased from 160.6 in June 1975 to 170.1 in June 1976. This is an increase of 9.5 points because

$$170.1 - 160.6 = 9.5.$$

But to find the *percent* increase in that one-year period, we express the 9.5 point increase as a percent of the value at the beginning of the period, which was 160.6. Since

$$\frac{9.5}{160.6} = 0.059,$$

the Consumer Price Index rose by 5.9% during that year.

Thus far it may seem that the fancy terminology of index numbers is little more than a plot to disguise simple statements in complicated language. Why say "The Consumer Price Index (1967 = 100) stood at 181.8 by June 1977" instead of "Consumer prices increased 81.8% between 1967 and June 1977?" In fact the term *index number* usually means more than a measure of change relative to a base; it also tells us the kind of quantity whose change we measure. That quantity is a weighted average of several variables, with fixed weights. This idea is best illustrated by an example of a simple price index.

Example 4. A homesteader striving for self-sufficiency purchases only salt, kerosene, and the services of a professional welder. In 1970 the quantities purchased and total costs were as follows. (The cost of an item is the price per unit multiplied by the number of units purchased.)

Good or service	1970 quantity	1970 price	1970 cost
salt	100 pounds	0.05/pound	$ 5.00
kerosene	50 gallons	0.36/gallon	$ 18.00
welding	10 hours	8.00/hour	$ 80.00
			$103.00

The total cost of this collection of goods and services in 1970 was $103. To find the "homesteader price index" in 1975, we compute the 1975 cost of this same collection of goods and services. Suppose that in 1975 we have

Good or service	1970 quantity	1975 price	1975 cost
salt	100 pounds	0.07/pound	$ 7.00
kerosene	50 gallons	0.50/gallons	$ 25.00
welding	10 hours	10.00/hour	$100.00
			$132.00

The same goods and services that cost $103 in 1970 cost $132 in 1975. So the homesteader price index (1970 = 100) for 1975 is

$$\frac{132}{103} \times 100 = 128.1$$

When prices of a collection of goods and services are being measured, as in Example 4 and also in the Consumer Price Index and the Producer Price Index[1] for wholesale prices, the kind of index number illustrated in Example 4 is called a *fixed market basket price index.* The variable for which an index is found is the total cost of a "fixed market basket" of goods and services. The makeup of the market basket is determined in the base year; in Example 4, the basket contained 100 pounds of salt, 50 gallons of kerosene, and 10 hours of a welder's services. By 1975 the homesteader may have changed his purchases, but no matter. The price index measures the relative change in the cost of the *same* market basket from 1970 to 1975.

The basic idea of a fixed market basket price index is that the weight given to each component (salt, kerosene, welding) remains fixed over time. This basic idea can be extended (we won't go into the details) to produce the general idea of an "aggregative weighted index number with fixed weights." The index numbers published by the federal government and featured in our economic news are almost all of this type. Thus the term *index number* carries two ideas.

- It is a measure of the change of a variable relative to a base value.
- The variable is an average of many quantities, with the weight given to each quantity remaining fixed over time.

2.   The Consumer Price Index

The Consumer Price Index (forever after abbreviated CPI), published monthly by the Bureau of Labor Statistics, is a fixed market basket index measuring changes in the prices of consumer goods and services. The CPI is the most important of all index numbers. Not only does the CPI make headlines as the most popular measure of inflation (the declining buying power of the dollar), but it directly affects the income of almost half of all Americans.[2] This is so because many sources of income are "indexed." That is, they are tied to the CPI and automatically increase when the CPI increases. (The CPI last decreased in 1955, so we can ignore that pleasant but unlikely possibility.) Since the United Auto Workers first won a "cost of living escalator clause" in 1948, indexing has become a standard feature of union contracts. Over 8.5 million workers now have such contracts. Social Security payments are indexed, and so are federal civil service and military pension payments. Even food stamp allowances are indexed. When dependents are included, the CPI influences the income of half the population. This state of affairs may well be economically foolish, for *every* rise in the CPI generates more inflation by driving up labor and pension costs. But it certainly focuses attention on the Consumer Price Index.

What does the CPI measure? It is a fixed market basket index covering the cost of a collection of over 400 goods and services. The CPI is computed just as in Example 4, though the arithmetic is a bit longer with 400 items. Prior to 1978, there was a single CPI, officially called the Consumer Price Index for Urban Wage Earners and Clerical Workers. The 400 items in the market basket, and their weights in the index, were chosen to represent the spending habits of families of city wage earners and clerical workers. The market basket did *not* represent the spending habits of rural families, or of professional and self-employed workers, or of the unemployed, or of people not in the labor force. So if you were a farmer, a teacher, a medical doctor, or unemployed, the CPI did not describe the change in prices of the goods and services typically consumed by people like you. Only about 45% of the population was covered by the pre-1978 CPI.

Because of the great importance of the CPI, the Bureau of Labor Statistics (BLS) decided to update and enlarge the market basket, choosing items and weights to represent the average purchases of all nonfarm households living in metropolitan areas. About 80% of the population live in such households. ("Metropolitan areas" as officially defined include most suburban regions and a good many rural regions in addition to cities.) The teacher, medical doctor, and unemployed are now included, but not the farmer. Labor leaders were unhappy with this idea because the old CPI described changes in the price of a market basket typical of union households, and was embedded in many labor contracts. As a result of their protests, the BLS decided to publish *two* CPI's beginning in 1978. One directly continues the old CPI for urban wage-earners and clerical workers, while the other is the new, broader CPI. To keep things simple, let's concentrate on the narrower CPI.

How was the market basket arrived at? By an exercise in probability sampling. From 1964 to 1977, the market basket was based on a survey of family buying habits in 1960–1961. Beginning in 1978 the market basket is based on a Consumer Expenditure Survey made in 1972–1973. Two samples were taken, each containing over 20,000 families. Each was a multistage probability sample, stratified by geographic area, occupation, and several other variables. You gained some insight into these complex sampling designs in Section 5 of Chapter 1.[3] The households in the samples kept careful records of their expenditures, so the survey produced detailed information on how Americans spend their money.

These expenditures were classified into groups, such as "Fruits and Vegetables," "Women's and Girls' Apparel," and "Fuel and Utilities." Then a stratified probability sample was taken to choose individual items to represent each group. These items make up the market basket. The weight given to each item in computing the index depends on the share of spending its group received in the Consumer Expenditure Survey. There are of course separate market baskets for the two CPI's, each reflecting the average spending habits for the target population of households.

How are the data for the monthly CPI collected? By another exercise in probability sampling. The 1972–1973 survey also asked *where* the sample households bought each item, so a sample of retail outlets can be chosen that gives proper weight to drug stores, department stores, discount stores, and so forth. Prices are collected each month in 85 metropolitan areas. These 85 areas are a probability sample of all the nation's metropolitan areas—a stratified sample consisting of 28 large metropolitan areas specified in advance and a probability sample of 57 others. (Recall from Chapter 1 that stratified samples auto-matically including all the largest units are common in economic sampling.) Then prices are obtained from a probability sample of over 18,000 retail outlets each month, distributed over the 85 metropolitan areas. It's a big job.

The result of all this sampling is the monthly CPI, both the two national CPI's and separate CPI's for the largest metropolitan areas. Probability sampling pro-duces results with little bias and quite high precision. Because the published CPI is rounded off to one decimal point (such as 181.3), a change of 0.1 may be due to rounding off. But a change of 0.2 in the CPI almost certainly reflects a real change in the price of the market basket.

Does the CPI have shortcomings? Indeed it does. The CPI is computed with great statistical expertise, but we have seen again and again that statistics is not a cure-all. The CPI is a fixed market basket price index, and all such indices have some problems with validity of measurement (recall Chapter 3). It is not really possible to keep the market basket fixed year after year. After all, a 1979 car is not the same as a 1969 car, so the "new car" item in the market basket changes each year. The BLS then must decide the issue of *changes in quality.* How much of the yearly rise in passenger car prices is due to the better quality of the product, and how much is a genuine price hike? In 1975, for example, manufac-turers' suggested retail prices for passenger cars rose an average of $386. The Bureau decided that $130 of this increase paid for higher quality, primarily for improved emission control systems. (Catalytic converters were added to most cars that year.) So only the remaining $256 was counted as a price increase in computing the CPI. There were *no* increases in auto prices in the CPI between 1959 and 1970. Ralph Nader and the United Auto Workers think that represents too much credit for better cars.

A related difficulty with the fixed market basket is *changing buying habits.* The "men's business shirts" in the 1960–1961 survey were white and 100% cotton. (Remember those days?) This item was outdated long before the new survey in 1972–1973. Once again the BLS is forced to fiddle with the market basket by substituting items and adjusting the prices. Shirts made of blends of synthetic fabrics entered the market basket in 1966, but colored business shirts were kept out until 1971. The BLS is somewhat slow to change the market basket as items become outdated because this is contrary to the fixed market basket principle.

Adjustment for quality and replacement of outdated items are carefully made and generally can be ignored in interpreting the CPI. What cannot be ignored is that a fixed market basket index does not measure changes in the cost of living. Our buying habits are directly affected by changing prices. We can keep our cost of living down by switching to substitutes when one item rises in price. If beef prices skyrocket, we eat less beef and more chicken. Or even more beans. The CPI measures price changes, not changes in the cost of living. It probably slightly overstates rises in the cost of living by ignoring our ability to change our buying habits. As evidence of this, we might note that in the year from September 1972 to September 1973, the CPI food component increased 21.5%, but total sales at grocery stores rose only 12.5%. Consumers were changing their choice of food items, especially switching away from expensive prepared foods. Thus the cost of the food they actually bought rose more slowly than the price of the CPI's fixed market basket of food.

How is the CPI used to adjust for the effects of inflation? A dollar in 1975 is not the same as a dollar in 1950, for the decrepit 1975 dollar could buy much less than the more robust 1950 dollar. Especially in times of rapid inflation, we can understand changes in our financial picture over time only by using "constant dollars" rather than "current dollars." Constant dollars are dollars of constant buying power, usually equal to the buying power of actual dollars in the base period of the CPI. The recipe for converting a current dollar amount into constant dollars (or "1967 dollars") is

$$\text{constant dollars} = \frac{\text{current dollars}}{\text{current CPI}} \times 100$$

Here is an example.

> **Example 5.** A worker earned $10,000 in 1967 and $14,000 in 1975. The average CPI (1967 = 100) for 1975 was 161.2. So an income of $14,000 in 1975 dollars was worth only
>
> $$\frac{\$14,000}{161.2} \times 100 = \$8685$$
>
> in 1967 dollars. The worker's real income, measured in terms of buying power, has dropped since 1967 because his raises did not keep pace with inflation. A worker must earn $16,120 in 1975 to have the same buying power as $10,000 had in 1967.

The value in constant 1967 dollars of amounts in dollars of earlier years can be found from the CPI (1967 = 100) for those years. Table 1 gives the CPI values needed.

> **Example 6.** In 1920, the median earnings of full-time manufacturing workers were $1532 per year. What is the value of that income in 1967 dollars? The CPI (1967 = 100) for 1920 was 60.0. So the 1967 buying power of $1532 in 1920 is
>
> $$\frac{\$1532}{60.0} \times 100 = \$2553.$$

Table 1

ANNUAL AVERAGE CPI (1967 = 100)

Year	CPI	Year	CPI	Year	CPI
1800	51	1940	42.0	1966	97.2
1825	34	1945	53.9	1967	100.0
1850	25	1950	72.1	1968	104.2
1860	27	1955	80.2	1969	109.8
1870	38	1956	81.4	1970	116.3
1880	29	1957	84.3	1971	121.3
1890	27	1958	86.6	1972	125.3
1900	25	1959	87.3	1973	133.1
1910	28	1960	88.7	1974	147.7
1915	30.4	1961	89.6	1975	161.2
1920	60.0	1962	90.6	1976	170.5
1925	52.5	1963	91.7	1977	181.5
1930	50.6	1964	92.9		
1935	41.1	1965	94.5		

SOURCES: *Handbook of Labor Statistics* 1975, and current issues of the *Monthly Labor Review*. Pre-1917 values are estimates made by the BLS. Post-1917 values come from previous versions of the CPI updated to 1967 = 100.

What is the value of that $1532 in 1920 in terms of (say) 1977 dollars instead of 1967 dollars? The answer requires another formula, one that actually includes the "constant dollars" recipe as a special case. Here it is: To convert an amount in current dollars at time A to the amount with the same buying power at time B,

$$\text{Dollars at time B} = (\text{Dollars at time A}) \times \frac{\text{CPI at time B}}{\text{CPI at time A}}$$

Example 7. The average manufacturing worker's 1920 income of $1532 is equal in buying power to a 1977 income of

$$\$1532 \times \frac{181.5}{60.0} = \$4634.$$

because the CPI (1967 = 100) was 60.0 in 1920 and 181.5 in 1977. The average manufacturing worker of 1920 didn't earn very much. Remember that when you next feel a yearning for the Good Old Days.

"Now this here's a genuine 1920 dollar. They don't make 'em like that anymore."

An advantage of the last recipe is that it is not affected by base changes for the CPI. So long as the same base is used for time A and time B, the recipe always gives the same answer. Because the CPI (1967 = 100) passed 200 in 1978, and would have passed 230 if the previous base (1957–1959 = 100) had continued in use, politicians prefer to have the base changed now and then to keep the index below the clouds. The base for the CPI was changed in 1935, 1953, 1961, and 1972.

Don't go away unhappy at the steep climb of the CPI in recent years. Remember my favorite index number: the Japanese urban land price index (1965 = 100) stood at 2286 by 1974.

3.   Economic and Social Indicators

The monthly Consumer Price Index, the monthly unemployment rate, and most other newsmaking government statistics are produced at regular time intervals. Indeed, frequently the *change* in prices or unemployment from month to month is the center of attention rather than the actual value of the CPI or the unemployment rate.

A sequence of measurements of the same variable made at different times is called a *time series*. Usually (but not always) the variable is measured at regular intervals of time, such as monthly.

The variable measured in a time series may be any of the many kinds we have studied—counts (such as the number of persons employed), rates (such as the unemployment rate), index numbers (such as the CPI), and other kinds of variables as well. The key idea of a time series is that each observation records both the value of the variable and the time when the observation was made.

An especially important set of time series are the *national economic indicators*. These time series, compiled by agencies of the Federal government, are designed to indicate the state of the economy. They are chosen for their importance according to economic theory, their validity as measures of significant economic facts, and their consistent behavior over time when compared with the behavior of the economy. We have already met important economic indicators in discussing the CPI and unemployment rate.* Until quite recently, the national economic indicators were of interest primarily to academicians and to government officials as a guide for economic policy. Now, however, legislation ties large transfers of money to the economic indicators. A 1% rise in the CPI, for example, triggers a billion-dollar hike in wages and other income payments. In 1977, over $16 billion in federal aid was allocated to states and communities on the basis of unemployment statistics. In all, about $30 billion each year are transferred on the basis of statistics compiled by the BLS.[4] The national economic indicators have moved from the business section of the newspaper to the front page.

The best-publicized economic indicators are those which, like the CPI and unemployment rate, measure the present state of the economy. These are called *coincident indicators* because their movements coincide with those of the economy as a whole. Less known to the public, but critical to business and government policy makers, are the *leading indicators*. These are economic time series whose movements tend to lead (occur before) movements of the overall economy; thus they can help to forecast future economic conditions.

There are 12 major leading economic indicators. In addition to fulfilling the criteria used to select all economic indicators, the leading indicators are chosen for their past success in changing direction ahead of turning points in overall economic activity. Most of the leading economic indicators are measures of *demand* for various kinds of economic output. Some are direct measures of demand, such as the number of new building permits issued for residential houses, or the dollar value of new orders for industrial plants and equipment (in 1967 dollars, of course). Others are indirect measures of demand, such as the average work week of manufacturing workers. (This is a leading indicator because manufacturers increase or reduce overtime quickly when demand for their

---

*More detail on economic indicators can be found in Geoffrey H. Moore and Julius Shiskin, "Early Warning Signals for the Economy," in J. M. Tanur et al. (eds.), *Statistics: A Guide to the Unknown* (San Francisco: Holden-Day, 1972).

products changes. They hire or lay off workers more slowly; measures of employment and unemployment are coincident indicators.)

The Department of Commerce has spared us from trying to make sense of 12 different time series at once by publishing the *Composite Index of Leading Indicators* (CLI) each month. This is a fixed weight index number of the kind we have seen already. It is a weighted average of the 12 leading indicators. Since combining several leading indicators usually results in better forecasts of the future, the CLI is not far behind the CPI in the attention it gets from the media. In Figure 3 of Chapter 4, for example, we compared two graphs of the CLI that appeared in different newspapers on the same day.

How well does the CLI predict future economic activity? Take the change in the CLI over a quarter (three-month period) as the independent variable. Let the percent change in the Gross National Product for the following quarter be the dependent variable. (The Gross National Product is the total value of all goods and services produced in the economy. It is the usual measure of overall economic activity.) For the period 1953 to 1970, these variables had $r^2 = 0.37$. That's pretty good by social science standards.[5] Another picture is given by Figure 1. Notice that the CLI turns down *before* a recession (shaded areas) and then turns up *during* the recession and before economic recovery. That's what "leading" means.

A question should now occur to any properly greedy reader. Can I use the

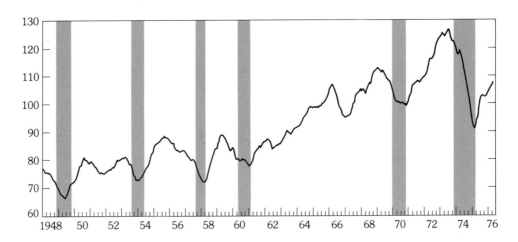

Figure 1. Composite index of leading indicators (seasonally adjusted; 1967 = 100). Shaded areas represent periods of recession as defined by the National Bureau of Economic Research, except for the latest recession, which is tentatively judged to have ended in March 1975. [United States Department of Commerce, Bureau of Economic Analysis. Reproduced by permission from Maury N. Harris and Deborah Jamroz, "Evaluating the Leading Indicators," *Federal Reserve Bank of New York Monthly Review,* June 1976, p. 169.]

CLI to forecast what will happen to the stock market and make a killing? Sorry. Stock prices are one of the 12 leading indicators in the CLI; they tend to move before the economy as a whole.

Social Indicators

The national economic indicators are well established with the government, the media, and the public. Social scientists have urged the adoption of a similarly authoritative series of *social indicators*. Social indicators are time series intended to provide statistical measures of social values and well-being. Such indicators might provide information for policy makers and for the public similar to the official economic information already available. The government has shown some interest in this idea. The Office of Management and Budget published a volume of statistics under the title *Social Indicators 1973* and another as *Social Indicators 1976*.

Many statistical measures of health, housing, crime, and other social concerns already are published by the government. But these are far less carefully collected than are our economic indicators. Economic statistics are more precise, are compiled more regularly, and are published with a shorter time lag. (*Social indicators 1976* appeared in December of 1977!) It is noteworthy that economic indicators such as the unemployment rate are based on regular large sample surveys of citizens. No such effort is expended on social statistics. Estimates of crime rates, for example, are compiled from data supplied by police agencies, not by asking a sample of citizens if they have been victims of a crime. That's not unlike studying unemployment by polling employers. Official social indicators would treat social variables with the level of statistical care now reserved for economic variables.

The suggestion that social indicators be added to economic indicators seems to bring up one new idea and several difficulties. The new idea is to add "subjective" or "opinion" information to improved versions of the "objective" social statistics now available. This is an attractive idea. It would be interesting to follow over time changes in the values Americans hold, their degree of satisfaction with their jobs, how much they are afraid of crime, and so on. Politicians and others now operate on hearsay in these areas. A well-designed sample survey, regularly repeated, would provide fascinating data.

Some of the difficulties in the proposal for official social indicators are directly related to the inclusion of subjective responses. Measuring even so objective a factor as "unemployment" is not entirely easy. How then shall we measure "satisfaction with the quality of life?" Any measure placed on an official list of social indicators will receive much attention, and so should be well chosen. To measure a factor, you recall, we must have a clear concept of what the factor is. For example, economists have a clear concept and definition of "money supply." They agree that money supply has an important influence on the economy. So money supply is regularly measured and is one of the leading economic indicators. Social scientists have no such agreement over the concept

"Have you ever thought of adding an indicator of how people feel about having their opinions asked every other day?"

of "quality of life." Many different measures of the quality of life, both objective and subjective, have been proposed, none of which commands the kind of respect that "money supply" has among economists. The measurement and conceptualization problems so common in the social sciences appear once again. It is probably necessary to begin with many measures of the quality of life, with the hope that regular data collection will clarify which are most useful. Certainly there is interesting information to be gained. One-time surveys suggest, for example, that satisfaction with the quality of life goes *down* as level of education increases. Has this dissatisfaction grown in recent years? Is there really a turning away from material things to things of the spirit as sources of satisfaction? I'd like to know.

Social indicators have problems other than conceptualization and measurement. The economic indicators serve as a basis for making short-term economic policy and for transferring large sums in government payments. That justifies the expense needed to compile the indicators at frequent intervals. Social indicators do not appear to have the same direct relation to policy making by either public or private bodies. I'd like to know if more Americans are looking for satisfaction in things of the spirit this year than last, but I'm not sure my curiosity justifies the kind of massive effort described for the CPI in Section 2. A considerable effort would be required to collect accurate social indicators. At least this would employ more statisticians. But perhaps by now you feel that there are statisticians enough already.

4. Interpreting Time Series

And so the CLI, the CPI, and other time series run on toward the future, providing us each month with new data. The goal of this machinery is in part to tell us where we are, but also to suggest where we are going. Predicting the future is always a risky business, and statistical time series do not remove the risk. The interpretation of time series is complicated by the fact that several types of movement are going on together. Let us look at each type separately.

Seasonal variations are regular changes that recur in periods of less than a year. Figure 2 (repeated from Chapter 4) shows a large seasonal variation in the frequency of civil disturbances, which regularly increase in the summer and decrease in winter. We must remove the effect of seasonal variation to see the underlying trend in the time series. In Figure 2 we can do this visually, and we find that underneath the seasonal variation the frequency of civil disturbances was decreasing during these years. Seasonal variation strongly affects some

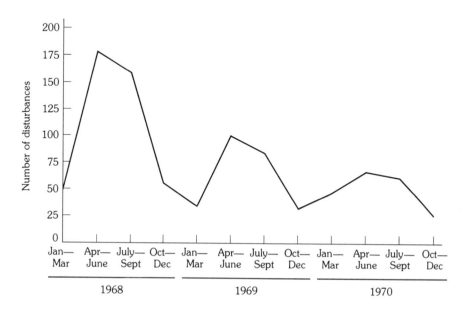

Figure 2. Trend and seasonal variation in a time series. Civil disturbances, 1968 to 1970. [From *Statistical Abstract of the United States*, 1971, p. 139.]

economic indicators. Retail sales peak at Christmas time. Unemployment usually drops between May and June, and rises between December and January. (In January, Christmas help are laid off and construction employment also drops. In June, construction and other good-weather work is increasing.)

Seasonal variation can confuse the interpretation of time series. A rise in unemployment in January need not mean that the economy is in trouble. Rising unemployment is expected in January when economic conditions remain unchanged from December. Only a larger than expected rise in unemployment is cause for concern. To avoid misinterpretation, the BLS reports a "seasonally adjusted" unemployment rate. An example will show how seasonal adjustment compensates for seasonal variation.

> **Example 8.** The unemployment rate in the state of Indiana this January is 7.1%. Looking at data for the past several years, we learn that on the average the January unemployment rate is 1.03 times the mean of the 12 monthly rates for the year. That is, in past years,
>
> $$\text{mean monthly rate} = \frac{\text{January rate}}{1.03}.$$
>
> Seasonal adjustment therefore reduces the actual Indiana unemployment rate for January by dividing by 1.03. A raw rate of 7.1% would be reported as 6.9% seasonally adjusted because
>
> $$\frac{7.1}{1.03} = 6.9.$$

As Example 8 indicates, a seasonally adjusted value is the average value for the year that is implied by the actual value for a shorter period.* Actual values are seasonally adjusted downward in periods typically above average, and upward in periods typically below average. Seasonal adjustment is often the first step in interpreting time series. Watch for that phrase in news reports.

Figure 1 displays the Composite Index of Leading Indicators over a 28-year period. Notice under the head that this time series has been seasonally adjusted, and so is free of seasonal variation. The remaining major movements shown in Figure 1 are trend and cycles. A *trend* is a persistent long-term movement. Cycles are up and down movements of irregular strength and duration. Figure 1 shows a continuing trend upward in the level of the CLI, on which are superimposed up and down cycles whose major bottoms occur in the shaded periods of economic recession.

---

*For national economic data the BLS uses a seasonal adjustment scheme much more complex than the simple calculation of Example 8. But the concept behind the arithmetic is similar.

The goal of analysis of a time series is usually the study of trend, cycles, or both. The upward trend in the CLI is probably a result of inflation and is of no particular interest. The cycles, however, reflect the up and down business cycles of the economy as a whole (in advance, since the CLI is composed of leading indicators). Analysis of the CLI therefore seeks to decide where we are in the current business cycle so proper economic policies can be adopted. Even with seasonal variation removed, this is not easy to do. First, business cycles are irregular in length and strength, so they cannot be systematically predicted as seasonal variation can be. Even isolating *past* business cycles in Figure 1 is quite subjective. Second, superimposed on trend, cycles, and seasonal variations in a time series are movements of a final type: *erratic fluctuations.* Storms, strikes, oil embargoes, and other chance occurrences large and small affect the economy and the CLI. It is extremely difficult to tell if a three-month flat spot in the CLI means that the business cycle has peaked and is about to turn down. Perhaps it is only a "pause" (to quote the president's chief economic advisor on one such occasion) caused by lack of rain in Nebraska, a strike at Ford Motor Company, and an upcoming presidential election.

Business cycles have been a center of attention for over a century, and a good

"Isn't it fascinating that you were ruined by a business cycle, while I was ruined by an erratic fluctuation?"

deal of nonsense (and some sense) has been written about them. The cycles present in other time series come in for attention as well, especially if they appear to repeat themselves at regular periods. As a witness to the attention some people pay to cycles, consider the following excerpts from an article in *The Wall Street Journal*.

> *One question frequently asked when good friends get together is, "How often do the thickness and thinness of the sedimentary deposits fluctuate on the bottom of Lake Saki in the Crimea?"*
>
> *The answer, as every schoolboy knows, is, "The thickness and thinness of the sedimentary deposits on the bottom of Lake Saki in the Crimea have fluctuated on a 17⅓-year cycle that has repeated itself over and over and over again for more than 4000 years—since 2295 B.C."*
>
> *Actually, not every schoolboy knows that. But Edward R. Dewey, who was a schoolboy 60 to 70 years ago, knows. He also knows that there is a close connection between the level of steel production, the price of butter and the abundance of red squirrels. That there are more grasshoppers about when the Dow Jones industrial average plunges. And that cotton prices, business failures, sunspots and the abundance of grouse all seem to be related.*

*   *   *

> *According to cyclists, there are "extraterrestrial forces" that govern the ebb and flow of daily life and influence everything from rainfall to the frequency of international battles. Furthermore, these occurrences are thought to oscillate in predictable patterns, which often coincide—thus the relationship among steel, butter and red squirrels. (An aside to readers in the central, eastern and southern United States: This theory does not hold for your squirrels. Your squirrels are grey. Sorry.)*

*   *   *

> *In his latest book (and his 648th published work), Cycles: The Mysterious Forces That Trigger Events, Mr. Dewey explains that many unrelated and different phenomena seem to operate on identical cycles as if guided by some unseen hand. How else, he asks, can one explain the regular 5.9-year cycle for cotton prices, grouse abundance, et al.? Or the identical 9.6-year cycles in the growth of tree rings, the abundance of bedbugs and the amount of runoff from the Son River in India?*[6] [Reprinted with permission of *The Wall Street Journal*. © Dow Jones & Company, Inc., 1972. All Rights Reserved.]

You may opt for "extraterrestrial forces," but I can tell you how else one can explain the identical 9.6-year cycles in bedbugs and Son River runoff. Mr. Dewey has clearly spent his life examining tens of thousands of time series. Many of these show no regular cycles. (Remember that most cycles, like business cycles, are irregular.) But some, perhaps thousands, *seem* to have regular cycles. (Remember that pinning down cycles in a time series is partly guesswork.) And among those which seem to have cycles, a few match—such as bedbug abundance and Son River runoff. There is nothing unexpected in this. It is a great truth that any large collection of data has some striking patterns in it, which enough searching will find. Those who notice these striking patterns too often imagine that they have found Reality when they have only stumbled over Accident. To begin to provide evidence of a real connection (extraterrestrial or not) between bedbugs and the Son River, we must follow both time series *after* the similar cycles are noticed and see if the regular cycles and their similarity continue. It is much more impressive to look for a pattern you chose in advance, and find it, than to sift the data searching for any pattern whatsoever. Yet even here, if we follow enough cycles from the past, some will persist into the future by accident alone. Consider, for example, the following list of presidents elected every twenty years since 1840.

1840	William H. Harrison
1860	Abraham Lincoln
1880	James A. Garfield
1900	William McKinley
1920	Warren G. Harding
1940	Franklin D. Roosevelt
1960	John F. Kennedy

Every one of these presidents died in office. I learned this from an account in a famous old newspaper feature, "Ripley's Believe It or Not!" Ripley published the list in the late forties, with a question mark following 1960. So the pattern has already persisted for one cycle after it was discovered. Now the question mark follows 1980. Should we warn the candidates that the extraterrestrial forces are out to get them?

NOTES

1. The Producer Price Index has replaced the long-familiar Wholesale Price Index in the Bureau of Labor Statistics' monthly reports on wholesale prices. The BLS feels that by pricing goods at all stages in the production pipeline, the WPI often counted the same price increase twice. The Producer Price Index samples only goods ready for sale to the final customer. Since 1978, the BLS has been engaged in a long-term revision of its wholesale price statistics. Details appear in John F. Early, "Improving the Measurement of Producer Price Change," *Monthly Labor Review,* April 1978, pp. 7–15. The *Monthly Labor Review,* published by the BLS, is a source of current information on many of the topics in this chapter.

2. This is the estimate in 1974 of the Commissioner of Labor Statistics, Julius Shiskin. His article "Updating the Consumer Price Index—An Overview," *Monthly Labor Review,* July 1974, pp. 3–20, is the source of much of the information in this section.

3. More detail can be found in Michael D. Carson, "The 1972–73 Consumer Expenditure Survey," *Monthly Labor Review,* December 1974, pp. 16–23.

4. These figures are again those of the Commissioner of Labor Statistics, from Julius Shiskin, "A New Role for Economic Indicators," *Monthly Labor Review,* November 1977, pp. 3–5.

5. This result is from Maury N. Harris and Deborah Jamroz, "Evaluating the Leading Indicators," *Federal Reserve Bank of New York Monthly Review,* June 1976, p. 170.

6. From Bob Harwood, "Of the Relationship Among Red Squirrels, Butter Prices, Steel," *The Wall Street Journal,* January 12, 1972.

Exercises

Section 1

1. A Bottecchia Giro d'Italia bicycle increases in price as follows:

1973	$275
1975	$325
1977	$350

Give the index numbers (1973 = 100) for 1973, 1975, and 1977.

2. The price received by a farmer for a bushel of soybeans fluctuates as follows:

1972	$4.00
1974	$6.00
1976	$5.00
1978	$7.00

Give a soybean price index (1974 = 100) for all four years.

3. In Exercise 2
   (a) How many points did the soybean price index rise between 1974 and 1978? What percent increase was this for 1978 over 1974?
   (b) How many points did the soybean price index rise between 1972 and 1978? What percent increase was this for 1978 over the 1972 value?

4. The Consumer Price Index (1967 = 100) stood at 170.1 in June 1976 and at 181.8 in June 1977.

   (a) How many points did the index gain between June 1967 and June 1977? What percentage increase was this?
   (b) How many points did the index gain between June 1976 and June 1977? What percentage increase was this?

5. The BLS publishes separate CPI's for major metropolitan areas in addition to the national index. The mean values of two of these indices for 1975 were (1967 = 100)

155.8 for Seattle

161.7 for Atlanta

Can you conclude from this that 1975 consumer prices were higher in Atlanta than in Seattle? Why or why not?

6. A bicycle racer must purchase a bicycle, helmet, riding shorts, and riding shoes with cleats to equip himself. His 1970 purchases and their prices in both 1970 and 1975 are given below.

Commodity	1970 quantity	1970 price	1975 price
Bicycle	2	$300 each	$350 each
Helmet	1	$30 each	$35 each
Shorts	3	$10 each	$10 each
Shoes (pair)	2	$20/pair	$25/pair

Compute a fixed market basket price index (1970 = 100) for 1975 by using these data.

7. A certain guru must purchase for his sustenance only olive oil, loincloths, and copies of the *Atharva Veda* from which to select mantras for his disciples. Here are the quantities and prices of his purchases in 1965 and 1975.

Commodity	1965 quantity	1965 price	1975 quantity	1975 price
Olive oil	20 pints	$0.50/pint	18 pints	$1.00/pint
Loincloth	2	$0.75 each	3	$0.80 each
Atharva Veda	1	$8.50	1	$8.40

From these data find the Guru Price Index (1965 = 100) for 1975.

Section 2

1. Tuition for Indiana residents at Purdue University has increased as follows:

Year	Tuition
1967	$400
1969	$700
1971	$700
1973	$700
1975	$750
1977	$820

Use the annual average CPI's given in Table 1 to restate the tuition in constant 1967 dollars. Make two line graphs on the same axes, one showing current dollar tuition for these years and the other showing constant dollar tuition.

2. A beginning policeman in a major city earned $8000 in 1967. The same job in 1977 paid $15,000. Express the 1977 salary in 1967 dollars. Did policemen's pay in this city keep up with inflation during the decade 1967–1977?

3. The median income of U.S. families in 1970 was $9876. How much is this in 1975 dollars? The median family income in 1975 was $14,094. Did a typical family gain or lose buying power between 1970 and 1975?

4. Much has been written about the inability of middle class families to buy houses at the high prices now prevailing. Here are median prices for new homes sold in each of three periods:

1965	$24,700
1971	$36,400
1977	$53,700

Express the 1965 and 1971 prices in 1977 dollars. Have housing costs increased beyond the overall rate of inflation?

5. The Ford Model T sold for $950 in 1910 and for $290 in 1925. Obtain the current value of the CPI, and use it to restate each of these prices in current dollars.

6. The official definition of "poverty level" is supposed to be adjusted for the effects of inflation. For a family of four, the poverty level was an income of $3743 in 1970 and $5050 in 1975.

   (a) Do these incomes have approximately equal buying power in their respective years, as they should if "poverty level" had the same meaning in both periods?
   (b) Obtain the current value of the CPI and use it to restate the 1975 poverty line in current dollars. That is approximately the current poverty level income for a family of four persons.

7. What would the CPI be in 1975 if the base period were 1930? (You can find this by changing $100 in 1930 dollars into 1975 dollars. The resulting number of 1975 dollars is the 1975 price index (1930 = 100).) What would the current CPI be if the base period were 1930?

8. Here are some examples of how the CPI is often said to overestimate price increases. Comment on each example. In particular, which can be corrected by a new consumer survey because they are due to out-of-date information?

   (a) Exterior house paint prices in the CPI are up, but buyers have switched from the oil paints of 1960 to latex water-base paints, a different product.

(b) Exterior house paint prices are up, but new paints cover better so that less paint is needed to paint a house once. New paints also last longer, so we need to buy them less often.

(c) Exterior house paint prices are up, but buyers have switched from small hardware stores (higher prices) to discount stores (lower prices). So the price actually paid is not up as much as the hardware store price.

(d) Exterior house paint prices are up, but new paints are much more convenient; they are easier to use and to clean up. This convenience has no direct money value, but it means we get greater satisfaction and would be willing to pay more than for less convenient paints.

9. Now that there is more than one CPI, political pressure may lead to creation of a whole family of price indices, each with a market basket tailored to a specific group. In particular, some congressmen want to set up an index for the aged, to be used in place of the general CPI to adjust Social Security payments. Briefly discuss the pros and cons of this proposal, and express your opinion.

Section 3

1. Choose one of the following economic indicators. Write a short essay describing what the indicator measures, why it is economically important, and what statistical procedures are used to compile the indicator. (To help you locate material in the library, the government agency responsible for each index is listed. Each agency publishes material describing the indicators for which it is responsible.)

   (a) Producer Price Indices (Bureau of Labor Statistics, U.S. Department of Labor)

   (b) The Gross National Product (Office of Business Economics, U.S. Department of Commerce)

   (c) The Index of Industrial Production (Federal Reserve Board)

2. As part of a set of social indicators, we wish to include measures of the amount of crime and of the impact of crime on people's attitudes and activities. Suggest some possible indicators in each of the following categories.

   (a) Statistics to be compiled from official sources

   (b) "Objective" information to be collected by a sample survey of citizens

   (c) "Subjective" information on opinions and attitudes to be collected by sample survey

3. The primary official statistics on crime in the United States are found in the *Uniform Crime Report* published by the Federal Bureau of Investigation. These reports provide social indicators of the first type (a) mentioned in Exercise 2, and they attract considerable public attention. Look up a copy of the *Uniform Crime Report* and discuss it in a short essay. What kinds of data

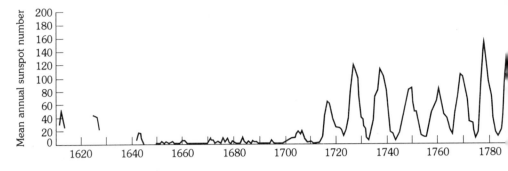

Figure 3. Sunspot numbers, 1610 to 1976. [From "The Case of the Missing Sunspots" by John A. Eddy. Copyright © 1977 by Scientific American, Inc. All rights reserved.]

does it contain? How were they obtained, and how does the collection process compare with the one for obtaining the CPI or unemployment rate? How often is the report published? (The answers to these questions suggest clearly how inferior our social statistics are in comparison with our economic statistics.)

Section 4

1. This is an exercise in seasonal adjustment of time series data. The basic data (from the BLS survey) on unemployment in the state of Indiana for three months in 1972 were:

Month	Labor force	Unemployed
January	2,129,900	120,000
May	2,231,800	115,700
June	2,257,300	139,000

Use these data to compute the unadjusted Indiana unemployment rate for each of these months.

Indiana takes data for the previous 10 years to make seasonal adjustments. For the 10 years prior to 1972,

January had 1.03 times the average monthly unemployment rate for the year;

May had 1.00 times the average monthly unemployment rate for the year;

June had 0.98 times the average monthly unemployment rate for the year.

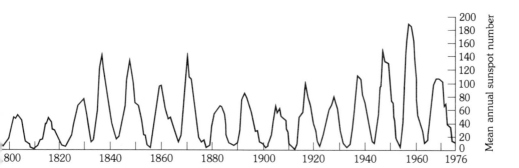

Use these facts to obtain seasonally adjusted Indiana unemployment rates for
January, May, and June 1972.

2. Sales volume for Sears, Roebuck and Co. in December is about 240% of the
average monthly sales volume for the year. (Cheers for Xmas!) This December, Sears' sales volume is $4 billion. What is the seasonally adjusted
sales volume for this December?

3. The BLS publishes the CPI both unadjusted and seasonally adjusted. There
is some seasonal variation owing to weather (food prices), holidays, and so
forth, so the two versions of the CPI often will be slightly different.

   (a) If you want to follow general price trends in the economy, would you
   use the seasonally adjusted or unadjusted version of the CPI? Why?

   (b) If you have a labor contract with an escalation clause tied to the CPI,
   you want your wages to keep pace with the actual prices you must
   pay. Which version of the CPI would you use for this purpose, and
   why?

4. Figure 3 is a plot of the "mean annual sunspot number" from 1610 to 1976.
Since the superstitious think that sunspots influence all manner of earthly
happenings, study of this time series should be interesting.

   (a) The sunspot cycle is the most obvious feature of this time series. About
   how long is the sunspot cycle from maximum to maximum? Does the
   length of the cycle remain constant over time, or are there significant
   variations in the length?

   (b) By tracing the curve of the sunspot maxima over many cycles, I think I
   can see a longer cycle superimposed on the sunspot cycle. Comment
   on this suggestion.

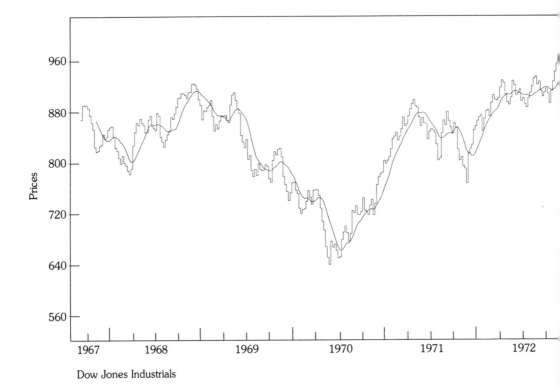

Dow Jones Industrials

Figure 4. The Dow Jones Industrial Average. Any point on the smooth curve represents the average of the Industrials over the previous 10 weeks. Any point on the step curve represents the midweek close for that week. [Graph provided by Dunn and Hargitt, Inc., investment advisors. Reproduced by permission.]

(c) Does this time series show any striking noncyclical phenomena? Describe any you notice.

5. Few time series are watched more closely than the Dow Jones Industrial Average, a weighted average of the prices of the common stocks of 30 major manufacturing corporations. Figure 4 is a plot of the DJIA over a recent 10½-year period. The smoother curve in Figure 4 gives at each point the

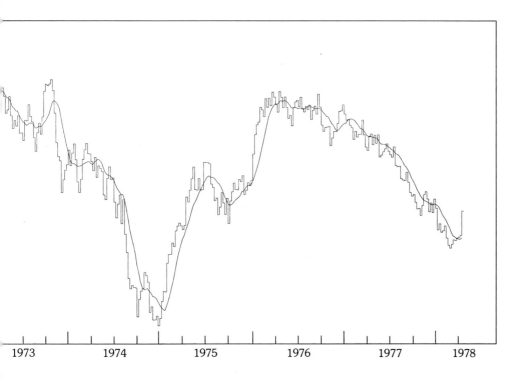

average of the DJIA over the past 10 weeks, which eliminates short-term fluctutations and makes broad movements more visible.

(a) Describe the trend of the DJIA over this period.
(b) Do you see any evidence of cycles that tend to recur at regular periods? If so, can you think of a possible explanation for the timing of the cycles?

Part **III**

Drawing Conclusions from Data

T he experiment was designed, the protocol tested, the subjects assembled, the myriad details dealt with, double-blind enforced, the diagnoses completed. The raw data have been graphed and tabled, averaged and correlated. And now you must state a conclusion that will stand the scrutiny of nitpicking journal editors and jealous rivals.

Sir Peter Medawar, a Nobel laureate, wrote that

> It is a truism to say that a "good" experiment is precisely that which spares us the exertion of thinking: the better it is, the less we have to worry about its interpretation, about what it "really" means.*

In recognition of this wisdom, your experiment was carefully controlled and randomized, so that any effect that appears must be due to your treatment. But wait. You assigned subjects to treatments at random, and while this eliminates systematic bias, there will still be differences between the groups due to the luck of the draw. Will someone charge that the good performance of your favored treatment is just an accidental result of the randomization? Alas, it isn't true that any effect that appears must be due to the treatment. In even the best experiment, the effect might be due to an unlucky randomization that happened to produce very unlike groups of subjects. You need still more statistics to argue convincingly that your effects really are due to the treatment. The methods of statistical inference are designed to draw conclusions taking into account the effects of randomization.

---

*Sir Peter Medawar, *Induction and Intuition in Scientific Thought* (Philadelphia: American Philosophical Society, 1969), p. 15.

We must study these effects of randomization in more detail. The study of randomness is called *probability theory,* a subject of interest to those who wish to understand such worldly pursuits as roulette and state lotteries, as well as to students of the lofty subject of statistics. Probability is the subject of Chapter 7. Since randomization is the foundation of statistical designs for collecting data, probability is the foundation of statistical methods for drawing conclusions from data. Chapter 8 presents some of the concepts behind statistical inference. The methods of inference are largely left to more traditional introductions to statistics, which usually begin where I leave off.

Probability: The Study of Randomness

Even the rules of football agree that tossing a coin avoids favoritism. Favoritism in choosing subjects for a sample survey or allotting patients to treatment and placebo groups is as undesirable as in awarding first possession of the ball in football. Statisticians therefore recommend probability samples and randomized experiments, which are fancy-dress versions of tossing a coin. The central idea of statistical data collection is the deliberate introduction of randomness into the choice or assignment of units. Both tossing a coin and choosing a SRS are *random* in the sense that

- The exact outcome is not predictable in advance.
- Nonetheless, a predictable long-term pattern exists and can be expressed by a relative frequency distribution of the outcomes after many trials.

The inventors of probability samples and randomized experiments in this century were not the first to notice that some phenomena are random in this sense. They were drawing upon a long history of the study of randomness and applying the results of that study to statistics.

Randomness is most easily noticed in many repetitions of games of chance—rolling dice, dealing shuffled cards, spinning a roulette wheel. Chance devices similar to these have been used from remote antiquity to discover the will of the gods. The most common method of randomization was "rolling the bones," tossing several *astragali*. The astragalus is a solid, quite regular bone from the heel of animals that, when thrown, will come to rest on any of four sides. (The other two sides are rounded.) Cubical dice, made of pottery or bone, came later, but even dice existed before 2000 B.C. Gambling on the throw of astragali or dice is, in contrast to divination, almost a modern development; there is no clear record of this vice before about 300 B.C. Gambling reached flood tide

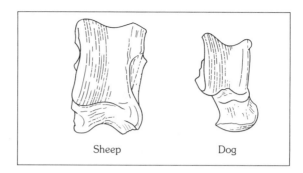

Animal astragali, actual size. [Reproduced by permission of the publishers, Charles Griffin & Company, Ltd., of London and High Wycombe. From F. N. David, *Games, Gods and Gambling,* 1962.]

in Roman times, then temporarily receded (along with divination) in the face of Christian displeasure. Clearly unpredictable outcomes have been noticed and used from the beginning of recorded time.[1]

But none of the great mathematicians of antiquity considered that the outcomes of throwing bones or dice have a clear pattern in many trials. Perhaps this is because astragali and most ancient dice were so irregular that each had a different pattern of outcomes. Or perhaps the reasons lie deeper in the classical reluctance to engage in systematic experimentation. Professional gamblers, not as inhibited as philosophers and mathematicians, must long have known something of the regular pattern of outcomes of dice or cards and adjusted their bets to the "odds" of success. These odds the gamblers often could not guess correctly from experience alone. The systematic study of randomness began (I oversimplify, but not too much) when seventeenth-century French gamblers asked French mathematicians for help. The mathematical study of randomness, *probability theory,* originated with Pierre de Fermat and Blaise Pascal in the seventeenth century and was well developed by the time statisticians took it over in the twentieth century. In this chapter we examine probability, but without mention of the actual mathematics that has grown from the first attempts of the French mathematicians to aid their gambler friends.

Probability is now important for many reasons having little to do with either gambling or collecting data. Many natural and artificial phenomena are random in the sense that they are not predictable in advance but have long-term patterns. For example, the science of genetics is based on Gregor Mendel's observation that for given parents the characteristics of offspring are random with long-run patterns that he began to uncover. And the emission of particles from a radioactive source occurs randomly over time, with a pattern which helped to suggest the cause of radioactivity. Probability theory is used to describe phenomena ("construct models" is the fashionable terminology) in genetics, physics, and many other fields of study. Although we will not meet such applications here, the ideas of this chapter shed light on these fields as well.

1. What is Probability?

Probability begins with the observed fact that some phenomena are random. We do not know whether a pair of dice will give 8 as their sum on the next roll, but by observation we can discover that an 8 will occur on about 14% of a long series of rolls. That 14% is part of the predictable pattern that emerges after many rolls. Since an 8 will appear in 14%, or in fraction form 14/100, of many rolls of two dice, we think of "14 in 100" as the chance of getting an 8 on any one roll. In more formal language, the probability of an 8 when two dice are rolled is 14/100, or in decimal form 0.14. Here is the vocabulary we will use.

Event—any specific collection of the possible outcomes of a random phenomenon.

Frequency of an event—the number of times the event occurs in a sequence of repetitions of the random phenomenon.

Relative frequency of an event—the fraction or proportion of repetitions on which the event occurs. A relative frequency is always a number between 0 and 1.

Probability of an event—if in a long sequence of repetitions the relative frequency of an event approaches a fixed number, that number is the probability of the event. A probability is always a number between 0 (the event never occurs) and 1 (the event always occurs).

We have met frequency and relative frequency before. *Probability* is succinctly defined as long-term relative frequency. Return once more to the bead-sampling experiment summarized in Figure 1 of Chapter 1. This experiment

"What kind of childish nonsense are you working on now?"

consisted of 200 trials of the random phenomenon of drawing a SRS of size 25 from a large box of beads, 20% of which were dark. The outcome "5 dark beads in the sample" had frequency 47 and relative frequency $^{47}/_{200} = 0.23$. The *event* "4, 5, or 6 dark beads in the sample" had frequency 111 and relative frequency $^{111}/_{200} = 0.55$ because on 111 of the 200 trials one of the outcomes 4, 5, or 6 occurred. The number 0.55 is not quite the probability of the event "4, 5, or 6 dark beads," but it is quite close because it is the relative frequency in 200 trials. Making more and more trials would give a relative frequency even closer to the probability. The first three exercises for this section are intended to give you some experience with the somewhat mysterious phenomenon of randomness.

Our "definition" of probability is not intended to satisfy either the mathematician or the philosopher. It merely builds on the observation that long-term relative frequencies often do settle down to fixed numbers, and it provides the terminology to describe this situation. I do not know why the world is made so that randomness exists, but it is an observed fact that it is so made. You should note that not all phenomena are random in our sense. Some (such as dropping a coin from a fixed height and measuring the time it takes to fall) are predictable. That is, repetitions give the same result time after time. Such phenomena we call *deterministic*. They are the subject of much of the older physical sciences. Other phenomena are unpredictable but display no long-term pattern. If, for example, the operator of a roulette wheel has a brake that he can apply at will, he can prevent the relative frequency of "red" from settling down to a fixed probability in the long run.

If an unpredictable phenomenon is to show a long-term pattern, it must at least be true that the *same* phenomenon is repeated, and repetitions are *independent* in the sense that the outcome of one repetition has no effect on the outcome of any other repetition. Both of these conditions are violated if the operator of a roulette wheel can apply a brake to it.

Here are some examples to help you think about probability as long-term relative frequency.

Example 1. If the same (or identical) pennies are tossed repeatedly, the conditions for making statements about probability are present: The *same* coin is being tossed, and since the coin has no memory, the repetitions cannot influence each other. Experience shows that the probability of a head is very close to $^1/_2$. For example, the eighteenth-century French naturalist Comte de Buffon tossed a coin 4040 times and got 2048 heads. That's a relative frequency of 0.507. The statistician Karl Pearson spent some time at the turn of the century making 24,000 tosses. He got 12,012 heads, for a relative frequency of 0.5005.

You may feel that it is obvious from the balance of the coin that the probability of a head is about ½. Such opinions are not always correct. You are invited to take a penny and, instead of tossing it, hold it on end on a hard surface with the index finger of one hand and snap it with the other index finger. The coin will spin for several seconds and then fall with either heads or tails showing. A long series of trials reveals that the probability of a head in this random experiment is not at all close to ½. Moral: We defined probability *empirically* (that is, in terms of observations), and only by observation can we be sure of the approximate value of the probability of an event.

Example 2. Insurance is based on the idea of probability. If, for instance, all males in the United States are observed during their twenty-first year, some will die during that year. Whether a certain 21-year-old male will die is not predictable, but observation of several million such men shows that about 0.18% of them (that's 0.0018 in decimal form) die each year. So if an insurance company sells many policies to 21-year-old men, it knows that it will have to pay off on about 0.18% of them and sets the premium high enough to cover this cost. The number 0.0018 is the *probability* that an American male will die in his twenty-first year.

The probability of an event is a measure of how likely the event is to occur, but does not make sense unless we can at least imagine many independent repetitions of the random phenomenon. When we say that a coin has probability ½ of coming up heads *on this toss* we are applying to a single toss a measure of the chance of a head based on what would happen in a long series of tosses.

The idea of probability is a bit subtle. Here are some fine points to set you thinking.

The "Law of Averages." If in tossing a fair coin we get 10 straight heads, is tails more likely on the next toss? Because the probability of tails is $^1/_2$, many people think that the "Law of Averages" demands that some tails now appear to balance the 10 heads. Are they right?

No. The coin has no memory, so it does not know that it has come up heads 10 straight times. Put more formally, because tosses are independent the probability of a tail on the next toss is still ½.

That answer is correct but not satisfying. It can be checked empirically if you have several years to waste: Toss a penny many times. Every time you get 10 straight heads, record whether the next toss gives heads or tails. In the long run you will find tails occurring about half the time after 10 heads. A better tactic is to seek to understand how the long-run relative frequency of tails can be ½ *without* making up for the 10 straight heads with some extra tails. To understand this, let us suppose that the next 10,000 tosses are evenly divided, giving 5000 heads and 5000 tails. Then the relative frequency of tails after 10,010 tosses is

$$\frac{5000}{10,010} = 0.4995.$$

This is very close to ½. The 10 straight heads are swamped by later tosses and need not be made up for by extra tails. (Of course, the next 10,000 tosses will not yield exactly 5000 tails, but the point is that if the fraction of tails in the long run is about ½, 10 straight heads will not affect this at all.)

Belief in this phony "Law of Averages" can lead to consequences close to disastrous, and not only for gamblers. A few years ago, "Dear Abby" published in her advice column a letter from a distraught mother of eight girls. It seems that she and her husband had planned to limit their family to four children. But when all four were girls, they tried again. And again, and again. After seven straight girls, even her doctor had assured her that "the law of averages was in our favor 100 to one." Unfortunately for this couple, having children is like tossing coins: Eight girls in a row is highly unlikely, but once seven girls have been born it is not at all unlikely that the next child will be a girl. And she was.

"So the law of averages doesn't guarantee me a girl after seven straight boys, but can't I at least get a group discount on the delivery fee?"

What Probability Doesn't Say. There is, you may think, little difference between the statements

(a) "In many tosses of a fair coin, the fraction of heads will be close to ½."

(b) "In many tosses of a fair coin, the number of heads will be close to
    one-half the number of tosses."

Alas. Statement (a) is true, and is what we mean by saying that the probability
of a head is ½. Statement (b) is false; in many tosses of a fair coin, the number of
heads is certain to deviate more and more from one-half the number of tosses.
This is, as Pooh would say, mystigious. To see why it is true, consider the
following example.

Number of tosses	Number of heads	Fraction of heads	Difference between number of heads and ½ number of tosses
100	51	0.51	1
1000	510	0.51	10
10,000	5100	0.51	100
100,000	51,000	0.51	1000

There it is: The *fraction* of heads stays close to ½ while the *number* of heads
departs more and more from one-half the number of tosses. (Again, this exact
outcome is unlikely, but it is typical of what happens in many repetitions.)

Probability versus Odds. Probability was born in a gambling hall, from
whence it climbed to more respectable status. Back in the gambling hall, the
chance of an event often is stated in terms of "odds" rather than probability. At
the risk of encouraging you to misapply your knowledge of probability, let us
learn to translate odds into probabilities.

Example 3. You are rolling two dice, a common way of losing money.
You would very much like to roll a 7, and you have heard that the odds
against this are 5 to 1. What's the probability of a 7? Odds of 5 to 1 means
that failing to roll a 7 happens five times as often as success. In the long
run, then, five of every six tries will fail, and one will succeed in rolling a 7.
The probability of a 7 is now clear. It is one out of six, or

$$\frac{1}{6} = 0.167.$$

Notice that odds of 5 to 1 are not the same as "1 in 5." The latter means
probability 1/5, while the former gives the probability as 1/6.

The recipe illustrated in Example 3 is

> **Odds of A to B against an outcome means that the probability of that outcome is $B/(A + B)$**

Thus if the odds against the favorite in a horse race are 3 to 2, this is equivalent to that horse having probability 2/5 of winning.

Enough of conceptualizing about probability. In practice, we often wish to describe a random phenomenon by assigning probabilities to its various outcomes. This is called giving a *probability model* for the phenomenon. Such a probability model is often based partly on observation and partly on our feeling about what the probability of the outcomes should be. These models are useful for thinking about random phenomena and for computing the probabilities of complicated events from probabilities of simple events. We shall soon meet some examples. But the correctness of the model must always be judged by comparing it with observations of the random phenomenon it is supposed to describe because probabilities are defined empirically.

The mathematics of probability begins by describing properties of all legitimate probability models. We need only two such properties.

A. The probability of any event must be a number between 0 and 1.

B. If we assign a probability to every possible outcome of a random phenomenon, the sum of these probabilities must be 1.

Properties A and B of any probability model follow from our understanding of probability as long-run relative frequency. Any relative frequency is a number between 0 and 1, and this is property A. Because some outcome must occur on each repetition, the sum of the relative frequencies of all possible outcomes must be 1, and this is property B. Here are some simple examples of probability models.

> **Example 4.** On the basis of several thousand repetitions of the experiment of randomly selecting a voter on October 31, 1972, the Harris polling organization gave the following probability model for voter presidential preferences.
>
> | Outcome | Probability |
> |---|---|
> | Would vote for Nixon | 0.60 |
> | Would vote for McGovern | 0.32 |
> | Undecided | 0.08 |

This example would be described more naturally as "relative frequencies in a sample." Instead we have thought of it as giving (from sample observations) a model for the random experiment of choosing an adult American at random on October 31, 1972 and asking for whom he or she would vote. Notice that all three outcomes have probabilities between 0 and 1 (property A), and that these probabilities add to 1 (property B).

Example 5. You are about to begin gambling with a die. (That's the singular of "dice." The study of "house-houses," "mouse-mice," "die-dice," and so on must set speakers of simpler languages muttering.) On inspection, you feel that the die is "fair," and so you assign each of the six faces the same probability of coming up. This is a legitimate probability model because it satisfies properties A and B. It is also correct for many dice. Whether or not it is correct for your die can be decided only by tossing the die many times and checking whether the long-term relative frequencies are close to $1/6$ for each face.

Outcome	Probability
⚀	1/6
⚁	1/6
⚂	1/6
⚃	1/6
⚄	1/6
⚅	1/6

Summing Up: What is Probability?

I have stressed that long-term stability of relative frequencies is an observed fact in some circumstances. This observation provided a way to think about probability in detail, coming at last to properties A and B, which characterize all legitimate probability models. But long-term relative frequency is not the only important interpretation of what probability is. We could instead define the probability of an event as a number between 0 and 1 that represents my personal assessment of the chance that the event will occur. ("I think Dallas has a 30% chance of going to the Superbowl this year.") Probabilities interpreted this way are called *personal probabilities* or *subjective probabilities* because they express personal opinion. Your personal probability for the event that Dallas will play in this year's Superbowl is no doubt not the same as mine.

Personal probability has several advantages over the relative frequency interpretation. The probability that Dallas will go to the Superbowl this year, or the probability that my firm's bid will be high enough to win a certain contract, cannot be thought of as long-term relative frequencies because these probabilities refer to a single, unrepeatable chance phenomenon. So personal probability has a wider scope than long-term relative frequency. The other advantage of a subjective interpretation of probability is that it provides a meaningful definition of probability, not just a way of thinking about randomness. Long-term relative frequency is not truly a definition of probability; we can never watch an endless series of trials to be certain that the relative frequency settles down to a probability. So "long-term relative frequency" refers to an ideal never quite attained. Personal probability, on the other hand, is exactly what it pretends to be: a subjective assessment of chance.

The disadvantage of personal probability is that it is personal. When long-term relative frequencies do exist, my personal assignment of probabilities may bear no relation to the pattern of outcomes actually observed. Which interpretation of probability is favored in applications varies with the weight accorded to these advantages and disadvantages. Personal probability predominates when the insight and partial information of a decision-maker are important, as in business decisions and gambling on horses. Frequency ideas rule when repeatable events are in question, as in quality control of mass-produced items and gambling on roulette wheels.

I prefer to keep the frequency interpretation of probability foremost in your mind, partly because of my own view of the relative usefulness of frequency versus subjective interpretations, and partly for pedagogic reasons. But we will meet both interpretations, not always sharply distinguished, through the rest of this book. The clash of interpretations can be played down because any assignment of probabilities must have properties A and B, whether interpreted as personal assessment of chance or as long-term relative frequency. The users of probability in science, business, gambling, and statistics begin by assigning probabilities to outcomes. However you interpret the notion of probability, the rules describing legitimate assignments of probabilities to outcomes stand forever firm.

2.   Finding Probabilities by Simulation

Suppose that a couple plans to have children until they have a girl or until they have four children, whichever comes first. What is the probability that they will have a girl among their children? To answer probability questions such as this, we first construct a probability model. In this case, it seems reasonable to assume that:

(a) Each child has probability ½ of being a girl and ½ of being a boy.

(b) The sexes of successive children are independent.

But how can we compute the probability of a somewhat complex event (having a girl in four tries) from this simple model?

There are two ways of finding the probability of complex events from known probabilities of simple events. One is to master the mathematics of probability theory, a worthwhile endeavor that we wish to avoid. The other is to *simulate* (imitate or run a small scale model of) the random phenomenon by using our trusty companion, the table of random digits. The idea is to imitate the probability model by using the properties of random digits, then use the table to simulate many repetitions of the phenomenon. The relative frequency of any event eventually will be close to its probability, so that many repetitions give a good estimate of probability.

We will simulate the child-bearing strategy of the couple discussed above.

Example 6. Step 1.   A single random digit simulates the sex of a single child as follows

$$0, 1, 2, 3, 4 \qquad \text{the child is a girl}$$
$$5, 6, 7, 8, 9 \qquad \text{the child is a boy.}$$

Step 2.   To simulate one repetition of the child-bearing experiment, use successive random digits until either a girl or four children are obtained. Using line 130 of Table A, we find

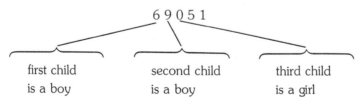

and the couple stops at three children, having obtained a girl.

Step 3.   Simulate many repetitions and use the relative frequency of the event "the couple has a girl" to estimate its probability. Here is the result of using line 130. To interpret the digits, we have written G for girl and B for boy under them, have drawn vertical lines between repetitions, and under each repetition have written "+" if a girl was born and "−" if not.

690	51	64	81	7871	74	0	951	784	53	4	0	64	8987
BBG	BG	BG	BG	BBBG	BG	G	BBG	BBG	BG	G	G	BG	BBBB
+	+	+	+	+	+	+	+	+	+	+	+	+	−

In 14 repetitions, a girl was born 13 times. So our estimate of the probability that this strategy will produce a girl is

$$\frac{13}{14} = 0.93.$$

"I've had it! Simulated wood, simulated leather, simulated coffee, and now simulated probabilities!"

This example of simulation deserves careful discussion. Step 1 simulates part (a) of the probability model because we assigned 5 of the 10 possible digits to the outcome "girl." Because all 10 are equally likely to occur at any point in the table, any one table entry has probability $5/10$ or $1/2$ of indicating "girl." Here are further examples of this idea.

Example 7. Simulate an event that has probability $3/10$ as follows

0, 1, 2	the event occurs
3, 4, 5, 6, 7, 8, 9	the event does not occur.

Example 8. To simulate an event that has probability 0.33, use *two* digits to simulate one repetition, with

00, 01, 02, . . . , 31, 32	the event occurs
33, 34, 35, . . . , 98, 99	the event does not occur.

Example 9. Simulate a random trial having *three* possible outcomes with probabilities $2/10$, $3/10$, and $5/10$ as follows:

0, 1	outcome A occurs
2, 3, 4	outcome B occurs
5, 6, 7, 8, 9	outcome C occurs.

Step 2 in Example 6 simulates one repetition of the child-bearing process because successive random digits are independent, and therefore simulate successive independent births. In Step 3, 14 repetitions were made, and the relative frequency of bearing a girl was found. The relative frequency 0.93 is not a very precise estimate of the probability because only 14 repetitions were made. With mathematics we could show that if the probability model given is correct, then the true probability of having a girl is 0.938. Our simulated answer came quite close.

Now that we have seen a first illustration of the mechanics of simulation, let's pause for a long look at some of the ideas.

The probability model is the foundation of any computation of probability, whether by simulation or by mathematics. It may appear a bit shady to begin the process of finding a probability by assuming that we already know some other probabilities, but not even mathematics can give you something for nothing. The idea is to state the basic structure of the random phenomenon, and then use simulation to move from the basics to the probabilities of more complicated events. The model is based on opinion and past experience; if it does not correctly describe the random phenomenon, the probabilities derived from it by simulation also will be incorrect. So will the probabilities a mathematician might obtain by his black arts, like that 0.938 in the childbearing example. That is the "true" probability of a girl only if the sexes of successive children are independent and each child is equally likely to be male or female.

The probability models we will meet have two parts:

(a) A simple random phenomenon with a small number of possible outcomes. These are assigned probabilities with properties A and B as discussed in Section 1.

(b) Independent trials of phenomena such as part (a) describes, sometimes repetitions of the same random phenomenon (like the successive children in Example 6), and sometimes independent trials of different random phenomena.

To Find the Probability of an Event by Simulation

(a) Specify a probability model for the random phenomenon by assigning probabilities to individual outcomes and assuming independence where appropriate.

(b) Decide how to simulate the basic outcomes of the phenomenon, using assignments of digits to match the assignment of probabilities (Step 1).

(c) Decide how to simulate a single repetition of the random phenomenon by combining simulations of the basic outcomes (Step 2).

(d) Estimate the probability of an event by the relative frequency of the event in many repetitions of the simulated phenomenon (Step 3).

The random digits play their usual role as substitutes for physical randomization. We could physically simulate the behavior of our probability model. The childbearing strategy might be simulated by an urn* with a number of balls, half red and half white. Red balls are female children and white balls are males. Draw a ball to represent the sex of the first child; you are equally likely to get a female or a male. Replace the ball (to maintain the half red and half white mixture), stir the urn well, and draw again. That's the second child. And so on. Urns and balls could always be used to do our simulations. But random digits have the same advantages in simulation as in random sampling; they are faster and more accurate than physical randomization. Thinking of physical models like urns full of balls does help to take the mystery out of random digits in simulation. Both the urn and the random digits make a manageable copy of the random phenomenon under study.

The precision of a simulation for estimating probabilities increases as more repetitions are used. This is simply a restatement of the "definition" of probability as long-term relative frequency. But there is a close connection with the precision of sample statistics from probability samples. Both statistics from large samples and probabilities simulated from many trials are highly precise in the sense that repeating the whole process would give nearly the same answer. Indeed, estimating an unknown probability p by a relative frequency $\hat{p}$ is substantially the same as estimating a population proportion p by a sample proportion $\hat{p}$.

More extensive simulations

Simulation is a common procedure for finding probabilities too difficult to compute, even for those who know probability theory. Such simulation is always done by a computer, which can be programmed to do thousands of repetitions in a short time. Large numbers of repetitions give very precise results, but the ideas remain those we have met. Simulations in science and engineering are usually accompanied by a statement of precision in the form of the standard deviation of the relative frequency used to estimate the unknown probability. Recall from Section 3 of Chapter 5 that the standard deviation of the sample statistic is a common way of stating precision in sampling as well. The next example illustrates the close connection between sampling and simulation by asking a probability question about a sampling procedure.

> **Example 10.** Suppose that 80% of all consumers prefer Brand A instant coffee to Brand B. If a SRS of 10 consumers is chosen, what is the probability that 7 or more of them prefer Brand A? (This is a question about the long-term pattern of results of a SRS. That long-term pattern, which has been with us since Chapter 1, can be described now in terms of the probability of various outcomes.)
>
> We first need a probability model. Here is the model we will simulate:

---

*I would like to call this container a pot, but protocol forbids. Pots full of balls of varying colors are officially called "urn models" in probability theory.

(a) Each consumer has probability 8/10 of preferring Brand A.

(b) The preferences of successive consumers are independent.

This is a good model for a SRS of size 10 from a population of which 80% (8/10) favor Brand A *if* the population is large.* Now for the simulation.

Step 1.   One digit simulates one consumer's preference:

> 0, 1, 2, 3, 4, 5, 6, 7   Brand A
>
> 8, 9   Brand B.

Step 2.   To simulate one repetition of the experiment, use 10 random digits. Count how many of these digits are 0, 1, ... , 7. This is the number of consumers in a sample of size 10 who prefer Brand A.

Step 3.   We do this 10 times starting at line 110 of Table A. Here are the 10 repetitions.:

38448	48789	5 prefer Brand A
ABAAB	ABABB	
18338	24697	7 prefer Brand A
ABAAB	AAABA	
39364	42006	9 prefer Brand A
ABAAA	AAAAA	
76688	08708	6 prefer Brand A
AAABB	ABAAB	
81486	69487	6 prefer Brand A
BAABA	ABABA	
60513	09297	8 prefer Brand A
AAAAA	ABABA	
00412	71238	9 prefer Brand A
AAAAA	AAAAB	
27649	39950	7 prefer Brand A
AAAAB	ABBAA	
59636	88804	6 prefer Brand A
ABAAA	BBBAA	
04634	71197	9 prefer Brand A
AAAAA	AAABA	

---

*That's a fine point. Think of an urn filled with 80% red balls (Brand A) and 20% white balls (Brand B). We begin to draw our SRS, and the first ball is red. Now the urn contains *less* than 80% red balls. So the preferences of the 10 consumers in our SRS are *not* independent because each consumer drawn changes the makeup of the remaining population. When the population is large, the dependence is so small we can neglect it. Drawing a red ball from an urn containing 80,000 reds and 20,000 whites does not noticeably change the chance of a red on the second draw.

The event "7 or more prefer Brand A" occurs in 6 of the 10 repetitions, so we estimate its probability to be

$$\frac{6}{10} = 0.6.$$

Ten repetitions gives quite poor precision. By mathematics or more extensive simulation we can find that the true probability that 7 or more of a SRS of 10 consumers prefer Brand A is 0.88. I did a set of 50 trials and got a relative frequency of $41/50 = 0.82$, which is closer to home.

The probability we estimated by simulation in Example 10 depends on the assumption that 80% of the population prefer Brand A. If that population proportion is different, the probabilities of various outcomes in the SRS are different. A complete study of probabilities for a SRS would include a description of how these probabilities change when the population proportion changes.

The building and simulation of random models is a powerful tool of contemporary science, yet a tool that can be understood in substance without advanced mathematics. What is more, several attempts to simulate simple random phenomena will increase your understanding of probability more than many pages of my prose. Having in mind these two goals of understanding simulation for itself and understanding simulation to understand probability, let us study a more extensive example.

Example 11. We are studying the Asian Stochastic Beetle, and we observe that females of this insect have the following pattern of reproduction

20% of females die without female offspring

30% have one female offspring

50% have two female offspring.

What will happen to the population of Asian Stochastic Beetles: Will they increase rapidly, barely hold their own, or die out? (Notice that we can ignore the male beetles in studying reproduction, as long as there are some around for certain essential purposes. Notice also that we are studying only a single population. It is common for ecologists to use probability models and simulation in their study of the interaction of several populations, such as predators and prey.)

The reproduction of a single female is simulated as follows

0, 1   dies without female offspring

2, 3, 4,   has one female offspring

5, 6, 7, 8, 9 has two female offspring.

Moreover, we will assume that female beetles reproduce independently of each other.

To answer the question "What is the future of the Asian Stochastic Beetle?" we will simulate the female descendents of several female beetles until they either die out or reach the fifth generation. Beginning in line 122 of the table of random digits,

$$13873 \qquad 81598 \qquad 95052 \qquad 90908 \qquad 73592,$$

the first beetle dies without offspring (1). The second has one offspring (3); she in turn has two offspring (8); the first of these has two (7) and the second has one (3) offspring. So the fourth generation of this family contains three female beetles.

We need a better way to record this simulation. Figure 1 records the female descendents of seven female Asian Stochastic Beetles. Each family is followed to the fifth generation. The two families on the left are those we just met, and the random digits beside each beetle in these families remind you how line 122 was used "from left to right in each generation of offspring." The fifth generation has 29 female beetles from the original seven. It is clear that the population of Asian Stochastic Beetles will increase rapidly until crowding, shortage of food, or increased predator populations change the reproductive pattern we have simulated.

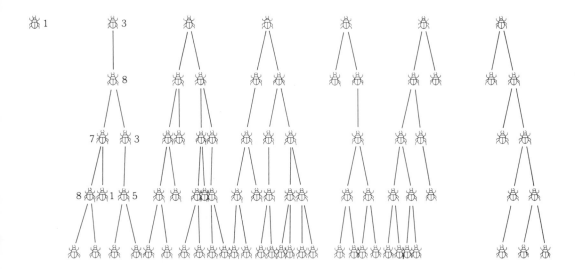

Figure 1. Simulation of the descendants of seven female stochastic beetles. 20% die without female offspring; 30% have one female offspring; 50% have two female offspring.

3.   State Lotteries and Expected Values

In 1964, the conservative state of New Hampshire caused a furor by introducing state-run gambling in the form of a lottery to raise public revenue without raising taxes. The furor subsided quickly as larger states adopted the idea, until almost a third of the states now sponsor lotteries. A lottery uses random selection to distribute prizes among those who have bought tickets. How can we measure the value of a lottery ticket, or compare the return we can expect from buying lottery tickets with that from gambling in Las Vegas? It is not enough to know the probability of winning. The amount won is also important because one lottery might offer many small prizes and another might award a few large prizes. The larger prizes might compensate for the lower probability of winning, making the second lottery a better bet. We need a way to take into account both the probability of winning and the amount won to compute the *expected value* of a lottery.

State lotteries have introduced ever more gimmicks and special prizes in an attempt to keep public interest high, and these make computation of the expected value of a ticket difficult. So let us go back a few years and study the original, uncluttered New York State Lottery.

> **Example 12.** The New York State Lottery awarded, for each one million tickets sold,
>
> | | |
> |---:|:---|
> | 1 | $50,000 prize |
> | 9 | $5000 prizes |
> | 90 | $500 prizes |
> | 900 | $50 prizes. |
>
> The winning tickets were drawn at random from those sold. The total value of these prizes is
>
> $$(\$50{,}000) + (9)\,(\$5000) + (90)\,(\$500) + (900)\,(\$50) = \$185{,}000.$$
>
> Since this amount is divided among 1,000,000 tickets, the average winnings per ticket is
>
> $$\frac{\$185{,}000}{1{,}000{,}000} = \$0.185$$
>
> or 18½ cents. This is the *expected value* of a ticket—the average value of an individual ticket.

Because lottery tickets cost 50 cents, New York State paid out a bit less than 40% (18½ over 50 is 0.37 or 37%) of the amount wagered by ticket buyers, and kept over 60%. This is typical of state lotteries. By way of comparison, gambling in Las Vegas pays out 85% to 92% of the amount wagered, depending on which game you choose. State lotteries are a poor bet. Professional gamblers avoid them, not wanting to waste money on so bad a bargain. Politicians avoid them for reasons nicely put by Nelson Rockefeller when he was Governor of New York: "I'm afraid I might win." Almost everyone else in lottery states plays. Surveys usually show that about 80% of the adult residents have purchased at least one lottery ticket. Why is such a poor bet so popular? Lack of knowledge of how poor the bet is plays a role. So does skillful advertising by the state. But the major attraction is probably the lure of possible wealth, no matter how unlikely the jackpot is. Many people find 50 cents a week a fair price for the entertainment value of imagining themselves rich. As one Carmen Brutto of Harrisburg, Pa., said in a newspaper interview, "My chances of winning a million are better than my chances of earning a million."[3]

There is another way of calculating the expected value of a New York State lottery ticket that can be applied more generally than the method of Example 12. (It gives the same answer; I just wish to organize the arithmetic differently.)

> **Example 13.** Buying a ticket in the New York State Lottery and observing how much you win is a random phenomenon. Because winning tickets are drawn at random, each ticket has 1 chance in 1,000,000 to win $50,000, 9 chances in 1,000,000 to win $5000, and so on. Here is a probability model for the amount won by one ticket

"I think the lottery is a great idea. If they raised taxes instead, we'd have to pay them."

Amount	Probability
$50,000	1/1,000,000
$5000	9/1,000,000
$500	90/1,000,000
$50	900/1,000,000
$0	999,000/1,000,000

The total probability of winning anything is 1/1000; that is, 1000 out of 1,000,000 tickets win something. The expected value can be found by multiplying each possible outcome by its probability, and summing.

$$(\$50,000)\left(\frac{1}{1,000,000}\right) + (\$5000)\left(\frac{9}{1,000,000}\right)$$

$$+ (\$500)\left(\frac{90}{1,000,000}\right) + (\$50)\left(\frac{900}{1,000,000}\right) + (\$0)\left(\frac{999,000}{1,000,000}\right)$$

$$= \$0.185 \text{ (just as before)}.$$

We have arrived at the following definition.

> **If a random phenomenon has numerical outcomes $a_1, a_2, \ldots, a_k$ that have probabilities $p_1, \ldots, p_k$, the *expected value* is found by multiplying each outcome by its probability and then summing over all possible outcomes. In symbols,**

$$\text{Expected value} = a_1 p_1 + a_2 p_2 + \ldots + a_k p_k.$$

The expected value is an average of the possible outcomes, but an average in which outcomes with higher probability count more. The expected value is the average outcome in another sense as well. *If the random phenomenon is repeated many times independently, the mean value of the outcomes approaches the expected value.* Statisticians call this fact the *law of large numbers.* Because of this law, the "house" in a gambling operation is not gambling at all. The average winnings of a large number of customers will be quite close to the expected value. The house has calculated the expected value ahead of time and knows what its take will be in the long run.

The law of large numbers is closely related to our definition of probability: In many independent repetitions, the relative frequencies of the possible outcomes will be close to their probabilities, and the average outcome obtained will be close to the expected value. Expected values, since they give the "average outcome" in two senses, are widely used. Some nongambling examples are given in the exercises. Here is another gambling example.

Example 14. The numbers racket is a well-entrenched illegal gambling operation in the poorer areas of most large cities. The New York City version works as follows. You choose any one of the 1000 three-digit numbers 000 to 999 and pay your friendly local numbers runner 50 cents to enter your bet. Each day, one three-digit number is chosen at random and pays off $300.

Amount	Probability
$300	1/1000
$0	999/1000

$$\text{Expected value} = (\$300) \left(\frac{1}{1000}\right) + (\$0) \left(\frac{999}{1000}\right) = \$0.30 .$$

Notice that this 30-cent expected value is considerably higher than the 18½-cent expected value of a 50-cent New York State Lottery ticket. Crime pays.

Because the criminal organization receives many thousands of bets through its runners each day, by the law of large numbers it will have to pay out very close to 30 cents per ticket. The rest is profit. This guaranteed profit might be endangered if bets were dependent, that is, if many customers chose to bet on the same number. Some numbers (such as 333) are so popular that they are "cut numbers"; a bet on such a number pays off less than $300 if it is the winning number. For a time in the good old days, Willie Mays' batting average was a cut number. The cut numbers protect the racket against very large payouts when a popular number wins.

You might trust the state lottery to conduct an honest random drawing, but perhaps you would not trust the local branch of organized crime.* How, then, does the numbers racket choose a three-digit number each day in a way its customers can trust? The winning number is the last three digits of a large number published every day in the newspaper. In New York, this number is the total amount bet at a local racetrack. If $1,454,123 was bet at the track, 123 is the winning number. The racetrack handle is printed in newspapers, so the winning number is publicly available. And the last three digits of a large number such as this are close to being random digits. (Can you see why the first three digits are not close to random?) There was a time when the numbers racket in Jersey City, New Jersey paid off on the winning New York State Lottery number. That's adding insult to the injury of a higher payout. In Cleveland, Pittsburgh, and Indianapolis the numbers game payoff is based on certain stock market tables printed in the regional edition of *The Wall Street Journal*. This edition is printed in Cleveland, and gamblers appear at the printing plant at

---

*Maybe you shouldn't trust anyone. The New York State Lottery was closed down for almost a year in 1975 and 1976 after it was discovered that ticket holders were being cheated by the inclusion of unsold ticket numbers in the prize drawings.

midnight to learn the winning number. A *Journal* official told a reporter "The cars line up bumper to bumper. You should see some of them—they're solid chrome."[4] Those, I suppose, are the racketeers, not the players. The law of large numbers guarantees the house a steady income and regular players a steady deficit.

As with probability, it is worth exploring a few fine points about expected values and the law of large numbers.

How large is a large number? The law of large numbers says that the empirical average of many trials will be close to the expected value; it doesn't say how many trials are needed to achieve this. That depends on the *variability* of the random phenomenon. Gambles with extremely variable outcomes (like state lotteries) require very large numbers of trials to ensure that the average outcome is close to the expected value. In 1977, Tom and Philomena Drake set out to invest $20,000 in lottery tickets in the hope of winning big. That would buy 40,000 tickets in the old New York lottery of Example 12. Even 40,000 tickets are not enough to be confident that their average winnings will be close to the expected value of 18½ cents. They might well either lose everything or make a profit.* Much of the psychological allure of gambling is its unpredictability for the player; the business of gambling rests on the fact that the result is not unpredictable for the house. Though most forms of gambling are less variable than state lotteries, the layman's answer to the applicability of the law of large numbers is usually that the house plays often enough to rely on it, but you don't.

Is there a winning system? Serious gamblers often follow a system of betting in which the amount bet on each play depends on the outcome of previous plays. You might, for example, double your bet on each spin of the roulette wheel until you win—or, of course, until your fortune is exhausted. Such a system tries to take advantage of the fact that you have a memory even though the roulette wheel doesn't. Can you beat the odds with a system? No. Mathematicians have established a stronger version of the law of large numbers which says that your average winnings (the expected value) remain the same so long as successive trials of the game (such as spins of the roulette wheel) are independent and you do not have an infinite fortune to gamble with. Sorry.

How can I find expected values? You know the mathematical recipe, but that requires that you know the probability of each outcome. Expected values too difficult to compute in this way can be found by simulation. The procedure is as before: Give a probability model and simulate many repetitions. By the law of large numbers, the average outcome of these repetitions will be close to the expected value.

> **Example 15.** If a fair coin is tossed repeatedly, what is the expected number of trials required to obtain the first head? (Here is the same question in a different disguise: What is the expected number of children a

---

*The Drakes actually invested in the Pennsylvania lottery, which like most present state lotteries has highly improbable "millionnaire drawings" that make them even more variable than the older versions. I learned about the Drakes in an Associated Press dispatch appearing in the *Lafayette Journal and Courier* of May 26, 1977.

couple must have in order to have a girl?) Each random digit simulates one toss, with odd meaning head and even meaning tail. One repetition is simulated by as many digits as are required to obtain the first odd digit. Here are simulated trials using line 131 of the table of random digits, with vertical bars dividing the repetitions.

$$05|007| \quad 1|663|2 \quad 81|1|9|4 \quad 1|487|3| \quad 041|9|7|$$

There are 13 trials, which required the following numbers of tosses to the first head:

$$2, 3, 1, 3, 3, 1, 1, 2, 3, 1, 3, 1, 1 .$$

The average number of tosses required was

$$(2 + 3 + 1 + \ldots + 1)/13 = 25/13 = 1.9 .$$

and this is our estimate of the expected value. (It is a good estimate; the true expected value is 2.)

A Summing Up

Probability and expected values give us a language to describe randomness. Random phenomena are not haphazard or chaotic, any more than random sampling is haphazard. Randomness is instead a kind of order in the world, a long-run regularity as opposed to either chaos or a determinism that fixes events in advance. When randomness is present, probability answers the question, "How often in the long run?" and expected value answers the question, "How much in the long run?" The two answers are tied together by the definition of expected value in terms of probabilities.

It appears more and more that randomness is embedded in the way the world is made. Albert Einstein reacted to the growing emphasis on randomness in physics by saying, "I cannot believe that God plays dice with the universe." Lest you have similar qualms, I remind you again that randomness is not chaos but a kind of order. Our immediate concern, however, is man-made randomness— not God's dice, but Reno's. In particular, statistical designs for data collection are founded on deliberate randomizing. The order thus introduced into the data is the basis for statistical inference, as we have noticed repeatedly and will study more thoroughly in the next chapter. If you understand probability, statistical inference is stripped of mystery. That may console you as you contemplate the remark of the great economist John Maynard Keynes on long-term orderliness: "In the long run, we are all dead."

NOTES

1. More detail can be found in the opening chapters of Florence N. David, *Games, Gods, and Gambling* (London: Charles Griffin and Co., 1962). The historical information given here comes from this excellent and entertaining book.

2. Stochastic Beetles are well known in the folklore of simulation, if not in entomology. They are said to be the invention of Arthur Engle of the School Mathematics Study Group.

3. Quoted in an article by Frank J. Prial in *The New York Times* of February 17, 1976.

4. Quoted in an Associated Press dispatch appearing in the *Lafayette Journal and Courier* of March 7, 1976.

5. The information in this exercise is again from Florence N. David, *Games, Gods, and Gambling* (London: Charles Griffin and Co., 1962), p. 7.

Exercises

Section 1

1. Hold a penny on edge on a flat surface with the index finger of one hand and snap it with your other index finger so it spins rapidly until finally falling with either heads or tails upward. Repeat this 50 times and record the number of heads. What is your estimate of the probability of a head in this random experiment? (In doing this experiment, disregard any trial in which the penny does not spin for several seconds or in which it hits an obstacle.)

2. Suppose that we toss a penny. Experience shows that the probability (long-term relative frequency) of a head is close to ½. Suppose, then, that we toss the penny repeatedly until we get a head. What is the probability that the first head comes up in an *odd* number of tosses (1, 3, 5, and so on)? To find out, repeat this experiment 50 times, and keep a record of the number of tosses needed to get a head on each of your 50 trials.

   (a) From your experiment, estimate the probability of a head on the first toss. What value should we expect this probability to have?

   (b) Use your empirical results to estimate the probability that the first head appears on an odd-numbered toss.

3. Roll a pair of dice 100 times and record the sum of the dots on the upward faces in each trial. What is the relative frequency of 8 among these 100 trials? (It is said in the text that in the long run this relative frequency will settle down to the probability of an 8, which is about 0.14.)

4. Probability is a measure of how likely an event is to occur. Match one of the probabilities that follow with each statement of likelihood given. (The probability is usually a much more exact measure of likelihood than is the verbal statement.)

$$0, 0.01, 0.3, 0.6, 0.99, 1$$

   (a) This event is impossible. It can never occur.

   (b) This event is certain. It will occur on every trial of the random phenomenon.

   (c) This event is very unlikely, but it will occur once in a while in a long sequence of trials.

   (d) This event will occur more often than not.

5. (a) A gambler knows that red and black are equally likely to occur on each spin of a roulette wheel. He observes 5 consecutive reds occur and bets heavily on black at the next spin. Asked why, he explains that black is "due by the law of averages." Explain to the gambler what is wrong with this reasoning.

(b) After hearing you explain why red and black are still equally likely after 5 reds on the roulette wheel, the gambler moves to a poker game. He is dealt 5 straight red cards. He remembers what you said, and assumes that the next card dealt in the same hand is equally likely to be red or black. Is the gambler right or wrong, and why?

6. The odds against being dealt three of a kind in a five-card poker hand are about 49-to-1. What is the probability of being dealt three of a kind?

7. An American roulette wheel contains compartments numbered 1 through 36 plus 0 and 00. Of the 38 compartments, 0 and 00 are colored green, 18 of the others are red, and 18 are black. A ball is spun in the direction opposite to the wheel's motion, and bets are made on the number where the ball comes to rest. A simple wager is *red-or-black*, in which you bet that the ball will stop in (say) a red compartment. If the wheel is fair, all 38 compartments are equally likely.

(a) What is the probability of a red?
(b) What are the odds against a red?

8. Below are four assignments of probability to the outcomes of rolling a die. Which, if any, is *correct* for this die can be discovered only by rolling the die. But some of the models are not *legitimate* assignments of probability. Which are legitimate and which are not, and why?

Probability

Outcome	Model 1	Model 2	Model 3	Model 4
⚀	1/7	1/3	1/3	1
⚁	1/7	1/6	1/6	1
⚂	1/7	1/6	1/6	2
⚃	1/7	0	1/6	1
⚄	1/7	1/6	1/6	1
⚅	1/7	1/6	1/6	2

9. Make an assignment of probabilities to outcomes in each of the following cases. Be sure that your assignment has properties A and B.

   (a) A coin is tossed and lands heads or tails. (Assume that the coin is balanced so that either face is equally likely to come up. Probability models are often based on assuming balance or symmetry. In this case, observation supports the assumption.)

   (b) A coin is spun and lands heads or tails. (Use the result of Exercise 1 to construct a probability model that is approximately correct.)

   (c) Two coins are tossed, the four possible outcomes being (head, head), (head, tail), (tail, head), and (tail, tail). (There are many legitimate models here, that is, assignments of probability satisfying properties A and B of the text. Try to assign approximately correct probabilities. Experiment if necessary.)

10. Using the understanding of probability as long-run relative frequency, explain carefully why the following rule is true in any legitimate probability model.

    "The probability that an event does not occur is one minus the probability that the event does occur."

11. You are gambling with a fair coin, which has probability ½ of coming up heads on each toss. You are allowed to choose either 10 or 100 tosses.

    (a) On the first bet, you win if the relative frequency of heads is between 0.4 and 0.6. Should you choose 10 tosses or 100 tosses?

    (b) On the second bet, you win if exactly half of the tosses are heads. Should you choose 10 tosses or 100 tosses?

Section 2

1. An opinion poll selects Americans over 18 at random and asks them, "If the election were held today, would you vote for Demo or Public?" Explain carefully how you would use Table A to simulate the response of one voter in each of the following situations.

   (a) Of all Americans over 18, 50% would vote for Demo and 50% for Public.

   (b) Of all Americans over 18, 60% would vote for Demo and 40% for Public.

   (c) Of all Americans over 18, 40% would vote for Demo, 40% would vote for Public, and 20% are undecided.

   (d) Of all Americans over 18, 53% would vote for Demo and 47% for Public.

2. Use Table A to simulate the responses of 10 independently chosen Americans over 18 in each of the four situations of Exercise 1.

   For situation (a), use line 110.

   For situation (b), use line 111.

For situation (c), use line 112.

For situation (d), use line 113.

3. A student is enrolled in a self-paced course that allows three attempts to take an examination on the material. To pass the course, the student must pass the examination. The student does not study and has probability 2/10 of passing on any one attempt by luck. What is the probability of passing on at least one of the three attempts? (Assume the attempts are independent because the student is given a different examination on each attempt.)

    (a) Explain how you would simulate the student's three tries by using random digits.

    (b) Simulate this experiment 50 times by using Table A beginning at line 120. What is your estimate of the student's probability of passing the course?

    (c) Do you think the assumption that the probability of passing is the same on each trial is realistic? Why or why not?

4. A wildcat oil driller estimates that the probability of finding a producing well when he drills a hole is 0.1. If he drills 10 holes without finding oil, he will be broke. What is the probability that he will go broke? Answer this question as follows.

    (a) State a simple probability model for drilling 10 holes.

    (b) Explain how you will use random digits to simulate drilling one hole and then explain how to simulate drilling 10 holes.

    (c) Use Table A beginning at line 140 to simulate 20 repetitions of drilling 10 holes. Estimate from this simulation the probability that the wildcatter will go broke.

5. Tossing four astragali was the most popular game of chance in Roman times. The scoring for the four possible outcomes of a single bone was

broad convex side of bone	4
broad concave side of bone	3
narrow flat side of bone	1
narrow hollow side of bone	6

Many throws of a present-day sheep's astragalus show that the approximate probability distribution for these scores is[5]

Score	Probability
1	1/10
3	4/10
4	4/10
6	1/10

The best throw of four astragali was the "Venus," when all the four upper-most sides were different.

(a) Explain how to simulate the throw of a single astragalus and of four independent astragali.

(b) Simulate 25 throws of four astragali. Estimate the probability of throwing a "Venus."

6. The Pennsylvania State Lottery (in 1974 and neglecting a few gimmicks) worked as follows. Each lottery ticket bears a six-digit number. Suppose that you have ticket 123456. A weekly winning number is drawn at random so every six-digit number has the same chance to be drawn. You win

$50,000 if the winning number is 123456

$2000 if the winning number is X23456 or 12345X

$200 if the winning number is XX3456 or 1234XX

$40 if the winning number is XXX456 or 123XXX

where X stands for any nonmatching number.

(a) Explain how to simulate one play of this lottery by using Table A to draw the weekly winning number.

(b) Simulate 20 plays of the lottery and record the weekly winning numbers drawn.

(c) On which plays did your ticket 123456 win a prize, and what were the values of the prizes won?

(d) Based on your 20 trials, what is your estimate of the probability of winning a prize if you hold one ticket in this lottery?

7. From your experience with random digits, you can find the exact value of the probability of winning the Pennsylvania lottery as it is given in Exercise 6.

(a) How many different six-digit numbers are there?

(b) How many of these will pay you each of

$50,000 $2000 $200 $40

if drawn as the weekly winning number?

(c) Now find the total number of winning numbers that will pay you a prize. From this and part (a) find the probability of winning a prize.

8. Females of the Benign Boiler Beetle have the following reproductive pattern

40% die without female offspring

40% have one female offspring

20% have two female offspring.

(a) Explain how you would use random digits to simulate the number of offspring of a single female Benign Boiler Beetle.

(b) Simulate the family trees to the fifth generation of enough of these beetles to decide whether the population will definitely die out, will definitely grow rapidly, or appears to barely hold its own. (Simulate the offspring of at least five beetles.)

9. A nuclear reactor is equipped with two independent automatic shutdown systems to shut down the reactor when the core temperature reaches the danger level. Neither system is perfect. System A shuts down the reactor 90% of the time when the danger level is reached. System B does so 80% of the time. The reactor is shut down if *either* system works.

   (a) Explain how to simulate the response of system A to a dangerous temperature level.
   (b) Explain how to simulate the response of system B to a dangerous temperature level.
   (c) Both systems are in operation simultaneously. Combine your answers to (a) and (b) to simulate the response of both systems to a dangerous temperature level. Explain why you cannot use the same random digit to simulate both responses.
   (d) Now simulate 100 trials of the reactor's response to an emergency of this kind. Estimate the probability that it will shut down.

10. The game of craps is played with two dice. The player rolls both dice, and wins immediately if the outcome (the sum of the faces) is 7 or 11. If the outcome is 2, 3, or 12 the player loses immediately. If he rolls any other outcome, he continues to throw the dice until he either wins by repeating the first outcome or loses by rolling a 7.

   (a) Explain how to simulate the roll of a single fair die. (It is easiest to use one digit and skip those not needed to represent outcomes.) Then explain how to simulate a roll of two fair dice.
   (b) Use Table A beginning at line 114 to simulate three plays of craps. Explain at each throw of the dice what the result was.
   (c) Now that you understand craps, simulate 25 plays and estimate the probability that the player wins.

11. A famous example in probability theory shows that the probability that at least two people in a room have the same birthday is already greater than ½ when 23 people are in the room. The probability model for this situation is

   (a) The birth date of a randomly chosen person is equally likely to be any of the 365 dates of the year.
   (b) The birth dates of different people in the room are independent.
   Explain carefully how you would simulate the birth dates of 23 people to see if any two have the same birthday. Do the simulation *once* by using line 139 of Table A. [*Comment:* This simulation is most easily done by letting three-digit groups stand for the birth dates of successive people. Some groups must be skipped in doing this. The simulation is too lengthy to ask you to repeat it many times, but in principle you can find the probability of

matching birthdays by routine repetition. This birthday problem is too hard for most of your math major friends to solve, so it shows the power of simulation.]

12. In Example 10, I commented that the responses of successive units drawn in a SRS are not truly independent but that the dependence is negligible if the population is large. Let's examine this comment.

   (a) An urn contains 10 balls, of which 8 are red and 2 are white. One ball is drawn at random. What is the probability that it is red? That it is white?

   (b) The first ball is the first unit in our SRS from this population of 10 balls. We set it aside, and draw a second ball from the urn at random. If the first ball was red, what is now the probability that the second is red? (*Hint:* What are the colors of the 9 balls left in the urn?)

   (c) If the first ball was white, what is now the probability that the second is red?

Because the probability that the second ball drawn is red when we know the color of the first ball drawn changes with the color of the first ball, the first and second responses in our SRS are *not* independent.

   (d) Now answer the questions of parts (a), (b), and (c) again, this time for an urn containing 100,000 balls, of which 80,000 are red and 20,000 white.

The probability of a red on the second draw still changes with the color of the first draw. But the difference is now so small that we can ignore it. That leaves us with the probability model of Example 10. No probability model exactly describes a real world random phenomenon, so we are satisfied with this one.

Section 3

1. The Connecticut State Lottery (in its original simple form and ignoring some gimmicks that raise the payout slightly) awarded at random, for each 100,000 50-cent tickets sold,

1	$5000 prize
18	$200 prizes
120	$25 prizes
270	$20 prizes.

What is the expected value of the winnings of one ticket in this lottery?

2. (a) What is the expected number of female offspring produced by a female Asian Stochastic Beetle? (See Example 11 of Section 2 for this insect's reproductive pattern.)

(b) What is the expected number of female offspring produced by a female Benign Boiler Beetle? (See Exercise 8 of Section 2.)

(c) Use the law of large numbers to explain why the population should grow if the expected number of female offspring is greater than 1, and die out if this expected value is less than 1. Do your expected values in parts (a) and (b) confirm the results of the simulations of these populations done in Section 2?

3. An insurance company sells a term life insurance policy that pays $10,000 if the insured dies within the next 5 years. The insured is a 21-year-old male, and the probability that he will die in each of the next 5 years can be found in *mortality tables* that record what fraction of men die at each age. Since the company collects a premium of $50 per year, the net payout if the insured dies is $10,000 less the premiums collected. Here is the table containing this information.

Outcome	Probability	Payout
Insured dies at 21	0.0018	$9950
Insured dies at 22	0.0018	$9900
Insured dies at 23	0.0019	$9850
Insured dies at 24	0.0019	$9800
Insured dies at 25	0.0020	$9750
Insured lives past 25	0.9906	0

What is the expected value of the payout on this policy?

4. Grocery store games are required by law to disclose the available prizes and the odds of winning each prize. From this information you can compute the expected value of the game. Here is the prize disclosure for one such game.

PRIZE DISCLOSURE

Prize values	Number of prizes	Odds of winning	
		With 1 card	With 13 cards
$1000	26	1 in 120,000	1 in 9231
$100	130	1 in 24,000	1 in 1847
$10	650	1 in 4800	1 in 370
$2	2600	1 in 1200	1 in 93
$1	49,400	1 in 64	1 in 5

A customer receives one card on each visit to the store.

(a) What is the expected value of one card?

(b) What is the expected value of 13 cards?

5. A "psychic" runs the following ad in a magazine.

   Expecting a baby? Renowned psychic will tell you the sex of the unborn child from any photograph of the mother. Cost $10. Money-back guarantee.

   This may be a profitable con game. Suppose that the psychic simply replies "girl" to each inquiry. In the worst case, everyone who has a boy will ask for her money back. Find the expected value of the psychic's profit by filling in the table below.

Sex of child	Probability	Profit in this case
Male		
Female		

6. Use the probability distribution of prizes for the Pennsylvania State Lottery (Exercise 7 in Section 2) to compute the expected value of the winnings from one ticket in this lottery.

7. Simulate the offspring (one generation only) of 100 female Asian Stochastic Beetles. What is your estimate of the expected number of offspring of one such beetle, based on this simulation? Compare the simulated value with the exact expected value you found in Exercise 2(a). Explain how your results illustrate the law of large numbers.

8. Section 2 opened with a discussion of a couple who plan to have children until they have either a girl or four children. What is the expected number of children that such a couple will have? (We don't know enough mathematics to find this expected value from the definition, so we must use simulation. Do the simulation as outlined in Section 2 and make 30 repetitions.)

9. If your state has a state lottery, find out what percent of the money bet is returned to the betters in the form of prizes. What percent of the money bet is used by the state to pay lottery expenses, and what percent is net revenue to the state that can be used for other purposes?

10. Write a brief essay giving arguments for and against state-run lotteries as a means of financing state government. Conclude the essay by explaining why you support or oppose such lotteries.

Chapter 8

Formal Statistical Reasoning

H ow shall we come to sound conclusions from empirical evidence? How shall we decide, for example, whether large doses of vitamin C reduce the incidence of colds and flu? Or how shall we decide whether the 1970 draft lottery was biased in favor of men born early in the year? It may happen that the evidence is so clear that no reasonable person would argue with our conclusion. If in a randomized and controlled experiment 80% of the placebo group caught colds during the winter, while only 30% of the vitamin C group did so, who would hesitate to recommend vitamin C? If in 1970 the 31 birthdates in December had all got draft numbers less than 50, the unfairness of the lottery would have been obvious. So it may happen that simply describing the data by graphs or descriptive statistics points to the conclusion. But it happens at least as often that the data only hint at the proper conclusion. In the Toronto vitamin C trial (Example 7 on page 64), 18% of the placebo group and 26% of the vitamin C group were free of illness. Is this good evidence that vitamin C prevents colds and flu? Or is the difference (26% versus 18%) so small that we should instead conclude that vitamin C is not noticeably more effective than a placebo? Common sense is not enough to answer such questions. We need systematic methods for drawing conclusions from data. Such methods make up the subject of *statistical inference.*

Drawing conclusions in pure mathematics is a matter of starting from a hypothesis and using accepted methods of logical argument to prove without doubt that the conclusion follows. Empirical science argues in almost the reverse order. If vitamin C prevents colds, we would expect the vitamin C group to have fewer colds than the placebo group; the vitamin C group did have fewer colds; so this is evidence in favor of vitamin C's effect. This is an *inductive argument* (from consequences back to a hypothesis) as opposed to the *deductive arguments* of pure mathematics (from hypothesis to consequences). Inductive arguments do not produce proof. The good health of the vitamin C group *might* be due to something other than the vitamin C they took. You have no doubt heard that "statistics cannot prove anything." True enough. Neither can any other kind of inductive argument. Outside mathematics there is no proof. But inductive arguments can be quite convincing, and statistical arguments are sometimes among the most convincing.

In Chapter 7 I side-stepped the heated philosophical argument over "What is probability?" by explaining probability theory simply as the vocabulary used to describe the observed phenomenon of randomness. Now we again face an area of controversy, controversy that this time we cannot quite ignore. Since inductive arguments seem in general harder to grasp than deductive arguments, it is not surprising that statisticians disagree over the proper kind of reasoning for drawing conclusions from data. I have chosen to give most of this chapter over to the kinds of statistical reasoning most favored by users of statistics. Even theoreticians who believe that the users have poor taste cannot fault me for a choice solidly based on such empirical grounds. The final section of the chapter will bring to light some of the controversies surrounding statistical inference by introducing a way of thinking about the subject quite different from those appearing in earlier sections.

One principle is agreed upon by all sides in the discussion about statistical inference: *Formal statistical reasoning is based on the laws of probability.* The views of statistics presented in this chapter are based on the approach to probability emphasized in Chapter 7. Probability there was long-term relative frequency.* So formal statistical reasoning is based on considering what would happen in many repetitions of the experiment or survey. This entire chapter is a working out of that idea.

Here is a distinction that you first met in Chapter 1 and that you absolutely must keep in mind when thinking about statistical inference.

> A *parameter* is a number describing the population. For example, the proportion of the population with some special property is a parameter that we call p. In a statistical inference problem, the population parameters are fixed numbers, but we do not know their values.
>
> A *statistic* is a number describing the sample data. For example, the proportion of the sample with some special property is a statistic that we call $\hat{p}$. Statistics change from sample to sample. We use the observed statistics to get information about the unknown parameters.

1.   Estimating with Confidence

Senator Bean wants very much to know what fraction of the voters in his state plan to vote for him in the election, now only a month away. (This unknown proportion of the population of voters is a *parameter p.*) He therefore commis-

*Another school of thought holds that statistical reasoning should begin with the "personal" or "subjective" idea of probability as a personal assessment of chance. Of this I will say nothing.

"It was a numbers explosion."

sions a poll. Being rich, he can afford a genuine SRS of 1000 registered voters. Of these voters, 570 say that they plan to vote for Bean. That's a reassuring 57% of those polled. (This observed proportion of the sample is a *statistic*, $\hat{p} = 0.57$.) But wait. Bean and his pollster know very well that a different sample of 1000 voters would no doubt have produced a different response. Perhaps 59% or 55%. Or perhaps even 51% or (horrors) 49%. How should the senator interpret the 57% sample result?

If you shouted "unbiasedness and precision" to the senator's dilemma, you may join the chorus of the wise. Unbiasedness tells us that the results of a simple random sample will be correct on the average; the mean of the $\hat{p}$'s from a large number of SRS's will be the true fraction p of voters who favor Bean. A statement of precision describes how variable the results of repeated sampling would be. Both unbiasedness and precision describe aspects of the distribution of results that would occur if many independent SRS's were taken from the same population. That distribution of results is the *sampling distribution* of the statistic $\hat{p}$, discussed in Section 3 of Chapter 4. There the sampling distribution was the long-run distribution of relative frequencies of the values of $\hat{p}$. Since long-run relative frequencies are probabilities, we can now think of the sampling distribution of a statistic as a *probability distribution*.

A probability distribution is interpreted exactly like a relative frequency distribution. Instead of describing a particular set of data, it describes the distribution that would arise after many, many repetitions. For example (to return to the senator), suppose that in fact 55% of the several million voters in Bean's state plan to vote for him. What would be the pattern (probability distribution) of the sample proportion $\hat{p}$ favoring Bean in many, many independent SRS's of size 1000?

We could discover this pattern by a very long simulation. Fortunately, it is also possible to discover the pattern by mathematics, and I will tell you the answer. The probability distribution of the sample proportion $\hat{p}$ favoring Bean in a SRS of size 1000 when 55% of the population favor Bean is very close to the normal distribution with mean 0.55 and standard deviation 0.015. If you don't believe me, go and simulate several thousand SRS's of size 1000 from such a population and make a histogram of the several thousand values of $\hat{p}$ you get. That histogram will look very much like the normal curve with mean 0.55 and standard deviation 0.015. (Because $\hat{p}$ is unbiased, you could guess that the mean of the distribution of $\hat{p}$ is 0.55 when the true p is 0.55.) We did a similar "simulation" in the bead-sampling experiment of Chapter 1, with results that appear in Figures 11 and 12 of Chapter 4. That the probability distribution of a sample proportion $\hat{p}$ is close to normal is not news to you.

Figure 1 shows the probability distribution of the sample proportion $\hat{p}$ in Senator Bean's case. This distribution shares the properties of all normal curves which were described in Section 3 of Chapter 5. But now we can use the language of probability instead of relative frequency. The 68-95-99.7 rule can be stated for Figure 1 as follows.

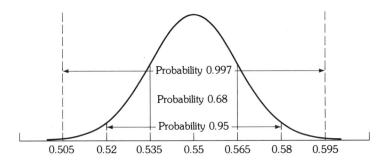

Figure 1. The probability distribution of a statistic. The sample proportion $\hat{p}$ of a SRS of size 1000 drawn from a population in which the population proportion is $p = 0.55$ has the normal probability distribution shown. The probability is 0.95 that $\hat{p}$ will fall within two standard deviations of p.

- The probability is 0.68 that a SRS of size 1000 from this population will have a $\hat{p}$ between 0.535 and 0.565 (because 0.535 is one standard deviation below the mean and 0.565 is one standard deviation above).

- The probability is 0.95 that a SRS of size 1000 from this population will have a $\hat{p}$ between 0.52 and 0.58, that is, within two standard deviations of the mean.

- The probability is 0.997 (almost certainty) that a SRS of size 1000 from this population will have a $\hat{p}$ between 0.505 and 0.595.

Senator Bean is becoming impatient. We are telling him how $\hat{p}$ behaves for a known population proportion p. He wants to know what he can say about p (the *unknown* fraction of voters who are for him) once he has taken a sample and observed $\hat{p} = 0.57$. Patience, senator. We're coming to that. Chew on this line of argument.

A. When a SRS of size 1000 is chosen from a large population of which a proportion p favor Bean, the proportion $\hat{p}$ of the sample who favor Bean has approximately the normal distribution with mean equal to p and standard deviation 0.015.*

B. By the 68-95-99.7 rule, the probability is 0.95 that $\hat{p}$ will be within 0.03 (two standard deviations) of its mean p.

C. That's exactly the same as saying that the probability is 0.95 that the unknown p is within 0.03 of the observed $\hat{p}$.

Aha! We see that 95% of all such SRS's produce a $\hat{p}$ within 0.03 of the true p. Bean's SRS had $p = 0.57$. So he can be quite confident that the true proportion of voters who favor him lies in the interval between

$$\hat{p} - 0.03 = 0.57 - 0.03 = 0.54$$

and

$$\hat{p} + 0.03 = 0.57 + 0.03 = 0.60.$$

Bean can be confident that he's favored by between 54% and 60% of the population.

Be sure you understand the ground of his confidence. There are only two possibilities. *Either* the true p lies between 0.54 and 0.60, *or* Bean's SRS was one of the few samples for which $\hat{p}$ is not within 0.03 of the true p. Only 5% of all samples give such inaccurate results because of the 95% rule. It is not impossible

---

*Actually the standard deviation changes when p changes. But for p anywhere between $p = 0.3$ and $p = 0.7$, the standard deviation of $\hat{p}$ is within 0.001 of 0.015. You can find more detailed information in Section 2.

that Bean had the bad luck to draw a sample for which $\hat{p}$ misses p by more than 0.03, but over many drawings this will happen only 5% of the time (probability 0.05). We say that Bean is "95% confident" that he is favored by between 54% and 60% of the voters.

Bean is a cautious man, and a method that will be right 95% of the time and wrong 5% of the time is not good enough for him. Very well, let's use the 99.7% rule. The probability is 0.997 that $\hat{p}$ falls within 0.045 (three standard deviations) of its mean p. So Bean can be 99.7% confident that the true p falls between

$$\hat{p} - 0.045 = 0.57 - 0.045 = 0.525$$

and

$$\hat{p} + 0.045 = 0.57 + 0.045 = 0.615.$$

Now he's smiling. A method that is correct 997 times in 1000 in the long run (probability 0.997) estimates that he is safely ahead.

You have just followed one of the most common lines of reasoning in formal statistical inference. Here it is in general terms.

A. **A statistic computed from a sample survey or a randomized experiment has a probability distribution (a regular long-term pattern of outcomes) because of the randomization used to collect the data.**

B. **This probability distribution changes when the population parameter changes. That is, the behavior of the sample statistic reflects the truth about the population.**

C. **Knowing this probability distribution, we can give a recipe for finding from the sample statistic an interval that has probability β of covering the unknown true parameter value. This is called a *confidence interval* with confidence level β.**

Step C is the definition of a confidence interval. (β is the Greek letter beta, the symbol commonly used in statistics to denote the confidence level.) Steps A and B show how confidence intervals are based on a knowledge of the probability distributions of sample statistics. This knowledge is obtained by mathematics and provides recipes for confidence intervals in many different settings. We saw two such recipes, and some of their background, in the case of Senator Bean. In our new vocabulary, if a SRS of size 1000 gives a sample proportion $\hat{p}$, we can make the following statements.

- A 95% confidence interval for the population proportion p is the interval from $\hat{p} - 0.03$ to $\hat{p} + 0.03$.

- A 99.7% confidence interval for the population proportion p is the interval from $\hat{p} - 0.045$ to $\hat{p} + 0.045$.

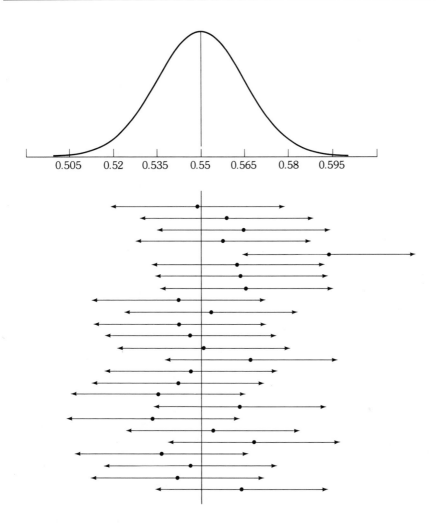

Figure 2. Behavior of confidence intervals in repeated sampling. The intervals above are 95% confidence intervals for p computed from 25 independent SRS's of size 1000 drawn from a population in which $p = 0.55$. The intervals vary from sample to sample, but all except one contain the true value of p.

The key idea of a 95% confidence interval is that the recipe gives a correct answer (an interval that covers the true parameter value) 95% of the time in the long run. A 90% confidence interval is right 90% of the time, and a 99.7% confidence interval is right 99.7% of the time. Figure 2 shows the results of simulating 25 trials of the 95% confidence interval $\hat{p} \pm 0.03$ based on a SRS of size 1000 from a population with $p = 0.55$. The normal curve at the top of the figure is the probability distribution of the sample proportion $\hat{p}$, in this case having a mean equal to 0.55 (the true value of p) and standard deviation 0.015.

Below are the confidence intervals resulting from 25 SRS's. The dot in the center of each interval is the observed value of $\hat{p}$ for that sample. The intervals shift from sample to sample, but only one of the 25 fails to cover the true p, represented by the vertical line. In the long run, the interval from $\hat{p} - 0.03$ to $\hat{p} + 0.03$ would cover the true p in 95% of all the samples drawn. This is the essential idea; as always, some fine points should be pondered. To these we now turn.

What confidence does not mean. For Senator Bean's poll, a method with probability 95% of being right estimated that he was favored by between 0.54 and 0.60 of the voters in his state. Be careful: We *cannot* say that the probability is 95% that the true p falls between 0.54 and 0.60. It either does or does not; we don't know which. No randomness is left after we draw a particular sample and get from it a particular interval, 0.54 to 0.60. So it makes no sense to give a probability. All we can say is that the interval 0.54 to 0.60 was obtained by a method that covers the true p in 95% of all possible samples. That's what we mean in saying we are 95% confident that p lies between 0.54 and 0.60.

High confidence is not free. Why would anyone use a 95% confidence interval when 99.7% confidence is available? Look again at Senator Bean. His 95% confidence interval was $\hat{p} \pm 0.03$, while 99.7% confidence required a wider interval, $\hat{p} \pm 0.045$. It is true in general that there is a tradeoff between the confidence level and the width of the interval. To obtain higher confidence from the same sample, you must be willing to accept a larger margin of error (wider interval). The way to get higher confidence and still have a short interval is to take a larger sample. The precision of a sample statistic increases as the sample size increases. That means that for a fixed level of confidence, the confidence interval grows ever shorter as the sample size increases. Or, if you prefer, the confidence level for an interval of the same length grows ever higher as the sample size increases.

It's a poor cook who uses the same recipe in every meal. The Gallup Poll's probability sampling method is such that when a sample of size 1000 is taken, we can be 95% confident that the announced sample proportion is within 4 points of the true population proportion. (Table 1 on page 18 gives this information in more detail. That table shows that the confidence statement I just made holds whenever the true population p falls between 0.3 and 0.7. Otherwise the margin of error is even smaller.) In more formal language a 95% confidence interval for the population proportion p based on a sample of size 1000 drawn by Gallup's probability sampling method is the interval from $\hat{p} - 0.04$ to $\hat{p} + 0.04$.

Now the 95% confidence interval for a SRS of size 1000 was $\hat{p} - 0.03$ to $\hat{p} + 0.03$. That recipe is wrong for the Gallup Poll because Gallup does not use a SRS. The recipe for a confidence interval depends on how the data were collected. Section 2 gives some more detailed recipes for use when you have a SRS. To use them when the data are not a SRS is tantamount to pouring catsup into your egg drop soup.

You might notice that Gallup's sampling method is less precise (has a wider 95% confidence interval) than a SRS of the same size. That is the price paid for the convenience of cluster sampling.

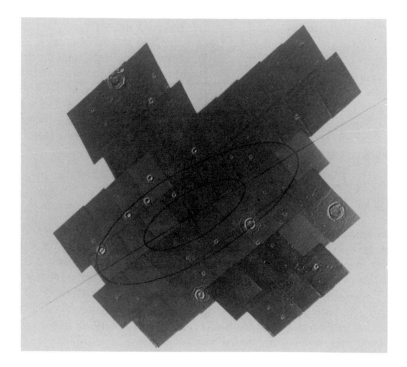

Confidence regions for a Mars landing. Predicting the landing site of an unmanned spacecraft is an exercise in estimation. The ellipses drawn on this photomosaic of the Chryse Planitia region of Mars represent NASA's before-the-act estimation of the landing site of the 1976 Viking 1 mission. The outer ellipse is a 99% confidence region; the probability was 50% that touchdown would occur within the inner ellipse. [Photo courtesy of NASA.]

Confidence intervals are used whenever statistical methods are applied, and some of the recipes are complicated indeed. But the idea of 95% confidence is always the same: The recipe employed catches the true parameter value 95% of the time when used repeatedly.

2.   Confidence Intervals for Proportions and Means*

Although the idea of a confidence interval remains ever the same, the specific recipes vary greatly. The form of a confidence interval depends first on the parameter you wish to estimate—a population proportion, or mean, or variance,

---

*This section is optional. It contains material more technical than the rest of the book and presents formulas that require a calculator for easy use.

or whatever. The second influence is the design of the sample or experiment; estimating a population proportion from a stratified sample requires a different recipe than if the data come from a SRS. The sampling design and the parameter to be estimated usually determine the form of the confidence interval. The final details depend on the sample size and the confidence level you choose. The two recipes in this section are quite useful, but in comparison with the statistician's full array of confidence intervals for all occasions, these two resemble a tool kit containing only a chisel and a roofing square. These are useful tools, but only sometimes.

Confidence Intervals for a Population Proportion

When a large SRS is selected from a population, the sampling distribution of the sample proportion $\hat{p}$ is close to a normal distribution. This normal sampling distribution has mean equal to the population proportion p because $\hat{p}$ is unbaised as an estimator of p. When the sample size n is 1000 and p is between 0.3 and 0.7, the standard deviation of $\hat{p}$ is close to 0.015. So by the 68-95-99.7 rule, $\hat{p} \pm (2)(0.015)$ is a 95% confidence interval for p. The same reasoning leads to the conclusion that whenever we know the standard deviation of the sampling distribution of $\hat{p}$, a 95% confidence interval for p is

$$\hat{p} \pm (2) \text{ (standard deviation of } \hat{p})$$

because 95% of the probability in the normal distribution of $\hat{p}$ falls within 2 standard deviations of the mean p.

By mathematics we can discover the standard deviation of the normal sampling distribution of $\hat{p}$. Here is the full story.

Sampling Distribution of a Sample Proportion

Suppose that a SRS of size n is drawn from a population in which the proportion p of the units have some special property. The proportion of units in the sample having this property is the statistic $\hat{p}$. When n is large, the sampling distribution $\hat{p}$ is approximately normal with mean p and standard deviation

$$\sqrt{\frac{p(1-p)}{n}}.$$

Figure 3 illustrates this sampling distribution. The standard deviation of $\hat{p}$ depends on the true p and on the sample size n. For example, when $n = 1000$ and $p = 0.5$, the standard deviation of $\hat{p}$ is

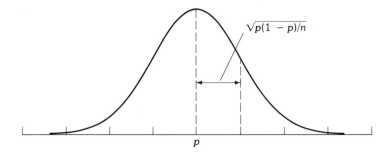

Figure 3. The distribution of $\hat{p}$ in a large SRS. The probability distribution of $\hat{p}$ is approximately normal with mean equal to the population proportion p. The standard deviation is $\sqrt{p(1-p)/n}$, which decreases as larger sample sizes n are chosen.

$$\sqrt{\frac{(0.5)(0.5)}{1000}} = (0.00025)^{\frac{1}{2}} = 0.0158$$

and when $p = 0.3$ (or 0.7), the standard deviation is

$$\sqrt{\frac{(0.3)(0.7)}{1000}} = (0.00021)^{\frac{1}{2}} = 0.0145.$$

These more exact results lie behind the statement in Section 1 that for p between 0.3 and 0.7 the standard error of $\hat{p}$ in a SRS of size 1000 is close to 0.015. We now know that a more accurate recipe for a 95% confidence interval for p, taking p and n into account, is

$$\hat{p} \pm 2 \sqrt{\frac{p(1-p)}{n}}.$$

But this formula is unusable because we don't know p. (If we did know p, we would not need to settle for 95% confidence!) When n is large, $\hat{p}$ is quite close to p. So at the cost of a further approximation, the estimated standard deviation formed by replacing p by $\hat{p}$ can be employed in the recipe. So the final version of a 95% confidence interval for p is

$$\hat{p} \pm 2 \sqrt{\frac{\hat{p}(1-\hat{p})}{n}}.$$

All of this started with the fact that in any normal distribution there is probability 0.95 within 2 standard deviations of the mean. What if we want a 90%

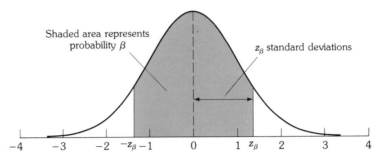

Standard deviations above and below the mean

Figure 4. Critical points of the normal distributions. The critical point z_β is the number such that any normal distribution assigns probability β to the interval from z_β standard deviations below the mean to z_β standard deviations above it.

confidence interval, or a 75% confidence interval? For any number β between 0 and 1 $(0 < \beta < 1)$ there is a number z_β such that any normal distribution has probability β within z_β standard deviations of the mean. Figure 4 illustrates the situation, and Table 1 lists the numbers z_β for various choices of β. These numbers are often called *critical points* for the normal distributions. For example, any normal distribution has probability 0.90 within 1.64 standard deviations of its mean. And any normal distribution has probability 0.95 within 1.96 standard deviations of its mean. (The number $z_{0.95} = 1.96$ was rounded off to 2 in giving the 68-95-99.7 rule.)

Table 1

NORMAL CRITICAL POINTS

β	z_β	β	z_β
0.50	0.67	0.80	1.28
0.55	0.76	0.85	1.44
0.60	0.84	0.90	1.64
0.65	0.93	0.95	1.96
0.70	1.04	0.99	2.58
0.75	1.15	0.999	3.29

NOTE: Any normal distribution has probability β within z_β standard deviations on either side of its mean.

Now for the final assault on p. The sample proportion $\hat{p}$ is within z_β standard deviations of p with probability β. This is the same as stating that the unknown p

is within z_β standard deviations of the observed $\hat{p}$ with probability β. Using the estimated standard deviation of $\hat{p}$ produces at last the following recipe.

Confidence Interval for a Population Proportion

Suppose that a SRS of size n is drawn from a population of units of which proportion p have some special characteristic. When n is large, an approximate level β confidence interval for p is

$$\hat{p} \pm z_\beta \sqrt{\frac{\hat{p}(1 - \hat{p})}{n}}.$$

Please note that this recipe is valid only when a SRS is chosen. Even then it is only approximately correct, for two reasons. First, the sampling distribution of $\hat{p}$ is only approximately normal. Second, the estimated standard deviation of $\hat{p}$ is only approximately equal to the exact standard deviation $\sqrt{p(1 - p)/n}$. Both of these approximations improve as the sample size n increases. For samples of size 100 and larger, the recipe given is quite accurate. It is often used for sample sizes as small as 25 or 30. If you have a small sample, or if your sample is not a SRS, please visit your friendly local statistician for advice. Now for some examples.

Example 1. Senator Bean, our acquaintance from Section 1, took a SRS of 1000 registered voters. Of these, 570 supported the Senator in his bid for re-election. So

$$\hat{p} = \frac{570}{1000} = 0.57$$

and the estimated standard deviation of $\hat{p}$ is

$$\sqrt{\frac{\hat{p}(1 - \hat{p})}{n}} = \sqrt{\frac{(0.57)(0.43)}{1000}} = 0.0156$$

A 95% confidence interval for the proportion p of all registered voters who support Bean is therefore

$$\hat{p} \pm z_{0.95} \sqrt{\frac{\hat{p}(1 - \hat{p})}{n}}$$

$$0.57 \pm (1.96)(0.0156)$$

$$0.57 \pm 0.030$$

or 0.54 to 0.60. This is the same result we found in Section 1. If Bean insists on 99% confidence, the interval is

$$\hat{p} \pm z_{0.99} \sqrt{\frac{p(1-\hat{p})}{n}}$$

$$0.57 \pm (2.58)(0.0156)$$

$$0.57 \pm 0.040$$

or 0.54 to 0.61. As usual, higher confidence exacts its price in the form of a larger margin of error.

Example 2. On page 45, a news article reports a Gallup Poll of 1506 adults. Thirty-three percent of these believed (incorrectly) that the United States is self-sufficient in oil. If Gallup had used a SRS, a 90% confidence interval for the proportion of American adults who share the delusion that we need not import oil would be

$$\hat{p} \pm z_{0.90} \sqrt{\frac{\hat{p}(1-\hat{p})}{n}}$$

$$0.33 \pm (1.64) \sqrt{\frac{(0.33)(0.67)}{1506}}$$

$$0.33 \pm 0.02.$$

(In fact, Gallup does not use a SRS, so this recipe is not appropriate. See Exercise 3 of Section 1 for Gallup's 95% confidence interval.)

Confidence Intervals for a Population Mean

Like the sample proportion $\hat{p}$, the sample mean $\bar{x}$ from a large SRS has a sampling distribution that is close to normal. Since the sample mean of a SRS is an unbiased estimator of the mean of the population, usually denoted by μ (the Greek letter mu), μ is the mean of the sampling distribution of $\bar{x}$. The standard deviation of $\bar{x}$ depends on the standard deviation of the population, which is usually denoted by σ (the Greek letter sigma). By mathematics we can discover the following fact.

Sampling Distribution of the Sample Mean

Suppose that a SRS of size n is drawn from a population having mean μ and standard deviation σ. The mean of the sample is the statistic $\bar{x}$. When n is large, the sampling distribution of $\bar{x}$ is approximately normal with mean μ and standard deviation $\sigma/\sqrt{n}$.

The standard deviation of $\bar{x}$ depends on both σ and the sample size n. We know n, but not σ. But when n is large, the sample standard deviation s is close to σ and can be used to estimate it. So the estimated standard deviation of x is $s/\sqrt{n}$. Now confidence intervals for μ can be found just as with p.

Confidence Interval for a Population Mean

Suppose that a SRS of size n is drawn from a population of units having mean μ. When n is large, an approximate level β confidence interval for μ is

$$\overline{x} \pm z_\beta \frac{s}{\sqrt{n}}.$$

The cautions cited in estimating p apply here as well: The recipe is valid only when a SRS is drawn and the sample size n is reasonably large

> **Example 3.** In Exercise 10 on page 156 there appears the count of col-iform bacteria per milliliter in each of 100 specimens of milk. Suppose that these specimens can be assumed to be a SRS of the milk sold in a certain region. Give a 90% confidence interval for the mean coliform count of all milk sold in that region.
>
> We first compute the sample mean and standard deviation for this set of data. The results are
>
> $$\overline{x} = 5.88 \quad s = 2.02$$
>
> so the 90% confidence interval is
>
> $$\overline{x} \pm z_{0.90} \frac{s}{\sqrt{n}}$$
>
> $$5.88 \pm (1.64) \frac{2.02}{\sqrt{100}}$$
>
> $$5.88 \pm 0.33.$$
>
> We are 90% confident that the mean coliform count in the population falls between 5.55 and 6.21 per milliliter.

3. Statistical Significance

Confidence intervals are one of the two most common types of statistical infer-ence. They are appropriate when our goal is to estimate a population parameter. The second common type of inference is directed at a quite different goal: to assess the evidence provided by the data in favor of a statement. An example will illustrate the reasoning used.

> **Example 4.** When the correlation coefficient between birth date (1 to 366) and draft number (1 to 366) for the 1970 draft lottery is calculated, we get $r = -0.226$. Is this correlation good evidence that the lottery was not random?
>
> *Formal Question:* Suppose for the sake of argument that the lottery were truly random. What is the probability that a random lottery would produce an r at least as far from 0 as the observed $r = -0.226$?
>
> *Answer* (from mathematics or simulation): The probability that a random draft lottery will have an r this far from 0 is less than 0.001 (one in a thousand).
>
> *Conclusion:* Since an r as far from 0 as that observed in 1970 would almost never occur in a random lottery, we have strong evidence that the 1970 draft lottery was not random.

In a random assignment of draft numbers to birth dates, we would expect the correlation to be close to 0. The correlation for the 1970 lottery was -0.226, showing that men born later in the year tended to get lower draft numbers. This is not a large correlation. The scatterplot (Figure 5) shows little association. Common sense is not enough to decide if $r = -0.226$ means the lottery was not random. After all, the correlation will almost never be exactly 0, and perhaps $r = -0.226$ is within the range that a random lottery would be expected to produce. So as an aid to answering the informal question "Is this good evidence of a nonrandom lottery?" we stated a formal question about probabilities. We asked just how often a random lottery would produce an r as far from 0 as the r observed in 1970. The answer could be obtained by many simulations of a random lottery, but I obtained it by mathematics. If a random draft lottery were run each year, a correlation as strong as that observed in 1970 would occur less than once in a thousand years! This convinces us that the 1970 lottery was biased.

Be sure you understand why this evidence is convincing. There are two possible explanations of that notorious $r = -0.226$:

(a) The lottery was random, and by bad luck a very unlikely outcome occurred.

(b) The lottery was biased, so that the outcome is about what would be expected from such a lottery.

We cannot be certain that explanation (a) is untrue. The 1970 results *could* be due to chance alone. But the probability that such results would occur by chance in a random lottery is so small (0.001) that we are quite confident that explanation (b) is right. Here is a second example of this reasoning.

> **Example 5.** The Toronto vitamin C experiment (Example 7 on page 64) was a randomized double-blind experiment with about 400 subjects in

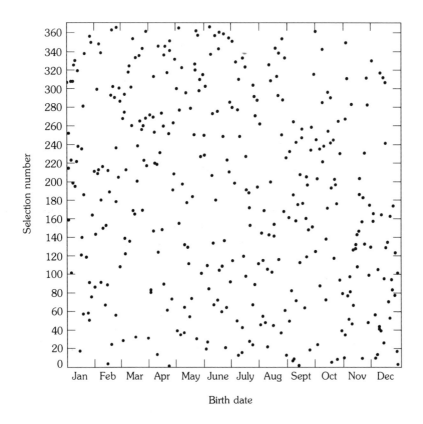

Figure 5. The 1970 draft lottery. The scatterplot shows the association between birth dates and draft numbers in the 1970 draft lottery. When birth dates are labeled from 1 (January 1, 1952) to 366 (December 31, 1952), their correlation with draft numbers 1 to 366 is $r = -0.266$.

each of two groups. In this study, 26% of the vitamin C group and 18% of the placebo group were free of illness through the winter. Is this good evidence that vitamin C prevents illness better than a placebo?

Formal Question: Suppose for the sake of argument that there is no difference between the effects of vitamin C and the placebo. That is, suppose that the only difference between the two groups of volunteers is due to the random allocation in the experimental design. What is the probability of observing an outcome favoring vitamin C by 26% versus 18% or more?

Answer: The probability that a difference this large would occur because of the random allocation alone is less than 0.01 (one in a hundred).

Conclusion: Since a difference as large as the one actually observed would occur only one time in a hundred if vitamin C has no more effect than a placebo, there is good evidence that vitamin C is more effective than a placebo.

The reasoning used in these examples is codified in *tests of significance*. In both examples, we hoped to show that an effect was present—that the draft lottery was biased in Example 4, and that vitamin C outperformed the placebo in Example 5. To do this, we began by supposing for the sake of argument that the effect we sought was not present. In Example 4, we supposed that the lottery was random, not biased. In Example 5, we supposed that a volunteer given vitamin C was no more likely to be free of illness than one given a placebo. We then looked for evidence against the supposition we made. Such evidence is also evidence in favor of the effect we hoped to find. But the first step in tests of significance is to state a claim that we will try to find evidence against.

> **The statement being tested in a test of significance is called the *null hypothesis*. The test of significance is designed to assess the strength of the evidence against the null hypothesis. Usually the null hypothesis is a statement of "no difference" or "no effect."**

The term "null hypothesis" is abbreviated as H_0, which is read "H-nought." It is usually stated in terms of some population parameter or parameters. For example, suppose that p_1 is the proportion of the whole population of North American males who would have been illness-free in 1971 if they had taken a gram of vitamin C each day, and let p_2 stand for the illness-free proportion if a placebo were given instead. Then the null hypothesis of Example 5 is

$$H_0: \quad p_1 = p_2$$

because this says that vitamin C has the same effectiveness as a placebo. It is useful to give a name to the statement we hope or suspect is true instead of H_0. This is called the *alternative hypothesis* and is abbreviated by H_1. In Example 5, the alternative hypothesis is that vitamin C is more effective than a placebo. In terms of population parameters this is

$$H_1: \quad p_1 > p_2.$$

A test of significance assesses the strength of the evidence against the null hypothesis in terms of probability. If the observed outcome is unlikely under the supposition that the null hypothesis is true, but is more probable if the alternative hypothesis is true, that outcome is evidence against H_0 in favor of H_1. The less probable the outcome is, the stronger is the evidence that H_0 is false. Now usually any individual outcome has low probability. It is unlikely that a random draft lottery would give exactly $r = 0$, but if we observed $r = 0$ we would certainly not have evidence against the null hypothesis that the lottery is random. Our procedure is therefore to say what kinds of outcomes would count as evidence against H_0 and in favor of H_1. In the draft lottery case, correlations r away from 0 (either positive or negative) count against the hypothesis of a random lottery. The farther from 0 the observed r is, the stronger the evidence.

The probability that measures the strength of the evidence that the 1970 lottery is nonrandom is therefore the probability that a random lottery would produce an r *at least as far from* 0 as the 1970 lottery did.

In general, we find the probability of getting an outcome at least as far as the actually observed outcome from what we would expect when H_0 is true. What counts as "far from what we would expect" depends on H_1 as well as H_0. In Example 4, an observed r away from 0 *in either direction* is evidence of a nonrandom lottery. In Example 5, we wanted to know if vitamin C was more effective than a placebo (that's H_1). So evidence against H_0 is measured by the probability that the percent illness-free in the vitamin C group *exceeds* that percent in the placebo group by as much as 26% versus 18%.

> **The probability of getting an outcome at least as far from what we would expect if H_0 were true as was the actually observed outcome is called the *P-value*. The smaller the *P*-value is, the stronger is the evidence against H_0 provided by the data.**

One final step is sometimes taken in assessing the evidence against H_0. We can compare the evidence we obtained with a fixed level of evidence that we regard as decisive. Because the strength of the evidence provided by the data is measured by the *P*-value, we need only say how small a *P*-value we insist on. This decisive value is called the *significance level*. It is always denoted by α, the Greek letter alpha. If we take $\alpha = 0.05$, we are requiring that the data give

The experimental evidence against the null hypothesis that Lucy did not act deliberately reaches a *P*-value of one in ten billion. Nevertheless, Charlie Brown repeats the experiment each year.

evidence against H_0 so strong that it would happen no more than 5% of the time (one time in twenty) when H_0 is really true. If we take $\alpha = 0.01$, we are insisting on stronger evidence against H_0, evidence so strong that it would appear only 1% of the time (one time in a hundred) if H_0 is really true. If the P-value is as small or smaller than α, we say that the data are *statistically significant at level α*. This is just a way of saying that the evidence against the null hypothesis reached the standard set by the level α. A common abbreviation for significance at (say) level 0.01 is "The results were significant $(P < 0.01)$." Here P stands for the P-value.

A recipe for testing the significance of the evidence against a null hypothesis H_0 is called a *test of significance* (or a *test of hypotheses,* but I will save that language for a slightly different kind of reasoning, which we will meet in Section 5.) Courses on statistical methods teach many such recipes for different hypotheses H_0 and H_1, for different significance levels α, and for different data-collection designs. An outline of what such a recipe must include appears in the boxed section. We are not concerned with any specific recipe, but rather with the reasoning that lies behind all such recipes. You are now well prepared to understand the meaning of conclusions stated in terms of statistical significance. "The results of the Toronto vitamin C experiment were significant at level $\alpha = 0.01$" summarizes in one sentence the long chain of reasoning we followed in discussing Example 5. It means that the experimental evidence favoring vitamin C was so strong that it would appear in less than 1% of a long series of experiments if the only difference between the experimental and control groups is due to random allocation of subjects.

Steps in a Test of Significance

(a) Choose the *null hypothesis H_0* and the *alternative hypothesis H_1*. The test is designed to assess the strength of the evidence against H_0. H_1 is a statement of the alternative we will accept if the evidence enables us to reject H_0.

(b) (Optional) Choose the *significance level α*. This states how much evidence against H_0 we will accept as decisive.

(c) Choose the *test statistic* on which the test will be based. This is a statistic which measures how well the data conform to H_0. In Example 1, the correlation coefficient was used because in a random lottery there should be little or no correlation between birth date and draft number.

(d) Find the *P-value* for the observed data. This is the probability that the test statistic would weigh against H_0 at least as strongly as it does for these data, if H_0 were in fact true. If the P-value is less than or equal to α, the test was *statistically significant at level α*.

To review and solidify this introduction to tests of significance, here is a concluding example.

Example 6. Is a new method of teaching reading to first graders (method B) more effective than the method now in use (method A)? An experiment is called for. We will use a *paired-sample experimental design:* 20 pairs of first graders are available, with the two children in each pair carefully matched in IQ, socioeconomic status, reading readiness score, and other variables that may influence their reading performance. One student from each pair is randomly assigned to method A, while the other student in the pair is taught by method B. At the end of first grade, all the children take a test of reading skill.

(a) We want to know if the new method B is superior to the old method A. So the null hypothesis is that method B and method A are equally effective. We will examine the experimental evidence against this H_0 in favor of the alternative that method B is more effective. To state H_0 and H_1 in terms of parameters, and later to do the necessary simulation, we must give a probability model for the experiment. The children in each pair are (as closely as possible) exactly identical as reading students. So if the two teaching methods are equally effective, each child has the same chance to score higher on the test. Let p stand for the proportion of all possible matched pairs of children for which the child taught by method B will have the higher score. The null hypothesis is

$$H_0: \quad p = \tfrac{1}{2}$$

and the alternative is

$$H_1: \quad p > \tfrac{1}{2}.$$

We can think of p as the probability that the method B child in any one pair will do better.

(b) We choose $\alpha = 0.10$. That is, we are willing to say that method B is better if it shows a superiority in the experiment that would occur no more than 10% of the time if the two methods were equally effective.

(c) The test statistic is the number of pairs out of 20 in which the child taught by method B has a higher score. The larger this number is, the stronger is the evidence that method B is better.

(d) Now we take a year off to do the experiment. The result is that method B gave the higher score in 12 of the 20 groups. The P-value for these data is the probability that 12 *or more* pairs out of 20 favor method B when H_0 is true. This is exactly the same as the probability of 12 or more heads in 20 tosses of a coin with heads and tails equally likely. We find this probability by simulation as follows.

Step 1. Each random digit simulates one pair of students:

odd   method A scores higher

even   method B scores higher

Step 2. One repetition requires 20 digits representing 20 pairs of students.

Step 3. Begin simulating in line 110 of Table A, recording for each repetition how many times B scored higher.

38448	48789	18338	24697	
ABBBB	BBABA	ABAAB	BBBAA	12 B's
39364	42006	76688	08708	
AAABB	BBBBB	ABBBB	BBABB	15 B's
81486	69487	60513	09297	
BABBB	BABBA	BBAAA	BABAA	11 B's
00412	71238	27649	39950	
BBBAB	AABAB	BABBA	AAAAB	10 B's

and so on. In these four trials the relative frequency of 12 or more B's was ½. Many more trials are needed to estimate the probability precisely. When they are made, the probability of 12 or more B's in 20 pairs of students is 0.25. This is the *P*-value. The *P*-value did not reach the required level of significance. The experimental results were not statistically significant at the $\alpha = 0.10$ level. We do not have adequate evidence that method B is superior to Method A.

4.   Use and Abuse of Tests of Significance

Tests of statistical significance are routinely used to assess the results of research in agriculture, medicine, education, psychology, sociology, and increasingly in other fields as well. Any tool used routinely is often used unthinkingly. This section therefore offers some comments for the thinking researcher on the use and abuse of this tool. Thinking consumers of research findings (such as students) might also ponder these comments.

1. *Choosing a level of significance.* The spirit of a test of significance is to give a clear statement of the degree of evidence against the null hypothesis obtained from the sample. This is best done by the *P*-value. But sometimes some action will be taken if the evidence reaches a certain standard. Such a standard is set by

giving a level of significance α. Perhaps you will announce a new scientific finding if your data are significant at the $\alpha = 0.05$ level. Or perhaps you will recommend using a new method of teaching reading if the evidence of its superiority is significant at the $\alpha = 0.01$ level. When α serves as a standard of evidence, we speak of *rejecting* H_0 *at level* α if the data are significant at that level.

The idea of using α as a criterion for taking some decision or action goes beyond the idea of a test of significance. But when you want to give such a rule, α is chosen by deciding how much evidence is required to reject H_0. This depends first on how plausible H_0 is. If H_0 represents an assumption that everyone in your field has believed for years, strong evidence (small α) will be needed to reject it. Second, the level of evidence required to reject H_0 depends on the consequences of such a decision. If rejecting H_0 in favor of H_1 means making an expensive changeover from one medical therapy or instructional method to another, strong evidence is needed. Both the plausibility of H_0 and H_1 and the consequences of any action that rejection may lead to are somewhat subjective. Different persons may feel that different levels of significance are appropriate. When this is the case, it is better to report the P-value, which leaves each of us to decide individually if the evidence is sufficiently strong.

When you really must make a decision with well-defined consequences, you should abandon the idea of testing significance and think about rules for making decisions. This approach to statistical inference is discussed in Section 5. It is different in spirit from testing significance, though the two are usually mixed in textbooks and are often mixed in practice. Choosing a level α in advance makes sense if you must make a decision, but not if you wish only to describe the strength of your evidence. In short: when a test of significance is what you want, don't set α in advance and do always report the P-value. This advice is easy to follow since the computer programs used for most statistical arithmetic automatically print out the P-value. It is acceptable to use "significant at level $\alpha = 0.01$" or the shorthand "$P < 0.01$" to describe your results. But the actual P-value is more informative.

Textbooks commonly stress certain standard levels of significance, such as 10%, 5%, and 1%. The 5% level ($\alpha = 0.05$) is particularly common. Significance at that level is still a widely accepted criterion for meaningful evidence in research work. Now there is no sharp border between "significant" and "insignificant," only increasingly strong evidence as the P-value decreases. It makes no sense to treat $\alpha = 0.05$ as a universal rule for what is significant. There is a reason for the common use of $\alpha = 0.05$—the great influence of Sir R. A. Fisher.* Fisher's ideas on statistical inference agreed with the reasoning behind tests of significance. Here is his opinion on level of significance.

---

*We met the great British statistician R. A. Fisher in Chapter 2 as the father of randomized experimental design. He was the father of much else in modern statistics as well, including the general use of regression (Chapter 5) and the mathematical derivation of the probability distributions of common test statistics. Fisher did not originate tests of significance. But since his writings organized statistics, especially as a tool of scientific research, his views on tests were enormously influential.

> . . . it is convenient to draw the line at about the level at which we can say:
> "Either there is something in the treatment, or a coincidence has occurred
> such as does not occur more than once in twenty trials. . . ."
>
> If one in twenty does not seem high enough odds, we may, if we prefer it,
> draw the line at one in fifty (the 2 percent point), or one in a hundred (the 1
> percent point). Personally, the writer prefers to set a low standard of
> significance at the 5 percent point, and ignore entirely all results which fail to
> reach that level. A scientific fact should be regarded as experimentally
> established only if a properly designed experiment rarely fails to give this level
> of significance.[1]

There you have it. Fisher thought 5% was about right, and who was to disagree
with the master?

2. *What statistical significance doesn't mean.* When a null hypothesis ("no
effect" or "no difference") can be rejected at the usual levels, $\alpha = 0.05$ or $\alpha =$
0.01, there is good evidence that an effect is present. But that effect may be
extremely small. When large samples are available, statistical tests are very
sensitive and will detect even tiny deviations from the null hypothesis. For
example, suppose that we are testing the hypothesis of no correlation between
two variables. With 1000 observations, an observed correlation of only $r = 0.08$
is significant evidence at the $\alpha = 0.01$ level that the correlation in the population
is not zero but positive. The low significance level does not mean there is a strong
association, only that there is strong evidence of some association. The true
population correlation is probably quite close to the observed sample value, $r =$
0.08. We might well conclude that for practical purposes there is no association
between these variables, even though we are confident (at the 1% level) that this
is not literally true.

Remember the wise saying: *Statistical significance is not the same thing as
practical significance.* I am tempted to interpret the results of the Toronto vitamin
C experiment in this light. Since the observed difference (that 26% versus 18%
again) was significant at the $\alpha = 0.01$ level, it does appear that vitamin C
prevented colds better than a placebo. But not much better. The difference
between an 18% chance of avoiding colds and a 26% chance is nothing to fuss
about.

The remedy for attaching too much importance to statistical significance is to
pay attention to the actual experimental results as well as to the P value. It is
usually wise to give a confidence interval for the population parameter you are
interested in. Confidence intervals are not used as often as they should be, while
tests of significance are perhaps overused.

3. *Don't ignore lack of significance.* Researchers typically have in mind the
research hypothesis that some effect exists. Following the peculiar logic of tests
of significance, they set up as H_0 the null hypothesis that no such effect exists,
and try their best to get evidence against H_0. Now a perverse legacy of Fisher's
opinion on $\alpha = 0.05$ is that research in some fields has rarely been published
unless significance at that level is attained. A survey of four journals of the

American Psychological Association published in 1959 showed that of 294 articles using statistical tests, only 8 did not attain the 5% significance level.[2]

Such a publication policy impedes the spread of knowledge. If a researcher has good reason to suspect that an effect is present, and then fails to find significant evidence of it, that may be interesting news. Perhaps more interesting than if evidence in favor of the effect at the 5% level had been found. If you follow the history of science, you will recall examples such as the famous Michelson–Morley experiment, which changed the course of physics by *not* detecting a change in the speed of light that they expected to find. (Of course, an experiment that fails only causes a stir if it is clear that the experiment would have detected the effect if it were really there. Such experiments are much rarer in psychology than in physics.) Keeping silent about negative results may condemn other researchers to repeat the attempt to find an effect that isn't there. Witness this parable.[3]

. . . There's this desert prison, see, with an old prisoner, resigned to his life, and a young one just arrived. The young one talks constantly of escape, and, after a few months, he makes a break. He's gone a week, and then he's brought back by the guards. He's half dead, crazy with hunger and thirst. He describes how awful it was to the old prisoner. The endless stretches of sand, no oasis, no signs of life anywhere. The old prisoner listens for a while, then says, "Yep. I know. I tried to escape myself, twenty years ago." The young prisoner says, "You did? Why didn't you tell me, all these months I was planning my escape? Why didn't you let me know it was impossible?" And the old prisoner shrugs, and says, "So who publishes negative results?"

4. *Statistical inference is not valid for all sets of data.* We learned long ago that badly designed surveys or experiments often produce invalid results. Formal statistical inference cannot correct basic flaws in the design. There is no doubt a significant difference in English vocabulary scores between high school seniors who have studied Latin and those who have not. (Recall Example 3 on page 59.) But so long as the effect of actually studying Latin is confounded with the differences between students who choose Latin and those who do not, this statistical significance has little meaning. It does indicate that the difference in English scores is greater than would often arise by chance alone. That leaves unsettled the issue of *what* other than chance caused the difference.

Both tests of significance and confidence intervals are based on the laws of probability. Randomization in sampling or experimentation assures that these laws apply. When these statistical strategies for collecting data cannot be used, statistical inference from the data obtained should be done only with extreme caution. Many data in the social sciences by necessity are collected without randomization. It is universal practice to use tests of significance on such data. It can be argued that significance at least points to the presence of an effect greater than would be likely by chance. But that indication alone is little evidence against

H_0 and in favor of the research hypothesis H_1. Do not allow the wonders of this chapter to obscure the common sense of Chapters 1 and 2.

5. *Beware of searching for significance.* Statistical significance is a commodity much sought after by researchers. It means (or ought to mean) that you have found something you were looking for. The reasoning behind statistical significance works well if you decide what effect you are seeking, design an experiment or sample to search for it, and use a test of significance to weigh the evidence you get. But because a successful search for a new scientific phenomenon often ends with statistical significance, it is all too easy to make significance itself the object of the search. There are several ways to do this, none of them acceptable in polite scientific society.

A common tactic is to make many tests on the same data. The story is told of three psychiatrists who studied a sample of schizophrenic persons in comparison with a sample of nonschizophrenic persons. They measured 77 variables for each subject—religion, family background, childhood experiences, and so on. Their goal was to discover what distinguishes persons who later become schizophrenic. Having measured 77 variables, they made 77 separate tests of the significance of the differences between the two groups of subjects. Now pause for a moment of reflection. If you made 77 tests at the 5% level, you would expect a few of them to be significant by chance alone, right? After all, results significant at the 5% level do occur five times in a hundred in the long run even when H_0 is true. Well, our psychiatrists found 2 of their 77 tests significant at the 5% level, and immediately published this exciting news.[4] Running one test and reaching the $\alpha = 0.05$ level is reasonably good evidence that you have found something; running 77 tests and reaching that level only twice is not.

The case of the 77 tests happened long ago, and such crimes are rarer now. Or at least better concealed, for some common practices are not very different. The computer has freed us from the labor of doing arithmetic, and this is surely a blessing in statistics, where the arithmetic can be long and complicated indeed. All computing centers maintain ''libraries'' of statistical programs, so a few simple commands will set the machine to work performing all manner of complicated tests and operations on your data. The result can be much like the 77 tests of old. I will state it as a law that any large set of data—even several pages of a table of random numbers—contains some unusual pattern. Sufficient computer time will discover that pattern, and when you test specifically for the pattern that turned up, the test will be significant. It also will mean exactly nothing.

One lesson here is not to be overawed by the computer. It is a wondrous tool that makes possible statistical analysis of large data sets and allows ever more complicated and sensitive statistical procedures to be used. The computer has greatly extended the range of statistical inference. But it has changed the logic of inference not one bit. Doing 77 tests and finding 2 significant at the $\alpha = 0.05$ level was not evidence of a real discovery. Neither is doing multiple regression analysis followed by principal components analysis followed by factor analysis and at last discovering a pattern in the data. Fancy words, and fancy computer programs, but still bad scientific logic. It is convincing to hypothesize that an effect or pattern will be present, design a study to look for it, and find it at a low

significance level. It is not convincing to search for any effect or pattern whatever, and find one.

Now I do not mean that searching data for suggestive patterns is not proper
scientific work. It certainly is. Many important discoveries have been made by
accident rather than by design. New computer-based methods of searching
through data are important in statistics. I do mean that the usual reasoning of
statistical inference does not apply when the search is successful. You cannot
legitimately test a hypothesis on the same data that first suggested that
hypothesis. After all, any data set has some peculiarity, and you may have found
only the peculiarity of this one set of data. The remedy is clear: Now that you
have a hypothesis, design a study to search specifically for the effect you now
think is there. If the result of this study is statistically significant, you have real
evidence at last.

5. Inference as Decision

Tests of significance were presented in Section 3 as methods for assessing the
strength of evidence against the null hypothesis. This assessment is made by the
P-value, which is a probability computed under the assumption that the null
hypothesis is true. The alternative hypothesis (the statement we seek evidence
for) enters the test only to help us see what outcomes count against the null
hypothesis. Such is the theory of tests of significance as advocated by Fisher, and
as practiced by many users of statistics.

But already in Section 4 signs of another way of thinking were present. A level
of significance α chosen in advance points to the outcome of the test as a
decision. If the P-value is less than α, we reject H_0 in favor of H_1; otherwise we
fail to reject H_0. The transition from measuring the strength of evidence to
making a decision is not a small step. It can be argued (and is argued by
followers of Fisher) that making decisions is too grand a goal, especially in
scientific inference. A decision is reached only after the evidence of many experiments is weighed, and indeed the goal of research is not "decision" but a
gradually evolving understanding. Better that statistical inference should content
itself with confidence intervals and tests of significance. Many users of statistics
are content with such methods. It is rare (outside textbooks) to set up a level α in
advance as a rule for making a decision in a scientific problem. More commonly,
users think of significance at level 0.05 as a description of good evidence. This is
made clearer by talking about P-values, and this newer language is spreading.

Yet there are circumstances in which a decision or action is called for as the
end result of inference. *Acceptance sampling* (Example 4 on page 4) is one such
circumstance. The supplier of bearings and the consumer of the bearings agree
that each carload lot shall meet certain quality standards. When a carload ar-
rives, the consumer chooses a sample of bearings to be inspected. On the basis
of the sample outcome, the consumer will either accept or reject the carload.
Fisher agreed that this is a genuine decision problem. But he insisted that acceptance sampling is completely different from scientific inference. Other eminent

statisticians have argued that if "decision" is given a broad meaning, almost all problems of statistical inference can be posed as problems of making decisions in the presence of uncertainty. I am not going to venture further into the arguments over how we ought to think about inference. I do want to show how a different concept—inference as decision—changes the ways of reasoning used in tests of significance.

Tests of significance fasten attention on H_0, the null hypothesis. If a decision is called for, however, there is no reason to single out H_0. There are simply two alternatives, and we must accept one and reject the other. It is convenient to call the two alternatives H_0 and H_1, but H_0 no longer has the special status (the statement we try to find evidence against) that it had in tests of significance. In the acceptance sampling problem, we must decide between

$$H_0: \quad \text{the lot of bearings meets standards}$$

$$H_1: \quad \text{the lot does not meet standards}$$

on the basis of a sample of bearings. There is no reason to put the burden of proof on the consumer by accepting H_0 unless we have strong evidence against it. It is equally sensible to put the burden of proof on the producer by accepting H_1 unless we have strong evidence that the lot meets standards. Producer and consumer must agree on where to place the burden of proof, but neither H_0 nor H_1 has any special status.

In a decision problem, we must give a *decision rule*—a recipe based on the sample that tells us what decision to make. Decision rules are expressed in terms of sample statistics, usually the same statistics we would use in a test of significance. In fact, we have seen already that a test of significance becomes a decision rule if we reject H_0 (accept H_1) when the sample statistic is statistically significant at level α, and otherwise accept H_0 (reject H_1).

Suppose, then, that we use statistical significance at level α as our criterion for decision. And suppose that the null hypothesis H_0 is really true. Then sample outcomes significant at level α will occur with probability α. (That's the definition of "significant at level α"; outcomes weighing this strongly against H_0 occur with probability α when H_0 is really true.) But now we make a *wrong decision* in all such outcomes, by rejecting H_0 when it is really true. That is, the significance level α now can be understood as the probability of a certain type of wrong decision.

Now H_1 requires equal attention. Just as rejecting H_0 (accepting H_1) when H_0 is really true is an error, so is accepting H_0 (rejecting H_1) when H_1 is really true. We can make two kinds of errors.

If we reject H_0 (accept H_1) when in fact H_0 is true, this is a *Type I* error.

If we accept H_0 (reject H_1) when in fact H_1 is true, this is a *Type II* error.

The possibilities are summed up in Figure 6. If H_0 is true, our decision is either correct (if we accept H_0) or is a Type I error. Only one error is possible at one time. Figure 7 applies these ideas to the acceptance sampling example.

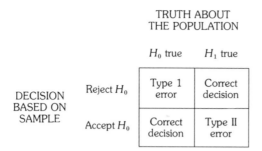

Figure 6. Possible outcomes of a two-action decision problem.

So the significant level α is the probability of a Type I error. In acceptance sampling, this is the probability that a good lot will be rejected. The probability of a Type II error is the probability that a bad lot will be accepted. A Type I error hurts the producer, while a Type II error hurts the consumer. *Any decision rule is assessed in terms of the probabilities of the two types of error.* This is in keeping with the idea that statistical inference is based on probability. We cannot (short of inspecting the whole lot) guarantee that good lots never will be rejected and bad lots never accepted. But by random sampling and the laws of probability, we can say what the probabilities of both kinds of error are. Because we can find out the monetary cost of accepting bad lots and of rejecting good ones, we can determine how much loss the producer and consumer each will suffer in the long run from wrong decisions.

Advocates of decision theory argue that the kind of "economic" thinking natural in acceptance sampling applies to all inference problems. Even a scientific researcher decides whether to announce results, or to do another experiment, or to give up the research as unproductive. Wrong decisions carry costs, though these costs are not always measured in dollars. A scientist suffers by announcing a false effect, and also by failing to detect a true effect. Decision theorists maintain that the scientist should try to give numerical weights (called *utilities*) to the consequences of the two types of wrong decision. Then he can

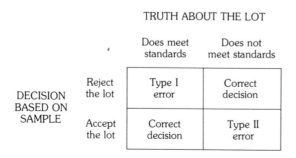

Figure 7. Possible outcomes of an acceptance sampling decision.

choose a decision rule with error probabilities that reflect how serious the two kinds of error are. This argument has won favor where utilities are easily expressed in money. Decision theory is widely used by business in making capital investment decisions, for example. But scientific researchers have been reluctant to take this approach to statistical inference.

To sum up, in a test of significance we focus on a single hypothesis (H_0) and a single probability (the P-value). The goal is to measure the strength of the sample evidence against H_0. If the same inference problem is thought of as a decision problem, we focus on two hypotheses and give a rule for deciding between them based on the sample evidence. We therefore must focus on two probabilities, the probabilities of the two types of error.

Such a clear distinction between the two ways of thinking is helpful for understanding. In practice, the two approaches often merge, to the dismay of partisans of one or the other. We continued to call one of the hypotheses in a decision problem H_0. In the common practice of *testing hypotheses,* we mix significance tests and decision rules as follows.

(a) Choose H_0 just as in a test of significance.

(b) Think of the problem as a decision problem, so the probabilities of Type I and Type II error are relevant.

(c) Because of Step (a), Type I errors are more serious. So choose an α (significance level) and consider only tests with probability of Type I error no greater than α.

(d) Among these tests, select one that makes the probability of a Type II error as small as possible. If this probability is too large, you will have to take a larger sample to reduce the chance of an error.

Testing hypotheses may seem to be a hybrid approach, or maybe a bastard approach. It was, historically, the effective beginning of decision-oriented ideas in statistics. Hypothesis testing was developed by Jerzy Neyman* and Egon S. Pearson in the years 1928–1938. The decision theory approach came later (1940s) and grew out of the Neyman–Pearson ideas. Because decision theory in its pure form leaves you with two error probabilities and no simple rule on how to balance them, it has been used less often than tests of significance. Decision theory ideas have been applied in testing problems mainly by way of the Neyman–Pearson theory. That theory asks you first to choose α, and the influence of Fisher often has led users of hypothesis testing comfortably back to $\alpha = 0.05$ or $\alpha = 0.01$ (and also back to the warnings of Section 4 about this state of affairs). Fisher, who was exceedingly argumentative, violently attacked the Neyman–Pearson decision-oriented ideas, and the argument still continues.

The reasoning in statistical inference is subtle, and the principles at issue are complex. I have (believe it or not) oversimplified the ideas of all the viewpoints

---

*Neyman was born in 1894 and at the age of 85 was not only still alive but still scientifically active. In addition to developing the decision-oriented approach to testing, Neyman was also the chief architect of the theory of confidence intervals.

mentioned and omitted several other viewpoints altogether. If you are feeling that you do not fully grasp all of the ideas in this chapter, you are in excellent company. Nonetheless, any user of statistics should make a serious effort to grasp the conflicting views on the nature of statistical inference. More than most other kinds of intellectual exercise, statistical inference can be done automatically, by recipe or by computer. These valuable shortcuts are of no worth without understanding. What Euclid said of his own science to King Ptolemy of Egypt long ago remains true of all knowledge: "There is no royal road to geometry."

NOTES

1. R. A. Fisher, "The Arrangement of Field Experiments," *Journal of the Ministry of Agriculture of Great Britain,* Volume 33 (1926), p. 504. Quoted in Leonard J. Savage, "On Rereading R. A. Fisher," *The Annals of Statistics,* Volume 4 (1976), p. 471.
2. Theodore D. Sterling, "Publication Decisions and their Possible Effects on Inferences Drawn from Tests of Significance-or Vice Versa," *Journal of the American Statistical Association,* Volume 54 (1959), pp. 30-34.
3. From Jeffrey Hudson, *A Case of Need* (New York: New American Library, 1968). Quoted by G. William Walster and T. Anne Cleary, "A Proposal for a New Editorial Policy in the Social Sciences," *The American Statistician,* April 1970, p. 16.
4. This example is cited by William Feller, "Are Life Scientists Overawed by Statistics?" *Scientific Research,* February 3, 1969, p. 26.

Exercises

Section 1

1. Suppose that Senator Bean's SRS of size 1000 produced 520 voters who plan to vote for Bean.

   (a) What is the 95% confidence interval for the population proportion p who plan to vote for Bean?
   (b) What is the 99.7% confidence interval for p?
   (c) Based on the sample results, can Bean be confident that he is leading the race?

2. A SRS of 1000 graduates of a university showed that 54% earned at least $20,000 a year. Give a 95% confidence interval for the proportion of all graduates of that university who earn at least $20,000 a year.

3. Table 1 on p. 18 is a table of margins of error for samples of several sizes drawn by the Gallup Poll's probability sampling procedure. We now can use that table to give 95% confidence intervals.

   Exercise 1 on p. 45 reports a 1977 Gallup Poll of 1506 American adults, of whom 33% thought (incorrectly) that the United States is self-sufficient in oil. Give a 95% confidence interval for the proportion of all American adults who believe this.

4. If Senator Bean took only a SRS of 25 voters, the probability distribution of the sample proportion $\hat{p}$ who favor him would be (very roughly) normal with mean equal to the population proportion p and standard deviation 0.1.

    (a) What property of this distribution shows that $\hat{p}$ is an unbiased estimate of p?

    (b) A sample of size 25 gives less precision than a sample of size 1000. How is this reflected in the distributions of $\hat{p}$ for the two sample sizes?

    (c) For the SRS of size 25, what is the number c such that the interval from $\hat{p} - c$ to $\hat{p} + c$ is a 95% confidence interval for p? Explain your answer.

    (d) If Senator Bean found 17 of 25 voters in a SRS favoring him, give a 95% confidence interval for the proportion of all voters who favor Bean.

5. In Senator Bean's SRS of 1000 voters, what is the number c such that the interval from $\hat{p} - c$ to $\hat{p} + c$ is a 68% confidence interval for p? Explain your answer.

6. We are going to simulate the performance of a 68% confidence interval for p based on a SRS of size 25.

    (a) Using the information given in Exercise 4, explain why the interval from $\hat{p} - 0.1$ to $\hat{p} + 0.1$ is a 68% confidence interval for p.

    (b) Suppose that in fact $p = 0.6$ (that is, 60% of all the voters favor Bean). Explain how to use Table A to simulate drawing a SRS of size 25.

    (c) Starting in line 101 of Table A, simulate drawing 10 SRS's of size 25 from this population. For each sample, compute the sample proportion $\hat{p}$ who favor Bean. Then compute the 68% confidence interval $\hat{p} - 0.1$ to $\hat{p} + 0.1$ for each sample. How many of the intervals covered the true $p = 0.6$? How many failed to cover p?

7. The recipes for confidence intervals depend on the probability distribution of the sample statistic used. In the text we considered only $\hat{p}$, the sample proportion. Here is a fact about the probability distribution of the sample mean, $\bar{x}$.

If a SRS of size 100 is chosen from a population that has variance 1 but unknown mean μ, the sample mean $\bar{x}$ has approximately the normal distribution with mean μ and variance 0.1.

From this fact, follow the argument given in the text for $\hat{p}$ step by step to derive the recipe for a 95% confidence interval for the unknown population mean μ.

8. A scientist measures the length in microns of a small object. (A micron is one-millionth of a meter.) Her measuring procedure is not perfectly accurate. In fact, repeated measurements follow the normal distribution with mean equal to the unknown true length μ (the measurement process is unbiased). The standard deviation of the distribution of measurements is 1

micron. (This is a statement of the reliability of the measuring process.)

(a) The results of 100 independent measurements can be thought of as a SRS of size 100 from the population of all possible measurements. If the mean of 100 measurements of the object is $\bar{x} = 21.3$ microns, use the result of Exercise 7 to give a 95% confidence interval for the true length μ.

(b) Suppose that only one measurement were taken and gave the result $x = 21.3$ microns. Give a 95% confidence interval for μ based on this single observation.

9. A poll taken immediately before the 1976 presidential election showed that 51% of the sample intended to vote for Carter. The polling organization announced that they were 95% confident that the sample result was within ±2 points of the true percent of all voters who favored Carter.

(a) Explain in plain language to someone who knows no statistics what "95% confident" means in this announcement.

(b) The poll showed Carter leading. Yet the polling organization said the election was too close to call. Explain why.

10. On hearing of the poll mentioned in Exercise 9, a nervous politician asked, "What is the probability that over half the voters prefer Carter?" A statistician said in reply that this question not only can't be answered from the poll results, it doesn't even make sense to talk about such a probability. Can you explain why?

Section 2

1. You are the polling consultant to a member of Congress. A SRS of 500 registered voters showed that 28% listed "energy problems" as the most important issue facing the nation. Give a 90% confidence interval for the proportion of all voters who hold this opinion.

2. In the setting of Exercise 1,

(a) Give a 75% confidence interval and a 99% confidence interval. Note how the confidence level affects the width of the interval.

(b) Suppose that the sample result $\hat{p} = 0.28$ had come from a SRS of 100 persons or a SRS of 4000 persons. Give a 90% confidence interval in both cases. Note how the sample size affects the width of the interval.

3. The Congressman receives 1310 pieces of mail on pending gun-control legislation. Of these, 86% oppose the legislation. Having learned from you about estimating with confidence, he asks you for an analysis of these opinions. What will you tell him?

4. An agricultural extension agent is concerned about hornworms infesting the tomatoes in the home gardens of her district. She checks a sample of 128 hornworms and is pleased to find 67 of them being parasitized by wasp larvae. Assuming these 128 can be regarded as a SRS, give an 80% confi-

dence interval for the proportion of hornworms in her district that are parasitized.

5. From Table 1, find the number c such that any normal distribution places 10% of its probability more than c standard deviations below the mean. (Figure 4 may help you to decide which number z_β is c.)

   A maker of light bulbs knows that the lifetime in service of his bulbs is normally distributed with mean 1500 hours and standard deviation 50 hours. He wants to advertise "Ninety percent of our bulbs last _____ hours or more." Fill in the blank, making use of the number c you just found.

6. The sampling distribution of $\hat{p}$ (the estimated proportion) for the Gallup Poll's probability sampling procedure is normal with mean equal to the population proportion p. But the standard deviation is *not* given by $\sqrt{p(1-p)/n}$, the SRS recipe. Be clever: Using Table 1 on p. 18 and your knowledge of normal distributions, find the standard deviation of $\hat{p}$ in a Gallup Poll sample of 1000 persons when the true p is 0.5. Compare your result with the standard deviation of $\hat{p}$ from a SRS of size 1000 from a population with $p = 0.5$.

7. The Congressman you advise knows from preliminary polls that about half the registered voters in his district favor his reelection. He wants to commission a poll that will estimate this proportion accurately. You, as his polling consultant, decide to take a SRS large enough to get a 95% confidence interval with margin of error ± 0.02. How large a sample must you take? (*Hint*: The margin of error is $\pm z_\beta \sqrt{p(1-p)/n}$, and p is close to 0.5.)

8. A SRS of 120 farmers in North Central Indiana is selected and asked their corn yield last year. The sample mean of the replies is $\bar{x} = 125$ bushels per acre, and the sample standard deviation is $s = 11$ bushels per acre. Give a 90% confidence interval for the mean corn yield of all North Central Indiana farmers.

9. Family income was one of the items included on only 20% of the forms in the 1970 census. Suppose (alas, it is too simple to be true) that the families who answer this question are a SRS of the families in each district. In Middletown, a city of 65,000 persons, 2621 families were asked their income. The mean of the responses was $\bar{x} = \$14,453$ and the standard deviation was \$3721. Give a 99% confidence interval for the 1970 mean family income in Middletown.

10. A laboratory scale is known to have errors of measurement normally distributed with mean 0 and standard deviation $\sigma = 0.0001$ gram. So repeated measurements of the same quantity are normally distributed with mean equal to the true weight and standard deviation $\sigma = 0.0001$ gram. A series of 25 weighings gives $\bar{x} = 2.3214$ grams and sample standard deviation $s = 0.00013$ gram.

    (a) Give a recipe for a level β confidence interval for the mean μ of a population having *known* standard deviation σ. Explain why you should use σ and ignore the sample standard deviation s.

(b) Use your recipe to give a 75% confidence interval for the true weight of the quantity weighed 25 times above.

11. Table 1 (and larger tables of normal probabilities) is useful for purposes other than obtaining confidence intervals. Suppose, for example, that the weight of tomato juice in mechanically filled cans varies from can to can according to a normal distribution with standard deviation 8 grams. This describes the precision of the canfilling machinery. The mean of the distribution can be set by adjusting the machine.

(a) A penalty is charged if more than 10% of the cans contain less than 454 grams. What mean should be set in order to have exactly 10% of the cans weigh less than 454 grams? (*Hint:* From Table 1, find the number c with 10% of a normal distribution falling more than c standard deviations below the mean.)

(b) Suppose instead that the penalty applies to the sample average weight $\bar{x}$ of a case of 12 cans. That is, no more than 10% of all cases may have $\bar{x}$ below 454 grams. To what value should the filling machine be set to produce just 10% of cases with average weight below 454 grams? (*Hint:* What is the standard deviation of the average weight $\bar{x}$ of the 12 cans in a case?)

Sections 3 and 4

1. In Exercise 10 on p. 92, an experiment was reported which used a paired-sample design like that of Example 3. Out of 6 pairs of plots, the experimental plot had a higher yield in five cases. We will assess the significance of this evidence against the null hypothesis that each plot in a pair is equally likely to have the higher yield. (This null hypothesis says that the experimental treatment—praying to the soybeans—had no effect.)

(a) Supposing that the null hypothesis is true, explain how to simulate for one pair whether the experimental or control plot has higher yield. Then explain how to simulate one repetition of the experiment with 6 independent pairs of plots.

(b) Simulate 20 repetitions of the experiment; begin in line 113 of Table A.

(c) The P-value is the probability that 5 or more (that is, either 5 or 6) out of 6 pairs favor the experimental plot. Estimate the P-value from your simulation. (Of course, 20 trials will not give a precise estimate.)

(d) About how low would the P-value have to be for you to conclude that prayer does increase yields? That is, what level of significance would you insist on to believe the result suggested by the experiment? Were the experimental results significant at that level?

2. For each of the following situations, state in words the proper null hypothesis H_0 and alternative hypothesis H_1.

(a) A sociologist asks a large sample of high school students which academic subject is their favorite. She suspects that a lower percentage of females than of males will say that mathematics is their favorite subject.

(b) An educational researcher randomly divides sixth-grade students into two groups for gym class. He teaches both groups basketball skills with the same methods of instruction. He encourages Group A with compliments and other positive behavior, but acts cool and neutral toward Group B. He hopes to show that Group A does better (on the average) than Group B on a test of basketball skills at the end of the instructional unit.

(c) A political scientist hypothesizes that among registered voters there is a negative correlation between age and the percent who actually vote. To test this, she draws a random sample from public records on registration and voting.

3. The classic experiment to detect ESP uses a shuffled deck of cards containing 5 suits (waves, stars, circles, squares, and crosses). As the experimenter turns over each card and concentrates on it, the subject guesses the suit of the card. If the subject has no ESP, he has probability 1/5 of being right by luck on each guess. If he does have ESP, he will be right more often. A subject is right in 5 of 10 tries. (Actual experiments naturally use much longer series of guesses so weak ESP could be spotted. No one has ever been right half the time in a long experiment!)

(a) Give H_0 and H_1 for a test to see if this result is significant evidence that the subject has ESP.

(b) Explain how to simulate the experiment; assume for the sake of argument that H_0 is true.

(c) Simulate 20 repetitions of the experiment; begin in line 121 of Table A.

(d) The actual experimental result was 5 right in 10 tries. Of what event is the P-value for this outcome the probability? Give a (not very precise) estimate of the P-value based on your simulation. How convincing is the experimental result?

4. An old farmer claims to be able to detect the presence of water with a bent stick. To test this claim, he is presented with 5 identical barrels, some containing water and some not. He is correct in 4 out of 5 cases. Assess the strength of this result as evidence of the farmer's special ability. (You must formulate the hypotheses and do a simulation to estimate the P-value.)

5. Read the article by Hans Zeisel and Harry Kalven, Jr., "Parking Tickets and Missing Women: Statistics and the Law," in *Statistics: A Guide to the Unknown*. These pages refer in nontechnical language to several tests of significance. In each of the following settings, state the null and alternative hypotheses. If a P-value is given in the article, state it also.

(a) The Swedish parking ticket case.

(b) The proportion of women in venires drawn by Dr. Spock's trial judge.

6. A study on predicting job performance reports that

An important predictor variable for later job performance was the score X on a screening test given to potential employees. The variable being predicted was the employee's score Y on an evaluation made after a year on the job. In a sample of 70 employees the correlation between X and Y was r = 0.4, which is statistically significant at the 1% level.

Answer the following questions.

(a) Explain to someone who knows no statistics what information "$r = 0.4$" carries about the connection between screening test and later evaluation score.

(b) The null hypothesis in the test reported above is that there is *no association* between X and Y when the population of all employees is considered. What value of the correlation for the entire population does this null hypothesis correspond to?

(c) Explain to someone who knows no statistics why "statistically significant at the 1% level" means there is good reason to think that there is association between the two scores.

7. A new vaccine for a virus that now has no vaccine is to be tested. Since the disease is usually not serious, 1000 volunteers will be used and will be exposed to the virus.

(a) Explain how you would use these 1000 volunteers in a designed experiment to test the vaccine. Include all important details of designing the experiment (but don't actually do any random allocation).

(b) We hope to show that the vaccine is more effective than a placebo. State H_0 and H_1.

(c) The experiment gave a P-value of 0.25. Explain carefully what this means.

(d) The researchers did not consider this evidence strong enough to recommend regular use of the vaccine. Do you agree?

8. A social psychologist reports that "In our sample, ethnocentrism was significantly higher ($P < 0.05$) among church attenders than among nonattenders." Explain to someone who knows no statistics what this means.

9. The article by Arie Y. Lewin and Linda Duchan, "Women in Academia," *Science*, Volume 173 (1971), pp. 892–5, reports an investigation in which applications of equally qualified male and female Ph.D.'s were sent to academic department chairmen. The chairmen were asked which applicant they would hire. The number who chose the male was somewhat greater than the number who would hire the female. The authors concluded that "The results, although not statistically significant, showed definite trends that confirm our hypothesis that discrimination against women does exist at the time of the hiring decision." This conclusion was strongly attacked in letters to the editor. One irate statistician wrote, "Are the standards of *Science* the standards of science?"

Discuss the validity of the conclusion that the survey results confirm the existence of discrimination. (If possible, read the entire article first.)

10. Return to Senator Bean's SRS of size 1000 in Section 1. The Senator wants to know if a sample proportion $\hat{p}$ is significant evidence that he is leading the contest. The null hypothesis is therefore

$$H_0: \quad p = \tfrac{1}{2}$$

where p is the proportion of all voters who favor Bean. The alternative hypothesis is

$$H_1: \quad p > \tfrac{1}{2}.$$

   (a) From Section 1, what is the probability distribution of $\hat{p}$ when H_0 is true?
   (b) Explain, using your knowledge of the normal distributions, why $\hat{p} = 0.53$ has a P-value of 0.025.
   (c) What is the P-value of $\hat{p} = 0.515$?

Section 5

1. A criminal trial can be thought of as a decision problem, the two possible decisions being "guilty" and "not guilty." Moreover, in a criminal trial there is a null hypothesis in the sense of an assertion that we will continue to hold until we have strong evidence against it. Criminal trials are therefore similar to hypothesis testing.

   (a) What are H_0 and H_1 in a criminal trial? Explain your choice of H_0.
   (b) Describe in words the meaning of Type I error and Type II error in this setting, and display the possible outcomes in a diagram like Figures 6 and 7.
   (c) Suppose that you are a jury member. Having studied statistics, you think in terms of a significance level α, the (subjective) probability of a Type I error. What considerations would affect your personal choice of α? (For example, would the difference between a charge of murder and a charge of shoplifting affect your personal α?)

2. A computerized medical diagnostic program is being designed that will scan the results of tests conducted by technicians (pulse rate, blood pressure, urinalysis, etc.) and either clear the patient or refer the case to the attention of a doctor. This program will be used to screen many thousands of persons who do not have specific medical complaints as part of a preventive medicine system.

   (a) What are the two hypotheses and the two types of error? Display the situation in a diagram like Figures 6 and 7.
   (b) Briefly discuss the costs of each of the two types of error. These costs are not entirely monetary.

(c) After considering these costs, which error probability would you choose to make smaller?

3. You are the consumer of bearings in an acceptance sampling situation. Your acceptance sampling plan has probability 0.01 of passing a lot of bearings that does not meet quality standards. You might think the lots that pass are almost all good. Alas, it is not so.

(a) Explain why low probabilities of error cannot ensure that lots which pass are mostly good. (*Hint:* What happens if your supplier ships all bad lots?)

(b) The paradox that most decisions can be correct (low error probabilities) and yet most lots that pass can be bad has important analogs in areas such as medical diagnosis. Explain why most conclusions that a patient has a rare disease can be false alarms even if the diagnostic system is correct 99% of the time.

4. A major advantage of the decision approach to inference is that it is not restricted to the two-decision situations characteristic of hypothesis testing. For example, suppose that three decisions are possible in an acceptance sampling setting.

Decision 1:   The lot of bearings is of high quality.
             Accept it at full price.

Decision 2:   The lot of bearings is of medium quality.
             Accept it at a lower price.

Decision 3:   The lot is of low quality.
             Reject it.

The performance of a decision rule is still assessed in terms of the probabilities of error. By filling in the display below, count the different types of error now possible.

TRUE QUALITY OF THE LOT

	High	Medium	Low
Accept at full price			
Accept at lower price			
Reject			

DECISION BASED ON SAMPLE

Table A

RANDOM DIGITS

Line								
101	19223	95034	05756	28713	96409	12531	42544	82853
102	73676	47150	99400	01927	27754	42648	82425	36290
103	45467	71709	77558	00095	32863	29485	82226	90056
104	52711	38889	93074	60227	40011	85848	48767	52573
105	95592	94007	69971	91481	60779	53791	17297	59335
106	68417	35013	15529	72765	85089	57067	50211	47487
107	82739	57890	20807	47511	81676	55300	94383	14893
108	60940	72024	17868	24943	61790	90656	87964	18883
109	36009	19365	15412	39638	85453	46816	83485	41979
110	38448	48789	18338	24697	39364	42006	76688	08708
111	81486	69487	60513	09297	00412	71238	27649	39950
112	59636	88804	04634	71197	19352	73089	84898	45785
113	62568	70206	40325	03699	71080	22553	11486	11776
114	45149	32992	75730	66280	03819	56202	02938	70915
115	61041	77684	94322	24709	73698	14526	31893	32592
116	14459	26056	31424	80371	65103	62253	50490	61181
117	38167	98532	62183	70632	23417	26185	41448	75532
118	73190	32533	04470	29669	84407	90785	65956	86382
119	95857	07118	87664	92099	58806	66979	98624	84826
120	35476	55972	39421	65850	04266	35435	43742	11937
121	71487	09984	29077	14863	61683	47052	62224	51025
122	13873	81598	95052	90908	73592	75186	87136	95761
123	54580	81507	27102	56027	55892	33063	41842	81868
124	71035	09001	43367	49497	72719	96758	27611	91596
125	96746	12149	37823	71868	18442	35119	62103	39244
126	96927	19931	36089	74192	77567	88741	48409	41903
127	43909	99477	25330	64359	40085	16925	85117	36071
128	15689	14227	06565	14374	13352	49367	81982	87209
129	36759	58984	68288	22913	18638	54303	00795	08727
130	69051	64817	87174	09517	84534	06489	87201	97245
131	05007	16632	81194	14873	04197	85576	45195	96565
132	68732	55259	84292	08796	43165	93739	31685	97150
133	45740	41807	65561	33302	07051	93623	18132	09547
134	27816	78416	18329	21337	35213	37741	04312	68508
135	66925	55658	39100	78458	11206	19876	87151	31260
136	08421	44753	77377	28744	75592	08563	79140	92454
137	53645	66812	61421	47836	12609	15373	98481	14592
138	66831	68908	40772	21558	47781	33586	79177	06928
139	55588	99404	70708	41098	43563	56934	48394	51719
140	12975	13258	13048	45144	72321	81940	00360	02428
141	96767	35964	23822	96012	94591	65194	50842	53372
142	72829	50232	97892	63408	77919	44575	24870	04178
143	88565	42628	17797	49376	61762	16953	88604	12724
144	62964	88145	83083	69453	46109	59505	69680	00900
145	19687	12633	57857	95806	09931	02150	43163	58636
146	37609	59057	66967	83401	60705	02384	90597	93600
147	54973	86278	88737	74351	47500	84552	19909	67181
148	00694	05977	19664	65441	20903	62371	22725	53340
149	71546	05233	53946	68743	72460	27601	45403	88692
150	07511	88915	41267	16853	84569	79367	32337	03316

Table B

SQUARE ROOTS

n	$\sqrt{n}$	n	$\sqrt{n}$	n	$\sqrt{n}$
1	1.0	21	4.6	41	6.4
2	1.4	22	4.7	42	6.5
3	1.7	23	4.8	43	6.6
4	2.0	24	4.9	44	6.6
5	2.2	25	5.0	45	6.7
6	2.4	26	5.1	46	6.8
7	2.6	27	5.2	47	6.9
8	2.8	28	5.3	48	6.9
9	3.0	29	5.4	49	7.0
10	3.2	30	5.5	50	7.1
11	3.3	31	5.6		
12	3.5	32	5.7		
13	3.6	33	5.7		
14	3.7	34	5.8		
15	3.9	35	5.9		
16	4.0	36	6.0		
17	4.1	37	6.1		
18	4.2	38	6.2		
19	4.3	39	6.2		
20	4.5	40	6.3		

NOTE: To find the square root of a fraction, use the rule that

$$\sqrt{a/b} = \sqrt{a}/\sqrt{b}.$$

For example, the square root of the fraction 10/6 is

$$\sqrt{10/6} = \sqrt{10}/\sqrt{6} = 3.2/2.4 = 1.3.$$

Index

Page references in *italics* refer to exercises.